The Referee's Survival Guide

ABOUT THE AUTHOR

JEFFREY CAMINSKY, a state referee emeritus, associate assessor, and former assignor, lives in Livonia, Michigan with his wife and family. In an alternate reality, he is a public prosecutor in Detroit.

His book *The Star Dancers*, the first in a series of science fiction adventure novels, is scheduled for publication in 2007.

The Referee's Survival Guide

Practical Suggestions
for Soccer Officials

Jeffrey Caminsky

NEW ALEXANDRIA PRESS
LIVONIA

Published by New Alexandria Press
PO Box 530516
Livonia, Michigan 48153
www.newalexandriapress.com

Portions of Chapter 6, "Dealing with Dissent," are adapted from materials first appearing in *Michigan Soccer* and *The Corsham Referee*.

ISBN   978-0-9790106-0-6
LCCN   2007900439

Printed in the United States of America
First Printing March 2007

Quantity discounts are available on bulk purchases of this book for educational or professional purposes. Special books or book excerpts can also be made available to fit specific needs. For information, please contact *sales@ newalexandriapress.com* or send written inquiries to New Alexandria Press, PO Box 530516, Livonia, Michigan 48153.

10 9 8 7 6 5 4 3 2 1
First Edition

To Jason and Julie,
who always keep their father young at heart....

Contents

Illustrations

Acknowledgments

IN MANY WAYS, LIFE IS a cooperative adventure, and few things in this world are possible without a great deal of help from others. While it would be impossible to note everyone whose advice and experience helped shape the pages that follow, there are a number of people to whom the author is specially indebted, most particularly:

- The YMCA soccer program, which graciously allowed me to serve as its assignor for many years...and especially Eileen Vesey, the former head of the program, whose tireless efforts on behalf of the local kids was a constant source of inspiration.

- The Michigan Wolves and Hawks, and the Livonia Meteors, whose fine youth programs let me develop whatever skills I came to possess as an official. They do, however, share some minor complicity in the series of field experiments I have conducted over the years, giving me a laboratory to discover many of the things that do not work for referees during a soccer game. They also generously provided a wealth of experience for an entire generation of gifted young officials in and around Livonia, Michigan. These fine young people are a source of personal pride to me, and professional pride to the entire state.

- The finest set of models ever to don a referee's uniform and wander around a soccer field doing their best to follow the incomprehensible directions of an incompetent photographer: Ramsey Allie, Ken Burcaw, Amie Musser, Patrick Pijls, Chris Seubert, and Maggie Vaillancourt.

- My cadre of conscripted proofreaders and editors: Ken Burcaw, who also loaned me the benefit of his many years of experience, on and off the pitch; my parents, Wallace and Alice Caminsky, who did not, as feared, faint with relief upon learning that their eldest son actually was capable of writing coherent sentences, but vainly tried to persuade him to include more of them in his writing; my wife, Nonie Caminsky, who also persuaded me that I might have some words of advice to offer others (although, if what follows strikes the reader as trifling or idiotic, her only fault in the matter was in trying to find something to keep her husband busy and out of trouble, and not in the lunacy that ensued); Chris Seubert, whose sense of humor and calm personality on and off the pitch help him solve problems without making them worse; and Kathleen Yanik, my sister-in-law, who tried her best to teach me the advantages of conventional punctuation.

- Julian Carosi, the learned webmaster of The Corsham Referee (www.corshamref.net), and the entire gang at SocRef-L, the online referee tent—who all provided outlets not only for many frustrations, but also for some developing thoughts of mine on the subject of soccer. It is not their fault that most of those thoughts were underexposed, or became garbled on their way to the printer.

And lastly, I need to thank and acknowledge the many fine authors and thinkers in the soccer world who preceded me, and whose fine writings and insights are largely responsible for any incidental clarity that appears in this book.

Unfortunately, despite everyone's best efforts to point them out ahead of time, the flaws in what follows are entirely mine.

Author's Note

LIKE MANY OF MY COLLEAGUES, I became a referee rather late in life. My soccer-playing son was finally old enough for his first part-time job, there was an appalling lack of officials for his favorite sport, and my wife and I decided that we didn't want him to face the barbarians we'd seen on the sidelines all by himself. I found that I enjoyed it immensely and have continued to the present day, all the while doing what I could to help the younger officials cope with the stresses and demands that come with *their* first jobs.

This book is an attempt to pass along some of what I have learned along the way, usually at no small cost to my pride and ego. I often wished there were materials available to help me through my own first couple of seasons. I hope others find this volume helpful.

A Special Note to Parents of Younger Referees

If your club is fortunate enough to have several different levels of play, it is common for new officials to receive assignments to non-competitive games involving young children.

After a few seasons, your son or daughter may begin to officiate more advanced soccer games. You will probably find that most of these games proceed smoothly. The participants are usually well-behaved, and most of the players display healthy doses of fair play.

There are, however, some participants along the sidelines whose sense of sportsmanship appears to come from watching too many *Godfather* movies, and whose own parents appear to have neglected some basic lessons in manners. Unfortunately, these people do not come with signs attached, and we can never be sure when they will appear, or which games they will infect.

Until your child is old enough to do premier- or travel-team matches involving teenaged players, you may wish to make sure that there is a friendly adult on hand, in the event of trouble. If an adult will be working the match, or serving as a "field marshal" for the venue, that will probably do; otherwise you may wish to stay and watch. Soccer is, after all, a wonderful spectator sport.

When your child begins doing adult games...well, people often don't know when to stop, myself included. But by then you can rest assured that your job is done. My mother still worries about me, of course, but she doesn't come to my games, either.

Jeff Caminsky
February, 2007

Introduction

YOU HAVE TAKEN THE referee course taught at your local club and are now ready to take on the world of soccer. You passed the test with flying colors, and everything should be downhill from here.

Unfortunately, too many of our new referees feel this way and don't realize that the classroom is only the first step toward becoming a soccer official. In fact it is, in many respects, the easiest step of all. Learning the Laws of the Game in a classroom is different than applying them on the soccer field. And passing the certification test only enables you to don your uniform and step onto the pitch. It does not teach you to read the temper of a game, or how to process the hundreds of bits of information that will pass before you every moment of every game that you officiate.

This book is not intended to be an all-encompassing volume on the rules of soccer, or how to perfect your craft as a referee. It does not reflect the official position of any organization or governing body, is not designed to be a collection of rules and procedures, and is hardly a comprehensive discussion on every aspect of soccer officiating. There are a number of books and resources, many of which appear at the end of this volume, which can help the official develop his skills and hone his insights into the game.* In addition, this book will not delve into the interpretation or mastery of various versions of the Laws of the Game. That is a topic left for the lawmakers, and the administrative bodies governing the many local, state, and national soccer associations. Rather, it is the author's hope that the ensuing pages provide some insight into the world of officiating soccer for the newer members of our fraternity, and some helpful tips to

---

* Or hers. There are, after all, a large number of female referees, and the intermittent use of the male pronoun is for grammatical precision, not to denigrate or insult half the human race.

guide you through your early years as a referee. It is written from the perspective of officials working amateur games affiliated with the United States Soccer Federation. Most of what passes for advice and assistance is based on real-world experience— either that of the author or of others— and is meant to provoke thought, and an occasional smile, as it helps the newly certified soccer referee adjust to life on the business side of a whistle.

Of course, if it does the same for anyone else along the way, and helps induce an occasional grizzled veteran to find the path leading out of the center circle, that would be fine, as well.

The Referee's Survival Guide

Chapter 1

Becoming a Referee

FOR MORE THAN A CENTURY, soccer has captured the affection and imagination of the world. Simple to understand and inexpensive to play, it has grown from its roots in ancient times to a modern game with standardized rules and organized leagues that span our planet. After a slow beginning in this country, it is now growing by leaps and bounds. While informal games need only a ball and players, formal competitions also require a neutral decision-maker, in order to settle the unavoidable disagreements that come during the course of any athletic competition. By officiating, you advance the growth and understanding of this wonderful sport in ways that future generations of players will come to appreciate. The level of play in any part of the world is often determined by the skill of the officials, and without skilled and dedicated referees, American soccer cannot continue to grow, and American players cannot hope to compete with the best the rest of the world has to offer.

While becoming certified as a soccer referee is an important step toward developing a deeper understanding of the sport, in many ways it is only a beginning. Taking a referee class and passing the examination just gives you a badge and whistle, and lets you get paid while running about the soccer field. The task of becoming a referee will last as long as you officiate, for no matter how good you become, you will always be learning, constantly improving your understanding of the game and the people around you, and continually refining your skills. The moment you stop learning, you will stop growing as an official. And the moment you stop growing, whatever skills you have developed will begin to fade.

Why am I Here?

One question each new referee needs to ask is "why do I want to be a referee?" The answers can be many and varied:

- Some—particularly younger officials, for whom refereeing may be their first job—are mainly interested in earning some extra spending money.

- Some want to officiate because they love soccer, others because they want some exercise.

- Some referee other sports as well, and want to add soccer to their schedule.

- Some may want to help their local club, or be there to help their son or daughter officiate.

- Others may like the thought of controlling events—or simply enjoy bossing other people around.

Whatever the reason, you can succeed as a referee with effort and dedication. But honest self-assessment is something every official needs, and your motivation for beginning a career as a paid referee may give you clues about possible strengths you will have as an official, as well as some weaknesses you may need to address.

For Love or Money?

Players and spectators will not care why we are officials—what motivates us, what drives us to become better, or what our particular circumstances might be. They want only a well-trained, competent, and impartial referee to keep the match safe, enjoyable, and fair. For our part, however, realizing what motivates us can help us understand what drives us to succeed, and what will sustain us through the challenges that lie ahead.

Success as an official will come from dedication and a sense of professional pride. Without both, the best intentions in the world will not help. Whatever our personal motive for becoming a referee, any one of us can excel. One official's willingness to work hard to earn the extra money that comes from working top-level matches can drive him toward excellence every bit as much as another's simple affection for the game her father taught her when she was young. What matters is not what brings us on to the pitch, but what keeps us there. In most cases, successful referees simply enjoy the job, enjoy the pride of a job well-done, and enjoy being of service to others. If we start with this, then we only need to apply ourselves and start developing the skills necessary to succeed.

Personality and Character

Over the course of our lives we will see an infinite variety of personalities. Some people are shy, some anger quickly. Some wear their hearts on their sleeves. Some never seem to lack for friends, or for a funny comeback.

There is, however, no single "referee personality" that can assure success on the field—nor, fortunately, any type of person who cannot become an outstanding soccer official. Each of us has our own unique strengths and weaknesses, and any one of us can become a great referee. But to do so, we must be able to look at ourselves honestly, and recognize the kind of person we are. This can remind us of the strengths we have that can help us, as well as the weaknesses we will need to overcome.

A referee's character will count for more than his personality, since it will be character that will determine how well the referee can stand up to the challenges on the pitch. But if we look at the referees we see beside us on the pitch, it will become apparent that many of best ones share some important characteristics that help them succeed. Some of these traits will come more naturally to us than others, but all of them need constant care and attention, and many of them will help us in other walks of life.

Common Traits of the Successful Referee

While any type of personality can result in a good soccer referee, many qualities are common to highly skilled officials around the world. Most of these traits are aspects of their character that they either had naturally or developed over time, and many of them are essential to success as a referee. What this means to the new officials is that there will be some aspects of your "on-field persona" that you must nurture and develop in order to feel at home on the pitch.

Integrity

Probably the most important character trait all referees share is a strong sense of personal integrity. Honesty on and off the field is essential to anyone hoping to convince others to trust him. A soccer match requires the players to rely upon the referee to make often-difficult decisions during hotly contested matches, and the Laws confer nearly total discretion on the officials to do what is best for the game *within the rules.* An official who lacks the personal integrity to see things honestly, and to see that everyone, including the officials, behaves according to the Laws of the Game will not get very far as a referee. Players and colleagues will come to be mistrustful of the official's intentions and impartiality, and if a referee loses the trust of the players, then the loss of match control is never far behind.

Though we often fail to appreciate it, players and spectators are willing to forgive an occasional mistake by the officials, so long as they seem to be trying their best to be fair to both sides. One thing they will not forgive is dishonesty.

Courage

As important as integrity is to a referee, it is meaningless without the courage to do what the official knows to be right.

Whether it is denying an appeal for a "handball" that the referee deems to be unintentional, turning a deaf ear to loud appeals for a penalty kick by a team whose star striker has tripped over the ball rather than a defender's foot, calling a penalty kick late in the game for a foul that only the referee and the defender know happened inside the penalty area, or keeping the offside flag down because a player who is racing ten yards past the last defender was onside when the ball was kicked, the referee cannot make the call that will cause the least amount of grief. Rather, he must make the call that he believes to be the right one.

Soccer is a game of energy and excitement, and disappointment over a call, or no-call, is often expressed angrily and loudly. But we have other tools for dealing with expressions of disappointment that get out of hand. Avoiding the problem by making the wrong call is not one of them.

Decisiveness

Courage and integrity will carry an official a long way. All the courage in the world will not matter, however, without the ability to make decisions quickly. Soccer is a fast-paced, highly intense game, where the play is ever-changing and the action can cover the whole field in a matter of seconds. A referee who takes too long to make up his mind about what has just happened may find play leaving him behind; and the referee who waits for prompting by the players to announce a decision will be seen as weak and easily persuaded.

Patience

While decisiveness is necessary, patience—on the soccer field, as in life—is a virtue.

Referees hoping to appear decisive and alert often have more time to announce a decision than they realize. Waiting an extra second or two before blowing the whistle can often prevent a great many problems:

- Waiting an extra second may allow a stumbling attacker to recover his footing, and continue on to score.

- Waiting an extra second may show whether the ball will go to the offender's teammate, or to the side that was fouled—and whether whistling will allow a tactical foul to succeed in disrupting an attack.

- Waiting an extra second may determine whether a goal will score despite a foul inside the penalty area, thereby sparing the referee the embarrassment of pulling the ball out of the net while explaining to an exasperated team that the goal is disallowed...but to punish the foul they will get a penalty kick, instead.

Patience involves more than waiting to see how play develops. A patient referee will often take his time dealing with a troublesome player or coach to maximize the effect of any card given for misconduct— perhaps giving the troublemaker the opportunity to bring his temper under control, or waiting until tempers have cooled before speaking to a player about a controversial call. This is because a wise referee will try to use every available tool—the voice, the whistle, the card, sometimes the "stare of death"—to keep the match under control. And a patient referee regards time as a resource to be used, avoiding the rush to take actions that will only make things worse.

The benefits of patience are many....up to a point. The challenge for the new official is learning when to be patient and when to be prompt.

Fair-mindedness

The reason that soccer confers so much discretion on its officials is because everyone presumes that the referee will be fair and impartial.

There is more to fairness, however, than simply treating both sides equally. A referee who relishes playing "gotcha" with the players—lowering the boom for trifling matters, or imposing disproportionate punishments for minor offenses—may be treating everyone the same, but is hardly being "fair" as far as the players are concerned. Unfairness to everyone is, after all, hardly a recommended path to success in any walk of life, and soccer is no exception.

Being "fair-minded" on the field means more than treating everyone consistently. It means that the referee treats everyone with respect, and avoids intruding needlessly on a game that rightly belongs to the players. There will be times when this will mean coming down sternly on a player or coach whose behavior is simply unacceptable. We do not, however, have the power to do so because soccer thinks that we are infallible. Rather, the game entrusts us with our authority because *someone* has to make a decision...and everyone is counting on us to be fair.

Empathy

Good referees will know all the rules and be able to apply them fairly and impartially. A great referee will understand the needs and motivations of the players, and empathize with the challenges that face them on the field of play.

Empathizing with the players does not mean that you are willing to tolerate rough or reckless play. It does mean that you will be able to sense a player's frustrations, whether caused by disappointment or a painful knock in the ankle, and use this knowledge to help you manage the game:

- A referee empathizing with a player will be able to tell the difference between a frustrated player who needs a moment to calm himself, and a nasty player who must be dealt with harshly.

- A referee able to empathize with the players will sense the difference between a game in which players accept hard, physical challenges with good spirits in the course of a sporting contest, and a game in which tempers are rising due to the level of contact.

- A referee who can empathize with the players will have the ability to distinguish between trifling fouls that have no effect on the game, and apparently minor contacts—such as a painful rap on the heel, or a routine-looking trip that disrupts a promising attack—that will make players angry unless they see justice being done.

Referees who have played the game have an advantage in this regard. Their on-field experience will help them read the body language of the players and let them understand instantly how a play is likely to affect tempers on the pitch. Those who have not played soccer, or some other sport at a competitive level of play, must find some way to develop this ability on their own.

Coolness under Fire

Ernest Hemingway once defined courage as "grace under pressure."[*] Though known for his love of bull-fighting, he may well have been talking about soccer referees.

Soccer has provoked riots as well as devotion among its fans, and has grown to become the most popular sport in the world largely because of its capacity to excite our passions. But soccer's ability to draw on raw human emotion presents a challenge for its referees, for while players and spectators watch the game with their hearts, referees watch with their eyes. If we allow our feelings to overwhelm our judgment, we risk chaos on the field. We are there to maintain order and keep everyone focused on the game. Everybody is counting on us to keep a level head, even when the disappointments of the moment have interrupted their own capacity for rational thought.

Some of us are naturally excitable. Most of us have a variable temperament, depending on our mood and on what is going on around us. Few of us are naturally inclined to relax in times of stress, or given to react to expressions of anger or insults by remaining calm and doing our best to ease whatever tensions are simmering around us. Developing this ability may be the biggest challenge to anyone striving to be a top-notch referee.

Humility

People who lack confidence often compensate for their insecurities by adopting an air of superiority. Looking down at the rest of the world may prop up a weak ego, but will never help a referee on the soccer field. While some can get away with being arrogant and brilliant, conceit by a referee can cause all sorts of self-inflicted problems, and being arrogant and clueless is a recipe for disaster in all walks of life.

Under the Laws of the Game, the referee's decision is final on all points concerning the fact of play. Soccer, in other words, regards the referee's judgment as infallible, so far as the game is concerned. Unfortunately,

---

[*]Interview with Dorothy Parker, *New Yorker*, November 30, 1929.

Actually, preferring short words to longer ones, Hemingway used the word "guts" rather than "courage," but his point was the same.

some referees take this to heart and approach the players with an attitude of arrogance and privilege, rather than with empathy and understanding.

A wise referee will realize that nobody is perfect, and that the reason he is blowing the whistle at the game is not because he knows more about soccer than anyone else, but because somebody has to make a decision on the field and that he, at least, has actually read the rules. Cultivating an attitude that the participants are inferior, because there is so much about soccer that they do not know, will not help a referee control himself, let alone the players. This, in turn, will limit how far the official's abilities can take him. On the other hand, the referee who develops an attitude of sympathetic understanding to the player's concerns—recognizing that we referee to help them play the game rather than the other way around—will have more success on the field and find no such limits on any future advancement.

Self-confidence

Unfortunately, humility is often well-deserved, and one whose ambitions far exceed his talents had best be humble, or be prepared to come to grief on or off the soccer field. But a strong ego and healthy confidence in ourselves and our abilities, tempered by the knowledge that we are not above making a mistake, can make us strong and resilient in our jobs as referees, and elsewhere.

Though perfection may have no need for improvement, the rest of us can all use a little work. Recognizing that we are not perfect can lead us to better ourselves. But modesty by itself is no path to success at any endeavor. Unless we have the confidence in ourselves to make the calls we know to be right and stand strong in the face of criticism, we will always be second-guessing ourselves. Perfection is an ideal that is probably beyond the grasp of any of us, but knowing that we have tried our best can give us pride in a job well-done.

Good Work Habits on the Field

Humans are creatures of habit and tend to revert to form during times of stress. It should come as no surprise that most accomplished officials have adopted and cultivated on-field habits that sharpen their performance.

Sloppiness is often a state of mind. While an official can often get away with cutting corners on the field—walking rather than running into position on the field; using weak or ambiguous mechanics; failing to run the ball to the end line, and the like—it is not an approach that leads to excellence. Many times, officials come to grief not because they are poor referees, but because their work habits have left them out of position at the critical "moment of truth" for the match, or because they made the right call but used a faulty signal which led to an unexpected turn of events on the pitch.

As a new official, it will be easier for you to begin training yourself to do things the right way from the outset, than it will be to break old, bad habits later in your career.

Hustle

In soccer, as in most sports, there is a premium on hustle. There are benefits gained by being alert and moving quickly into position and penalties to suffer by being slow to react to changing events. Officiating soccer is no different. The official who can anticipate and react to play as it is developing will usually be in place to spot a foul and prevent trouble. The official who always lags behind play will need luck and well-behaved players to maintain order on the field.

Hustle depends more on habit and mind-set than it does on raw physical speed. Many older referees somehow manage always to be in position wherever they are needed, even though their younger colleagues could leave them far behind in a foot race. Experience, though, can only teach us where we *need to be*. It is hustle that will get us there in time.

A Commitment to Fitness

Of course, all the best intentions in the world often founder when confronted with the real world. For the referee—even a referee blessed with an abundance of talent, resourcefulness, courage, and the patience of a saint—the determination to hustle into position is useless without the legs to get there.

Soccer is a physically challenging game, demanding a high level of fitness from its officials. Referees often run more than six miles during a game. Assistant referees may find themselves doing three or more miles worth of running, often sprinting at flank speed. Some referees try to use officiating to give them the chance for some fresh air and exercise. Successful referees all have some form of fitness regimen to keep them in condition, to enable them to officiate at their best. Experience teaches all of us that it is much easier to *stay* in shape than to *get* into shape.

Knowledge of the Game

Lastly, all good referees need a thorough knowledge of the game. While "facts of play" are often judged at the discretion of the referee, a misapplication of the law is a violation of the rules. If it affects the outcome, the mistake can cause a match to be replayed.

Knowing and understanding the Laws of the Game is necessary for anyone who wants to officiate the sport. Immersing yourself in the game's history and traditions is a good way to continue your education as a referee. It will give you a more complete understanding of the "whys" and "wherefores' of the game, and deeper insight into some of the fine points of the rules. More importantly, understanding the reason for each rule will let you apply them all at the right time. Knowing why a particular Law exists lets you keep things moving smoothly on the field, helping you sense when to apply which rule, as well as when an infraction can be overlooked as too trivial to stop play. And being able to place each rule in its proper context is essential in order to make each rule work as it is intended.

Watching as much soccer as you can, whether live or on television, will show you how other referees react to events on the field and hone your sense of when a contact is a foul, and when a foul is so trifling that it is safe to let it pass. It will also sustain you when you encounter the dilemma every soccer official confronts at some time—the unexpected, whether in the form of an event not covered in the rules, never covered in your training, or one which simply leaves you scratching your head in wonder. When this happens, the deeper your understanding of the game, the better equipped you will be to solve whatever problem confronts you. You may not remember the rule, but you may very well remember the solution.

Chapter 2

Ref'ing 101

HAVING DECIDED TO BECOME A REFEREE, and after completing the course requirements and basic training needed to do so, there is still the pesky question that each new official must face before starting to officiate: *now what?*

Unfortunately, you will soon discover that your course work only taught you the rules. Most likely, it did not teach you what to do when you actually get to the field and barely touched upon field protocol and game mechanics. For that, you must begin to educate yourself, and there is plenty of help available to you along the way. Books, videos, and more experienced officials are resources that will always be available to you, and you should use them whenever possible. But before you start, you should try to master a few basic concepts that are the key to survival in any number of endeavors, soccer included.

Basic Rules of Survival
Developing the skills, knowledge, and experience needed to master the art of officiating is a task that will never end and one that will last as long as you continue to referee. Some tools of survival on the pitch, however, can be digested quickly and easily— though applying them in practice, under the stress of excitement during a game, may prove a bit more difficult. It starts with recognizing a few fundamental ideas and, more importantly, actually coming to believe them:

Rule #1:

Keep reminding yourself that they are not yelling at you; they are yelling at your uniform.

People often react to someone else's anger by becoming defensive. On the soccer field, the shouts and groans along the sidelines may cause an inexperienced referee to doubt herself, come to believe that the cruel things people are saying about her are all too true, and make her start thinking:

- Did I miss that offside call that everyone is screaming about?

- Everybody else thought that was a push! What's wrong with me that I didn't see it?

- No matter what I do, everyone is still angry. Maybe they're right...maybe I really don't belong out here.

Soccer is a game of joy and passion. Unfortunately, passion sometimes leads the crowd to blame the referees for everything that goes wrong on the field. But since everyone else is watching the ball, they don't always see what the officials see. Even when they do, they often confuse the "right" call with the one that favors their own team. As disheartening this may be to referees, it is simply a reflection of human nature. Soccer is a game played, watched, and officiated by people, and we cannot avoid our common reactions to disappointment or frustration.

When things are falling apart, human beings often blame whoever is at hand for whatever is going wrong. Teenagers blame their parents; husbands blame their wives; bosses blame their secretaries. and at the end of the day, the secretary may go home and take it out on the cat. You should not take it personally when the crowd shows their disappointment over an unlucky break, or when their favorite team is struggling on the field. Many times, they are simply looking for someone to blame. If their lack of sportsmanship leads them to direct their disappointment at you, it is probably nothing personal. All they see is a uniform; they do not see the person inside it. If they did, they would do a better job of behaving themselves.

Rule #2:

Remember that no matter how isolated you feel, you are not alone.

It can be very lonely in the middle of the field, or running along a sideline filled with coaches and spectators. You may come to feel that everyone is watching you, and if things start going badly you may start thinking that there is nothing to keep them from starting a riot. If you do, take a deep breath and consider:

- Not everyone is a barbarian. If things get ugly, there will be plenty of good people there to assist you, including your fellow referees.

- Organized soccer takes referee abuse very seriously. There are dire consequences for those who verbally abuse or physically threaten a referee.

- Many states have laws protecting sports officials, and the police are only a phone call away.

- All you have to do to protect yourself is to keep calm, take names or numbers, and remember to file a report. Your state soccer association will take it from there.

Rule #3:

Keeping your sense of humor can go a long way toward relieving stress.

If you can relax enough not to feel threatened, you will find that many of the complaints you hear being loudly directed your way at the soccer field are really quite funny. Hearing spectators try to describe the offside rule can be the best antidote to a case of pre-game jitters that anyone can prescribe. And the first time you hear someone demand that the referee "call it both ways" after the first foul of the match, you may realize that most of the yelling at a soccer game is the product of ignorance. While it would be impolite to laugh out loud when a spectator makes a fool of himself, no book of etiquette would begrudge you a quiet smile, or prevent you from sharing what you have heard with your colleagues.

Rule #4:

Soccer, like life, can be a thing of joy and beauty...so try to relax, don't be afraid to smile, and have fun on the field.

Soccer is loved throughout the world because it is a game of beauty as well as athleticism. Watching a star striker execute a bicycle kick, seeing a keeper flying through the air to make an impossible save, or following the battles between attackers and defenders is what keeps fans and partisans cheering and groaning throughout the match, and always coming back for more.

As a referee, you have the best view of the action imaginable. You get to run around the field, sharing the game with an intimacy and intensity that nobody else can match, and sharing the victories and setbacks side-by-side with the players. You must never allow your enthusiasm or admiration for the skills you see color your judgment on the field. That does not mean that you cannot enjoy watching the show unfold.

Rule #5

To be a success, you will have better luck by solving problems rather than by creating them.

Law 18, the unwritten Rule of Common Sense, is a large tool in the successful referee's kit. It begins with the premise that the game is for the players, includes the realization that there are many ways to solve a problem, and ends with the realization that the referee who insists on making everybody mad is digging himself a very deep hole.

We are at the field to ensure a safe, fair, and enjoyable contest within the appropriate rules, and our sport gives us wide discretion in handling and resolving problems as they arise. If something is not exactly against the rules, and nobody is complaining, the wise referee will simply let it go. We will have enough problems simply officiating the match. We do not have to create any more of them simply to remind everyone that we have a badge and whistle. And if there are two legitimate ways to solve a problem—one which will make people angry, and another which will leave everyone satisfied—only a fool would insist on making things needlessly difficult.

Recognizing that racing toward avoidable trouble is not a path to success in any field leads us to two important corollaries, which also fall within Law 18:

- *Intelligence is not the same thing as wisdom.*

- *Knowing that you are right is more important than making everyone else admit it.*

A referee should be more interested in getting people to behave on the soccer field than in impressing people with mastery over the most arcane aspects of the rules.

Rule #6:
You cannot get out of a hole until you stop digging.

In times of stress it is easy to lose our focus and start reacting out of anger, frustration, or instinct.

As referees, surrounded by twenty-two other people—not including what sometimes sounds like a clamorous mob along the sidelines—we will often feel the need simply to dig in our heels and continue whatever we are doing. We do not, after all, want to seem weak, or appear influenced by the complaints of others. Courage is a necessary trait of a referee; stubbornness, however, is not. And as the captain of the *Titanic* discovered, sometimes it is better to change course than to continue rushing headlong toward disaster.

You should never change a call merely because somebody complains. You should, however, be open to the possibility that you are the one who should adjust to the situation around you, rather than insisting that the rest of the world change because you, after all, have a whistle.

- If you make a mistake, you should have the integrity to correct it if you can. If unsure of yourself, your colleagues on the sidelines may help you decide if your actions are well-considered, or whether you would be wise to consider a mid-course correction.

- If a player or coach complains that you are calling the game too loosely, or too tightly, you are under no obligation to change and may be within your rights to issue a caution for dissent. But if *everyone* around you seems angry and frustrated, you may want to consider the wisdom of a change in your approach to the particular game.

- Strength in the face of adversity can be a sign of courage and integrity. Persistence despite clear signs that you have made a mistake may be equally courageous, but is usually described as pig-headedness.

Rule #7:

When surrounded by flames, do not apply gasoline.

Humans, being proud creatures, are often stubborn when provoked. Some of us—men in particular, although women are not immune from the need to save face or the urge to have the last word in an argument—will simply refuse to back down under pressure no matter how foolish or mistaken we may be. A referee who cannot resist the temptation toward "one-upmanship," however, may keep escalating an incident until it blows up in his face.

On the highway, a game of "chicken" rarely leads to anything but disaster. We should not be surprised to see the same thing happen on the pitch. Remember that you hold all the cards and have all the power on the soccer field. It costs you nothing simply to walk away from a disagreement, and letting someone else have the "last word" is often a good way of letting a coach or player begin to cool off.

Rule #8

When you smell gas, don't light a match.

There will be times in your career when you will sense the tension building around you. Late in a close match, for example, the players may become frantic trying to score. When a game is being played for a divisional title, or between two arch-rivals, tempers often rise at the field for reasons unrelated to anything the officials might be doing. Or perhaps a nasty tackle, or a controversial call at a critical moment of the game, will cause people to lose their focus on the match and lead them to focus on the referee instead.

Whatever the cause, the temper of a match often ebbs and flows quite naturally. Usually, the game itself leads everyone to forget what happened five minutes ago, as they concentrate on whatever is happening at the moment. Be careful, during those times of stress, that you do nothing to heighten already-high emotions or aggravate feelings of anger or disappointment. Often, just keeping the game flowing is all you need to do, but you should always try to avoid making things worse by thoughtless actions or comments.

This does not mean that you should be afraid do your duties on the field, or that you should adjust your calls to suit whichever team is making the biggest fuss. But since you are there to solve problems, whenever possible you should try to calm tempers, and not inflame them.

Basic Equipment

Before your first game, you will need to assemble a referee kit. Most of your basic equipment will be available at your local soccer store, and you can find anything that is not is available locally through a number of catalogs or online suppliers. The checklist at the end of this chapter should be a good starting point for any beginning referee.

While equipment can get quite expensive, the beginning referee has no real need for multiple jerseys or four different kinds of cleats. A set of flags, proper socks, a whistle, and a proper jersey and shorts are all that is really needed. Most soccer players already have a set of black cleats, and any pair of black shorts will do for the beginner. Other equipment—paper and pen to record events occurring during the game, and a watch to keep track of time—are available in any number of places, including the utility drawer of most kitchens. In fact, you can probably adapt much of what you need from things you already have at home.

In any event, your referee kit should contain the following, which you should bring to every game:

- A full uniform, including a jersey, black shorts, referee socks, and shoes.

- Two whistles, each with a different pitch.

- A notebook, and pen or pencil.

- Assistant referee or "Linesman" flags.

- A set of red and yellow cards.

- Change for a five-dollar bill.

You should also get into the habit of taking a spare referee kit with you every time you go to a soccer field. Like the family doctor, you never know when you will be needed.

Assignors

Generally speaking, the Law regards referees as independent contractors, much like a babysitter, or the kid who cuts the grass. A benefit of this is the freedom to accept or decline assignments. The downside is that because assignments do not grow on trees, you must arrange for them on your own.

Most leagues or soccer clubs, as well as some referee associations, have someone designated as a "referee assignor," whose job is to give officials their assignments. Some assignors are paid, and some are volunteers, but they all have to stretch their limited resources to cover the games that are their responsibility. Most will balance assignments among their officials, and all do their best to match the game with the appropriate officials.

Before you can receive an assignment, however, the assignor must know that you are qualified and available. Many state associations have websites that can link officials with area assignors. In other parts of the country, you will have to contact them by mail or telephone to let them know that you would like to work for them. In many areas, the assignor will be a senior referee, who can serve as a mentor and confidante as well as a scheduler. In all parts of the country, though, the assignor will need to know about problems and conflicts you may have with any team, and is among the people you should contact in the event of trouble on the field.

Assignors try to be professional about their duties and expect their referees to act professionally as well. This means, among other things:

- When you accept an assignment, they will expect you to keep it.

- When you decline an assignment, they will expect you to do so promptly.

- If circumstances change, and you must turn back a game that you have already accepted, they will expect you to do so in a timely manner—which will not, except in the case of death, natural disaster, or similar type of dire emergency, be the night before—or the day of—the match.

- They will appreciate it if you keep them apprised of changes in your personal schedule or availability, since their duties do not end once the games begin, and they will be juggling schedules and referees for the entire season.

- And lastly, they will remember people who help them out of tight spots...as well as those who cause them.

Assignors will also help ambitious referees gain experience as they advance through the ranks. Referees comfortable with their present level of officiating, who want to push their own limits, should let their assignors know. There are always more challenges for the adventuresome referee who wants to keep improving.

Appearance and Deportment

While it is unwise to judge a book by its cover, the fact remains that people will begin to size up a referee from the moment they see him. This means that the first thing they will notice about you when you arrive at the field will be your appearance.

Referees should arrive at the field in a timely manner. You should show up at least thirty minutes before the start of the match, appropriately dressed and conducting yourself in a professional manner. While the professional game demands a stricter dress code (and even gives the referees their own dressing room), officials working at amateur or youth levels of play have no official pre-game guidelines. This does not mean that you should not do your best to look professional.

- A warmup or jogging outfit will always be acceptable upon arrival. Predominantly black clothing usually works best.

- Because we do not always know the team colors ahead of time, it is best to bring alternate jerseys to the field and decide which uniform to wear upon arrival. Younger officials, and those who cannot afford alternate jerseys, should at least have a different colored shirt available in case it is needed to avoid a conflict with the teams.

- If possible, referees should enter and leave the area as a team.

- Ideally, the referee crew will wear different-colored uniforms than either team, and either goalkeeper. If a conflict is unavoidable, the crew should choose the alternative that minimizes any confusion on the field.

- The referee makes the final decision on jersey conflicts between the teams. The League, or other competition authorities, may have their own priorities, however, such as directing that one side or the other change to an alternate jersey. If so, you should follow whatever rules are in force.

- Referees should, however, take care not to manufacture problems. Where practical, it is more helpful for the officials, rather than the players, to change uniforms.

- You should always strive to be neatly and professionally dressed. This means a proper uniform, with socks pulled up, shirt tucked in, and a current referee badge.

- Concessions made to inclement weather are at the discretion of the match referee. The higher the level of play, however, the fewer such liberties are allowed for the officials, as well as the players.

Your attitude upon arriving at the field also says a lot about how you approach your duties and will affect how the participants perceive you. A helpful, professional, and approachable attitude will usually serve you much better than an air of officiousness or superiority. Maintaining this attitude throughout the match, though sometimes difficult, is usually more beneficial to officials and participants alike.

Your First Games

Having purchased your equipment, and having your assignment in hand, you are now ready to go to the field to begin your career as a soccer referee. If you are like most people, at this moment you will start struggling with two questions that, surprisingly enough, you have never considered before:

- What in God's name was I thinking when I got myself into this?

- What in the world am I supposed to do when I get to the field?

Nerves

Nervousness is a common and expected human reaction to the unknown. Since you are new to officiating and don't know what to expect when you step on the field, you should not be surprised if you have a case of jitters or an attack of self-doubt. After all, even if you have played the game yourself, officiating is quite different than playing. You will be watching unfamiliar things and making split-second decisions under a new kind of pressure, which means that your finely honed competitive instincts will need some adjustment. And you may very well have heard stories about the lunatics at the field and be wondering if they are true. However uncomfortable you feel walking onto the field for the first time as an official, you will find that most of what you fear is not worth the worry:

- You will, most likely, be doing a lower-level, non-competitive match for which your training, however incomplete it might be, is probably sufficient.

- You may feel awkward and uncomfortable moving about the field, but this is perfectly natural.

- You may have a tendency to freeze, trying to recall the rule that applies or wondering if you saw the play correctly. This, too, is common.

- You may find yourself questioning your judgment and your senses. This, is also very common.

Remember that this is all new to you, and there is no reason why you should not feel uncomfortable. Experience does not, unfortunately, come without the bother of actually living through it, and every referee must start somewhere. If you are fortunate, everything will go well: you and the rest of your crew will have performed admirably (or, at least, nobody else will have noticed your blunders), and you will emerge from the game with increased confidence. If you are less fortunate, you will make some obvious mistakes, which some of the less civilized people along the sidelines may choose not to let pass without comment.

In either case, the sun will still rise the next day; your family will still love you; and there will be another game and another chance to learn. You will live through the experience. And, if you keep at it, this will be only the first of many similar experiences to come.

Oddly enough, as you gain experience and continue to grow as an official, you may come to find that you still become slightly anxious before a challenging match. By then, you will identify this as anticipation, rather than nerves, and it will not keep you from looking forward to the game. And you may be surprised to discover that you still kick yourself for making mistakes. If you learn your lessons, they will be different mistakes, but the real difference between a beginning referee and a skilled and experienced one is not that the veteran makes no mistakes. Rather, the veteran's mistakes simply pass unnoticed by most, since he makes the kinds of mistakes that only other veterans can detect.

When you get to the field

At a soccer field, everyone expects the referee to know precisely what to do at all times, and to be intimately familiar with the competition's etiquette and protocol. This can be intimidating for the new referee, who may very well know what a player or coach is supposed to be doing before the game, but never paid much attention to the referees until the game was about to start.

Customs and traditions may vary in different parts of the country and even from league-to-league or club-to-club, but in all cases, there are some duties that a referee needs to fulfil. Until you are comfortable within your own soccer community, here are some basic pre-game guidelines that you may find useful:

The Parking Lot

The referee's authority begins when he (or she) arrives at the game site, and continues until the official leaves at the end of the game. As a rule, for most games you should arrive at least thirty minutes before the scheduled kick-off.

Younger referees being driven to the field should have their parents (or whoever is providing a ride) wait at least until the game is confirmed. On occasion, a befuddled assignor may over-book the officials, or the club may double-book a field. You do not want to be stranded at the field, and unless you are within walking distance of home or rode your own bicycle to the field, you may want to double-check your assignment before your ride leaves you there.

Older referees who are adventurous enough to accept adult men's games should remember to park their cars facing *outward*...just in case.

The Field

Because it is the referee who determines whether the field is safe and conforms to the Laws of the Game, one of your first duties at the field will be to conduct an inspection of the grounds.

Ideally, by coming to the field thirty minutes early, you will have arrived early enough to conduct a thorough inspection of the grounds. This means walking or jogging[*] around the field, noting the condition of both

---

[*] Many officials take the opportunity to kill two birds with the same stone, and will conduct their field inspection by jogging around the field once or twice as a way of warming up.

goal areas and all field markings (and noticing whether they are authorized or illegal), checking both nets, and noticing any wet or low spots as well as anything else that seems out of the ordinary. You will be able to oversee corrections of any and all deficiencies by game time, and the match will proceed—on schedule, and in accordance with all aspects of Law 1.

As a practical matter, many fields serve as the venue for multiple games on a given day, and during a typical weekend in mid-season the demands of a fixed schedule will leave us pressed for time. While you should try to ensure that every aspect of the field is in accordance with the Laws, there will be times when this will be impossible. For example, a groundskeeper may not be available to remark the field; the team's corner flags may be locked in the trunk of the assistant coach—who is presently driving to Toronto on a business trip; and except at the professional level, it is unrealistic to expect goal posts that are two inches too low to be repaired by game time.

If a defect in the field can be corrected, it is your job to see that someone corrects it, even if it delays the start of the match for a short period of time. If it cannot be corrected within a reasonable period of time, you need to decide whether the deficiency presents an issue of safety. If it does, then the match cannot proceed; if it does not, then you should simply note the problem on your game report and let the game begin.

A Word on Playability

Weather conditions often affect field conditions, both before and during the game.

Until game time, conditions relating to field playability are the prerogative of the local authorities. The local recreation department may close the field due to flooding, for instance, or in less-competitive leagues, the local clubs may decide to reschedule a match that is scheduled for a soggy field. When that happens, they are supposed to notify the officials, who are freed from further responsibilities for the match.

Once game time arrives, and you are at the field, the playability of the field becomes *your* responsibility as the match official. While nobody wants to cancel a game when both teams are ready and willing to play, you must assess the condition of the field to determine whether it poses a safety risk or hazard to the players. If it does, then you must decline to officiate the match.

While there are no firm rules to guide you, many factors can help you make your decision:

- How much standing water is there, and in which parts of the field?

- Is any standing water deep enough to stop the ball, possibly turning the match from a game of skill into a farce?

- Will the ball bounce, if dropped from shoulder-height?

- Are there muddy areas on the field which are too slick to run through safely?

- Are either or both of the penalty areas—and in particular, the goal-mouths—too muddy to permit safe play?

- Is it likely that the field can be made playable by available means, such as adding some sand or trying to drain the water?

The Crowd

The rules of some competitions direct that the teams and spectators take different sides of the field. Other competitions put the teams on opposite sides and direct that spectators stay on the same side as their team. Still others array the fans in bleachers or grandstands, some distance away from the pitch.

All approaches have logic to them. Some make substitutions easier, and spare the coaches the problem of directing their team with two dozen would-be assistants looking over their shoulder. Others place a premium on teams controlling their own fans, making it easier for the referee to hold each team responsible for the behavior of its supporters.

In the end, it does not really matter what your local league does in this regard, as long as you know which practice to follow. In the cosmic scheme of things, the Universe does not care whether we drive on the left side of the road (as in England) or the right (as almost everywhere else), so long as everyone in the same place follows the same rule. Similarly, soccer does not care where everyone at the field is sitting—as long as everyone agrees.

The Players

At all levels of play, the referee is responsible for making sure that the players are properly equipped and wearing nothing that might pose a danger to themselves or anyone else. Mandatory equipment includes an appropriate uniform, shin guards, and shoes; forbidden equipment will include jewelry, and anything that the referee determines to be potentially dangerous.

At some point before the game begins, the match referee will need to make sure that the players and their equipment comply with Law IV, and to see if there will be enough players under Law III to let the match begin. Many officials conduct a "lineup" style inspection, standing the players in a row where their equipment is visible, and checking off the players against the team roster. Some teams even come to expect this sort of check-in, and the coach may start lining up the players when the officials draw near. This is not mandatory, however, and a referee who conducts the pre-game inspection without interfering with the team's warm-ups—walking among the players, unobtrusively noting their numbers and observing whether their equipment is acceptable—may find that he has pleasantly surprised everyone with his thoughtfulness. Whether or not this leads to similar civility once play begins, it is unlikely to get things off on the wrong foot.

At some levels of play, check-ins are informal and relaxed. House teams, particularly involving very young players, may not even keep score. For these games the referee's job can be a simple one: make sure the players are properly equipped, and help them have fun. Here, uniforms may consist of nothing more than similar T-shirts and the keeper's jersey may reach nearly to the ankles. Other, more competitive levels of play require greater levels of oversight and formality. Pass cards are often required, and the referee must document the players present or absent, in order to comply with league rules concerning eligibility and disciplinary sanctions for misconduct.

Whatever the level of play, you should adjust to the needs of the game and be as informal, or as meticulous, as circumstances require:

- If the match is an in-house game that will not report a result, you should nevertheless make an official report of any noteworthy incident that may occur.

- If the match is part of a competition requiring pass cards, you should check the cards against the roster. If the league wants you to turn in the pass card of any player who is sent off for a misconduct, you should retain the cards until the end of the match. If not, wise officials usually return the cards to the respective teams once they are checked-in. You do not, after all, want to force a coach to come looking for you the day after you have walked away with his team's pass cards.

Many referees find it useful to introduce themselves and their crew to the teams or their respective captains before the game. This helps establish a rapport with the players and may even permit a civil word or two before the match begins. It is often easier to keep a match under control if the participants see you as a human being, rather than just a uniform.

It is also customary for some referees, particularly beginners, to give a thorough briefing to both teams detailing what will and will not be allowed on the pitch. Generally speaking, this is not a wise thing to do. Invariably, something unexpected will happen on the field, or you will miss something that everyone else has seen, and you are likely to find your words coming back to haunt you. It is, after all, well and good to make a point of protecting the keeper from foul play, but informing the teams that you will be doing so will not spare you grief if the keeper bobbles the ball and a goal scores from the ensuing scramble in the goal mouth. It only gives the unlucky keeper's team someone to blame for the goal, and that someone will be you. Beyond this, however, before the game the players will be concentrating on getting ready for the match and unlikely to listen to anything you have to say. Unless there is a particular reason to do so—a potentially confusing change in the rules, for example, that may have an effect on play[*]—you are usually better off simply wishing them luck and calling for captains as soon as you are ready.

Unless you have already done so, the pre-game player inspection and check-in is the time for you to get the team rosters and game reports from the respective teams. You will also have to make sure that the team uniforms will not conflict, or cause confusion on the field.

This is also a good time to get the ball from the home team.

---

[*] An example of this occurred in 1992, when the "backpass" rule was changed to combat time-wasting, preventing the keeper from handling a ball deliberately kicked to him by a teammate.

In addition to the rule changes, differences in seasonal calendars and referee training schedules will occasionally delay implementation of rules from league-to-league, or country-to-country. In these situations, a pre-game clarification by the referee may help prevent needless trouble from arising during the match.

The Ball

The home team provides the ball for each game, and the referee must make sure that it is the correct size for the players, not lop-sided or defective, and inflated to a proper pressure. In most circumstances—but especially at fields adjacent to woods, cow pastures, golf courses, or fenced back yards—it is a good idea to have another ball or two in reserve, to keep the game rolling merrily along when someone kicks the ball into the next county.

Some referees use a pressure gauge when they inspect the ball, to ensure that it is inflated to the proper specifications. Others will simply use the "touch and feel" method. In either case, experienced officials often adjust the ball pressure to accommodate field conditions, increasing the pressure on a soggy field, decreasing it slightly when the field takes on the characteristics of sun-baked concrete. Whatever method you use, someone will probably complain about the ball, claiming that it is either too soft or too hard. When that happens, you are free to keep it, since you know that it is perfectly fine, or replace it, if you think that doing so will make everyone happy. Whatever you decide, you should at least take the time to recheck the ball, if only to be polite.

The Game Report

Most leagues have an official form that teams give to the officials before the game begins. Listed on the form will be the date, the field, the scheduled start time for the match, the teams playing, and the team rosters. There will also be places to record the officials present, the score of the match, goals scored, and a place to enter any misconducts or other noteworthy events that arise during the game, such as injuries or weather-related stoppages. Sometimes, the information will be listed on a single piece of paper; other times, each team will provide a separate report. Most often, there will be a place to indicate which players are present, and which are not playing. This can be very important, since misconducts can result in disciplinary action against a coach or player, and a team may need to document that a suspended player actually served his suspension.

Before the match begins, you will have to collect the appropriate game reports and record any pre-game information needed. You will need to note all goals and misconducts issued during the game, and transfer the information to the report when the match is over. Then, after checking the report for accuracy, you and the coaches should all sign the report and distribute copies according to the League's rules.

Some leagues prefer that the referee turn in the report. If so, the home team usually provides an envelope for mailing the documents to the League Office. Other leagues entrust the winning coach or, in case of a tie, the home team, with the responsibility for doing so. In any case the teams, and usually the referee, will receive a copy of the report for their records. Many competitive leagues that require pass cards instruct the match officials to withhold the cards of any players sent off during the game, and to forward the card to the league along with the game report. Be sure that you know your local league's rules and preferences *before* the match begins. You do not want to be in the position of trying to retrieve a pass card from a team who has just had their star player sent off.

The Crew

Each official should arrive at the field at least thirty minutes before game time. This allows the official to warm up before the game—a ritual often neglected by the young, which takes on added importance as the years slip by. It also gives the crew a chance to get acquainted, conduct a thorough pre-game conference, inspect the field as a team, and tune to the same wave-length for the upcoming game. Try to choose a secluded spot, away from players and spectators, where you can have a bit of privacy to discuss the game. A similar conference usually takes place at half-time, to discuss issues that arose during the first half and expectations for the rest of the match, and at game's-end, which can occur on- or off-site, depending upon the preferences of the officials.

Ideally, the whole crew should enter and leave together, as a team. As a practical matter, officials in amateur soccer do not always make this easy, sometimes arriving just before, or just after, the kickoff. You should take it upon yourself always to arrive in plenty of time, at least 30 minutes before game time, ready to begin your duties. Do not let the sloppy habits of others tempt you to cut corners yourself. The pre-game conference is an important time for the crew to get to know one another, and develop a common understanding about how they will be handling the game. This is impossible to do if one or more of the officials is late.

The Money

Game fees vary from league-to-league and state-to-state. In some leagues the home team pays the entire game fee, while in others the teams split the cost of the officials. To prevent needless disagreements from getting the game off to a bad start, it is best to sort out such details before you get to the field. Having the appropriate fee schedules and distribution in writing can often settle any disputes before they become problems.

One thing remains a constant for all officials, everywhere, across the country. Unless you will be paid later by the people who arranged for your appointment, *be sure to get paid before starting the game.* You do not want to be in the position of asking for money, hat in hand, from a coach who blames you for the outcome of the game.

It is the referee's responsibility to make sure that the game fee is distributed properly among the officials. Adults and more experienced officials should ensure that the younger referees receive their fair share before taking care of themselves.

The Coin Toss

Before the game begins, you will need to conduct a coin toss to see which team will be kicking off. The team losing the coin toss will kick off to start the match. The team winning the coin toss will get the choice of sides and will kick off to start the second half.

The coin toss need not be a drawn-out ritual, and you can use any coin. You are free to catch it in the air, or let it fall to the ground. Just be sure that the coin you use is big enough to find in the grass.

Traditionally, the entire referee crew participates in the coin toss at or near midfield, along with the captains from both teams. In practice—particularly at adult games, where most players arrive right at game time and things can be quite chaotic as the kick-off nears—the referee may conduct the coin toss while the rest of the crew is busy herding the teams together to start the match. The referee should remember to make a note of which side takes the opening kick-off, so that the right team gets the ball to start the second half. If you forget, just remember that the second half kick-off will go in the same direction as it did to start the game.

The Kick-off

Once the crew is prepared, the field is deemed adequate, and the players are ready, then it is time to start the match.

If the coin toss occurs just before kick-off, the officials will already be assembled in the center circle. If the coin toss occurred ahead of time, the officials should walk as a group to the middle of the field. It is customary for the crew to shake hands and wish each other luck. Then, the assistant referees move off to check the nets before taking their position on either sideline, while the referee waits patiently in or near the center circle.

After making sure that the players are all on the proper side of the field, the referee should hand the ball to a player from the team that lost the coin toss. That player will place the ball in the middle of the center circle. You should be sure that each player on the opposing team is at least ten yards away (which, you will recall from your basic referee class, is the diameter of the center circle), and check to make sure that the assistant referees are ready. When one side has the correct number of players and the keeper is ready, the assistant referee will unfurl the flag to show that there is nothing to prevent things from getting underway. When both assistant referees signal that their side of the field is prepared for kick-off, then the game is ready to begin. Blow your whistle, remember to start the clock, and try to have fun.

Half-time

When the first half ends, the referee (or one of the assistants) should collect the ball, the assistant referees should furl their flags, and the officials should assemble in the middle of the field. You should then go to wherever you have stored your equipment— ideally, a place offering both shade and a bit of privacy—where you can rest, have some water, and discuss the events of the first half. This also lets you make adjustments for the second half of the match.

Half-time usually lasts about ten minutes. Younger players, who are often refreshed in a heart-beat, are often ready to start the second half well before the officials.

At the end of half-time, the teams switch sides and the game resumes with another kick-off.

After the Game

Once the game is over, the officials still have work to do before their job is done. They must gather and return the game ball, then fill out and distribute the game reports, and return any collected pass cards to the respective teams.

Usually, the official nearest to the ball will run to fetch it before joining the other officials in the middle of the field. Typically, they all walk to their area of the game site to help the referee fill out the report. Goals and cards for misconduct must be recorded, and the result of the match needs to be reported. Typically, all send-offs require an explanation, to help the League determine the appropriate sanction. These explanations need not be long, but they must be objective and specific enough to convey the nature and circumstances of the offense. The officials, and a representative of each team, will then sign the form, and copies are dispersed according to the league rules. And then, unless there is another game to do, the officials are free to leave. Officials should always try to leave the field together, however. It not only looks more professional; it sometimes helps prevent trouble.

Different Levels of Play

It will not take long before you notice a substantial disparity in the playing styles and skill-levels of the players. The level of play will often determine how you should officiate the match, as well as how you interact with the participants.

Recreational games are played mostly for fun. At this level, problems with players will be few and far between, usually involving either competitive players who are "playing down" and insist on showing off, or refugees from other sports where the players crash into each other.* Spectators and players alike are generally well intentioned but often quite ignorant about the game. On occasion, ignorance and bad manners will merge, creating Fans from Hell— who, unfortunately, sometimes roam in packs. In most cases, the referee's authority will go unchallenged because nobody else knows the rules, coaches and players included. Exceptions are handballs (on which everyone is an expert) and, every once in a while, the six-second rule (since everyone can count). From the referee's perspective, fouls at this level are often clumsy, but rarely malicious; from the perspective of the players and most spectators, fouls occur whenever someone falls down.

Open, or Select games involve players who are more skilled, and games that are more intensely competitive than those at the recreational level. Players at this level and beyond generally try out for positions on their

---

* Hockey or American football come readily to mind.

teams and often travel a considerable distance for a competitive match. Players and spectators are usually more sophisticated about the game and may challenge the referee who seems to lack confidence or exhibits an occasional unfamiliarity with the rules (which everybody knows perfectly, even though few have actually read them). Physical play ranges from gentle to very rough, and games at this level of play will sometimes get quite nasty.

Premier games are intensely competitive, for the players as well as the officials. At this level of play the participants—players, coaches, and many spectators—are often highly sophisticated about the game. A number of them will be referees themselves, although some may occasionally let their emotions interfere with their otherwise sound judgment. While the games are challenging and exciting, officiating at this level is not for the faint of heart, and the new referee who tries to do so is likely to find his head spinning and his confidence sinking to new lows. On the other hand, the participants are usually knowledgeable enough to appreciate a well-officiated match. Most, but not all, premier-level players dislike rough or reckless play, preferring to win by skill rather than brute force, and even strong, physical teams will be disciplined and well-controlled in their contests for the ball. At times, however, the intensity of the matches will induce some players to seek an unfair advantage when they can, and "diving" can be rampant, especially if the players sense that they have a referee who is easily fooled.

Ages of the players can range from small children all the way up to adults, and some states have senior leagues for players in their 60s and beyond. Referees should try to calibrate their officiating to match the skill- and age-level of the players. Younger children are usually more interested in having fun than in winning and are unlikely to commit dangerous fouls or to fake injuries. Teenagers may need a firmer hand. And adults, especially adult men, can get out of hand quickly if the referee appears to be weak, but usually respond well to firm guidance so long as the officials seem to be trying their best. There will remain, however, similar distinctions among the three principal levels of play. Youth games at the premier level will be taken very seriously; recreational games at the adult level are usually played for fun. At any level, however, the players will not be happy if we do not take our job seriously.

Gender differences are the subject of debate among referees and others. While generalizations are often inaccurate, and the spread of women's soccer is calling many old assumptions into question, there appear to be marked differences between the games played by men and boys as compared to women and girls. While there will be wide differences between individual teams and players, as a group these distinctions seem to remain the same within comparable levels of play.

- While both sexes can be equally skilled, and their games can be equally intense, men are physically stronger, and their play tends to be faster and more physical. At the youth level, boys' games tend to be faster-paced, with more rough-housing, than girls' games.

- At all levels, males tend to cause more on-field trouble than females. On the other hand, they also tend to be more predictable—at least to the typical male referee.

A man, or older boy, who is hacked may come to his feet looking for revenge, and the referee will be alert to signs of trouble. By and large, though, the demands of an on-going game are often (though not invariably) a major distraction to him, and if a few minutes pass without retaliation he may very well forget which player hacked him as his mind returns to the game.

A woman, on the other hand, will get just as angry during the game, but the referee—especially a male referee, who may be looking for a typically male response to a nasty foul—can be misled if she does not rise to confront the source and may relax if she does not avenge herself at once. It is possible that she may not strike back at all, deeming retaliation to be the mark of a barbarian. It is also possible that, being an intelligent player, she has no intention of getting even when everyone is watching her, and will wait until the next run of play...or the next half...or the following week...or the following season...before exacting her revenge.

In this situation, a referee wishing to prevent trouble might consider having a quiet word with the player during a subsequent stoppage, commenting on the foul, asking if it still hurts, and promising to keep an eye on things for her (and, by inference, on her as well). This may be enough to keep her from striking back, at least during the one match. After that, it will be some other referee's problem.

Co-ed soccer games, though relatively new, present interesting challenges to the referee, whether veteran or rookie. Since many of the games are played at lower levels of intensity and skill, beginning referees often find themselves asked to officiate at these matches.

On the soccer field, as often in Life, the presence of women tends to exert a civilizing effect on the men around them. Generally, co-ed games are recreational in nature, and are played in a low-keyed environment in which the players are intent mostly on having fun.

There are, however, traps for the unwary referee, even in such otherwise peaceful matches. Most male players tend to shy away from tough physical challenges against female opponents, either for reasons of chivalry or because most referees tend to whistle them for fouls if they do not. In many cases, the reason for this is simple self-preservation by the referee. As a general rule, the quickest way for a co-ed match to get out of hand is for the men from one team to start bullying the other team's female players. If, rightly or wrongly, this is the perception on the field, their opponents—who will usually refrain from targeting the other team's women—will retaliate directly against the fouling team's men, usually (though not always) against the players who are causing the trouble. Once this happens, things can quickly get out of hand, which is why some referees will avoid the problem altogether by calling fouls very tightly, and sometimes unfairly, against the men.

This does not, of course, address the other source of occasional tension on a co-ed soccer field, namely the tendency of some men to hog the ball, rather than passing it to female players on their own team. This, however, is a problem that the referee is powerless to address.

Mentors, and more experienced officials

Assignors will usually try to pair inexperienced officials with veteran referees. This lets the newcomer benefit from the experience of others and affords a measure of protection during his early days as a referee.

Most experienced officials are proud and flattered to share their experiences with newer ones. Some soccer clubs have established "mentor programs" to help new or younger officials to learn their craft, and many state or local associations sponsor clinics or training programs to pass along information, techniques, and useful tips. The new referee should take advantage of these resources whenever the chance arises.

Advancing as an Official

As you gain experience as a referee, you will find that opportunities abound for those with the drive, energy, and dedication to develop their skills as officials. Some of these opportunities require years of training and a bit of luck. Others are close at hand, and need only a phone call or a few hours of your time.

Training—Formal and Informal

As a certified soccer official, you have already had a basic level of classroom training in order to obtain your badge. You will have to complete additional class work yearly in order to retain your certification. Some soccer clubs will also offer informal clinics for officials to hone their skills on the field.

As a referee, the best thing you can do to further your education is to immerse yourself in the game. Read as much as you can about the game's history and traditions, and watch as much soccer as you can find—whether at the pitch, at the stadium, or on television. Soccer is a dynamic sport in which the action is non-stop, and many decisions you need to make as a referee will involve observing and interpreting the ever-changing actions of the players. Without a thorough understanding of the way the game is played, you will be at a disadvantage when called upon to evaluate a player's actions on the field. And the more familiar you are with tactics, styles of play, and what is and is not generally accepted on the pitch, the more effective you will be as a referee.

In addition, you should view each game as a chance to learn. If paired with a good official as a crewmate, you can learn what others do to excel and get ideas for handling your own matches; if paired with a poor one, you can learn what doesn't work, and learn what to avoid. Mentors, and other senior officials, can also prove to be an invaluable resource for you.

Assessors

Each state runs its own program to teach, develop, and assess officials. Some programs are formalized and rigid, others are relaxed and less structured. In all cases, the assessor is charged with teaching proper mechanics, determining when an referee is ready for advancement, and helping officials reach their highest potential as referees. Unfortunately, some officials come to regard a visit from the assessor as no more welcome than a trip to the dentist, or a routine proctology examination.

As with every craft, there is an art to assessing, and some people are better at it than others. While a few assessors view their job as one of finding fault and deem tact to be a needless distraction, the vast majority are sympathetic and only want to help. All assessors can offer constructive criticism to the referee willing to listen, but some have a tendency to make referees behave differently, and some referees will start officiating not for the players, but to impress the man (or woman) with the clipboard. This not only undermines the very reason for the assessment, but can poison a relationship that should be more like mentor and student, and less like adversaries. As a result, there are two things to remember when dealing with an assessor:

(1) The assessor is always right; and

(2) If the assessor seems to be mistaken, unhelpful, or strikes you as an idiot, remember Rule Number 1—then take a deep breath, talk to a senior referee that you trust, and don't get discouraged.

Assessors can be one of your best resources as you learn the art of officiating. A poor assessor may only have criticism to offer you, but a good assessor will teach, and a great assessor can inspire.

Formal Advancement
All governing bodies have their own career pathways for soccer officials. The United States Soccer Foundation and American Youth Soccer Organization, for example, both have several grades of officials, each with its own age and experience requirements. Referees who advance through the ranks gain valuable experience during the process of upgrading, and get the chance to be assessed by more experienced officials.

Referees interested in formal upgrades should contact their local referee organizations. Presently, referees working within the United States Soccer Federation can start doing so at age 17, as long as they have the necessary game experience to begin the process.

Sample Game Report

Local Soccer League

Game Report   For_____

Date: _____ Game Start Time: _____   Field Location: _____

Home Team: _____   Colors: Shirt: _____ Shorts: _____

Visiting Team: _____   Colors: Shirt: _____ Shorts: _____

Team Name: _____   Manager: _____

Referee: _____   Referee Asst. 1: _____

Referee Asst. 2: _____   *Home teams call in the score to Division Commissioners within 24 hrs.*

Num.	First Name	Last Name	Goal	Yellow	Red	Infractions

Suspended Players:

First Name	Last Name	Date Beginning	Date Ending	ID Number

Referee Comments: _____

_____

Final Score: Home: _____ **Visitors:** _____

White Copy League   Canary Copy: Home Team   Pink Copy: Visiting Team

Referee Checklist

Standard Game Kit
Standard Dress
Gold Referee Jersey
Black Shorts
Black Referee Socks
Predominantly Black Shoes
Current Referee Badge

Optional Dress
Alternate Referee Jerseys
Warmup Clothing

Standard Equipment
Whistle
Watch or timer
Pen or pencil
Paper
Red and yellow cards
AR Flags
Coin
FIFA Rule Book
Rain & Cold Weather Gear
  (as needed)
Plastic Bag
  or Waterproof Pouch
  (To keep equipment dry in case of monsoon)

Misc.
Directions to Game
Assignor's Phone Number

Pregame Checklist
Park Car Facing Out
Pre-game Meeting
  with Ref'ing Crew
Inspect Field
Collect Game Fee
Collect Game Sheets
Player Check-in
  Equipment & Saftey Check
  Player Passes, if required
  Boring Speech to Players (Optional)
Inspect Game Ball
Coin Toss

Halftime Checklist
Halftime Conference
  with Ref'ing Crew
Rehydrate

Postgame Checklist
Return Ball
Fill out Game Report
Return Game Reports
  to respective teams
Return Cards
  to respective teams
Postgame Conference
  with Ref'ing Crew

Optional Equipment

Optional Game Equipment
Clipboard
   or Looseleaf Binder
Referee Wallet
   & Game Sheets
Extra Cards
Extra Whistles,
   Watches, and Pens
Ball Pump & Needles
Pressure Gauge
Cable Ties
   (To mend nets; not presently approved for use as supplement to cards when dealing with unruly players)

Emergency Equipment
First Aid Kit
Cellular Telephone
Disguise
   (if needed for quick get-away)

Misc.
Water Bottle
Snacks
Folding Chair

Chapter 3

Running the Line

MOST OFFICIALS BEGIN THEIR CAREERS as assistant referees, running the lines for more experienced officials.* While this helps ease new officials into their jobs, serving as an assistant referee calls upon special skills and, at higher levels of play, is a task every bit as challenging as being a center referee.

A new referee will probably begin at the recreational level of play, doing matches involving younger players. Even so, running a line at any level of play employs the same techniques, uses the same standard mechanics, and requires the official to master the same basic skills.

The Job of an Assistant Referee

Our basic referee training teaches us that assistant referees are there to *as*-sist, rather than *in*-sist. This means that while the whole team is there to help manage the game, it is the *referee's* decision that will be final. Assistant referees should do their best to follow the instructions given during the pre-game conference, and to follow the referee's lead during the match. The crew is, after all, a team, and part of their job is to make one another look good.

---

* Given modern trends favoring small-sided games for younger players, this may be changing. Small-sided, non-competitive matches are ideal for the new referee to get comfortable on the field and used to blowing the whistle.

The new official fortunate enough to work for a club with a well-developed program for young players should take every opportunity to develop his (or her) skills in the middle of a small-sided game. Most of the suggestions in the next chapter dealing with duties of a center referee should apply to these small-sided matches as well.

When running the line, it does not matter whether you agree with the way the referee is handling things on the field, whether you would handle a particular incident or call fouls the same way, or whether you would take a completely different approach to the match or to the players. Your turn will come soon enough, and when you are in the middle you should expect, and receive, the same support from the rest of your crew that you provide when you are on the line.

Signaling the Referee

Soccer uses a single whistle on the field for a basic reason: to keep disagreements among the officials from disrupting the game. The Laws direct that one official, the referee, will take responsibility for all final decisions on the field. As a result, only the referee may stop play directly, which is done by blowing the whistle. The other officials—the assistant referees and, in some games, the fourth official—may convey information leading to a stoppage, but the final decision is always the referee's.

The flag is the assistant referee's main way of conveying information, and each new official has to master several basic signals. Some signals are sequential, others are separate and distinct. Each communicates a specific piece of information to the referee for a specific purpose. Most are, in one form or another, a recommendation to the referee to stop play. Because the referee needs to see your flag at all times, you should keep your flag in the hand closest to the field and nearest to the referee, changing hands as needed as you move up and down the field. You should also try to avoid raising the flag part-way, only to change your mind when things turn out differently than you expect. Doing otherwise can confuse the players, the spectators, and occasionally the referee. It is better to train yourself to wait until you are certain of a call before starting to raise your flag.

Ready to Play

While you may store them as you see fit, once removed from your equipment bag flags should be kept in one of two conditions: furled, or unfurled. This tells the referee when you are ready for play to begin, and when the game needs to wait a bit longer.

Mechanics—Not Ready

Before and after each half, and whenever the referee has occasion to suspend or terminate the match, the assistant referee keeps the flag furled.

Mechanics—Ready to Play

The assistant referee signals that everything is ready to begin play in her half of the field by unfurling the flag.

To avoid misunderstandings, most referees will try to make eye contact with each assistant referee, and often exchange a wave or other hand signal before blowing the whistle to begin each half. You, too, should be looking to make eye contact with the center referee often during the match—at all stoppages of play, and before each restart.

Request for Stoppage

While the referee stops play by blowing the whistle, the assistant referee can only recommend a stoppage by raising the flag.

3.1 Ready to Play

Mechanics—Request for Stoppage

Having observed an incident that calls for play to stop, the assistant referee comes square to the field, raises the flag vertically, and looks to make eye contact with the referee. Once play is stopped, the assistant conveys the reason for the stoppage by using the appropriate signal.

3.2 Request for Stoppage

Offside Infractions

Among the most contentious aspects of many soccer games are the offside calls, or no-calls, that arise during a match. The offside rule is only meant to prevent cherry-picking by the attackers. For this reason, officials give the benefit of the doubt to the team with the ball whenever an offside call is uncertain. This means little to the defensive team or their spectators, of course, who will clamor loudly whenever an attacking player past the last defender gets the ball. But as the only person at the field positioned to see the play, it is the assistant referee's job to make the call accurately, penalizing only those offside players who participate in the next phase of play by moving to play the ball, by interfering with an opponent, or by capitalizing on a misplay by the defenders.

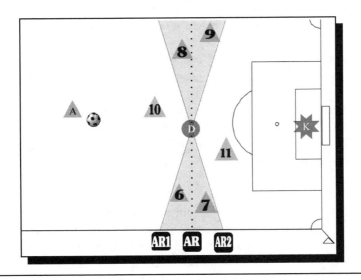

3.3

PARALLAX AND THE IMPORTANCE OF POSITIONING

While an assistant referee either trailing or ahead of the offside line (AR1 or AR2) will be able to see that #11 is offside, and #10 is onside, only a properly positioned assistant (AR) even with the next-to-last defender (D) can see which players to penalize if they receive the ball from the attacking player near midfield (A). From the perspective of an assistant lagging behind the play (AR1), an offside player near the far sideline may appear onside (#9), while a nearby onside player (#6) may appear to be past the offside line. For an assistant too far downfield (AR2), the perspective is reversed—and it is the far side attacker (#8) who is at risk for an inaccurate offside flag, while his impatient teammate on the near sideline (#7) may benefit from AR2's inaccurate line of sight.

No matter how far up- or downfield the AR may stray, the shaded area shows where players run the highest risk of an inaccurate decision by the assistant referee—especially if the assistant referee is unaware that he is out of position. Simple geometry ensures that the closer we are to the correct position, the smaller the area of risk will be.

While the nuances of the offside rule are beyond the scope of this book and may require years of experience to master, there are several basic tips that can help you avoid some of the common pitfalls and help minimize the grumbling you will have to endure along the touchline.

- Because the referee cannot un-blow the whistle, a slow flag is better than an early one, but a *timely* flag is best of all.

- While a player need not actually touch the ball to be flagged as offside, in most cases you should wait to see who will actually reach the ball first.

- Rather than constantly moving your head or shifting your body, remaining square to the field will let you focus on the next-to-last defender while permitting you to use your peripheral vision (or your ears) to determine the moment the ball is struck.

3.4 Player Offside

- As shown in Figure 3.3, to see the distorting effects of mispositioning, you only have to see how a straight line looks when viewed from a yard up- or down-field. This shows how critical it is for you to remain in position on the offside line—even with the ball, or the next-to-last defender.

- You do not have to signal "on-side" by making an affirmative gesture. Simply keeping your flag at your side indicates that play should continue.

- By the same token, while you are under no obligation to explain your calls, a quiet word to a coach or spectator who is complaining—such as "Number Six kept him onside," "He was onside when the ball was kicked," or "Number Twelve wasn't involved in the play"—can often go a long way toward keeping tempers under control along the sidelines.

Mechanics—Player Offside

Having determined that an offside player has interfered with active play, the assistant referee

3.5   *Spotting the Restart*
Far side, Middle of Field, Near Side

stops, comes square to the field, raises the flag vertically, and looks to make eye contact with the referee. Once the referee signals to stop play, the assistant indicates the spot of the infraction by pointing toward the field—holding the flag at a forty-five degree angle up to signal an offside player on the far side of the field, parallel to the ground to signal an offside player in the middle of the field, and a forty-five degree angle downward to signal an offside player on the near side of the field. After signaling the proper placement of the restart, the assistant referee should assume the appropriate position on the field — even with the ball, or the next-to-last defender.

Out of Bounds

One of the assistant referee's most basic tasks is to signal when the ball is out of play—meaning, under Law IX, that the whole of the ball has crossed one of the boundary lines on the pitch. As needed, the assistant can also help insure that the ball is correctly placed for the restart.

3.6   *Goal Kick*

Mechanics—Goal Kick or Corner Kick If the ball crosses the end line, it will be either a goal kick (if last touched by the attacking team) or a corner kick (if last touched by the defenders):

• To signal a goal kick, the assistant referee should go to the end line, come square to the field, and point directly toward the goal.

- To signal a corner kick, the assistant referee should go to the corner arc, come square to the field, and point down toward the corner flag at a 45-degree angle.

In both cases, the assistant referee should make sure to follow the ball to the end line. This not only enhances the credibility of the call, but ensures that the assistant is in the right position to see an unexpected deflection or incident occurring deep in the defensive end of the field. It is also important to look at the referee, and not at the flag. It helps develop a sense of team-

3.7   Corner Kick

work and camaraderie...and keeps us from looking confused or inattentive.

3.8   Throw-in

Mechanics—Throw-in

If the ball crosses the touch line, it will be a throw-in for one team or the other:

- At or near the point where the ball left the field, the assistant referee should come square to the field and point upward at a 45-degree angle, toward the goal defended by the team that kicked the ball out of bounds (or, toward the goal being attacked by the team entitled to the throw-in—whichever is easier for you to remember).

Mechanics—Ball out of Play

Sometimes, an out-of-bounds call may not be entirely clear: when a player is dribbling along the touchline, for example, the ball may leave the field of play and return very quickly, or a cross or corner kick may sail out of bounds, before curving back onto the field of play. If it would help clarify things, the assistant referee should use a sequenced signal:

- Having determined that ball has gone out of play, but sensing that confusion may exist about whether it actually went out of bounds, the assistant referee stops, comes square to the field, raises the flag vertically, and looks to make eye contact with the referee. Once the referee signals to stop

3.9   Sequenced Signal: Ball Out of Play

play, the assistant referee indicates the appropriate restart.

As with all signals, flag mechanics should be crisp and unambiguous. Sequenced signals should be clearly separated to eliminate any confusion, and the assistant referee should never signal across the body with the flag.

Goals

The culmination of all the players' running about the field occurs when one team puts the ball into the goal—which, they all hope, will be the *other* team's goal. As this is a highlight and match-critical event in any soccer game, there are a number of prescribed signals for you to use.

3.10 Improper Mechanics Flag Across Body

Mechanics—Goal Scored

When the ball is clearly inside the goal, the assistant referee runs a short distance upfield to confirm the goal, while trying to make eye contact with the referee. Upon seeing confirmation of the goal, the referee will point to the center circle.

3.11   Goal Scored

Mechanics—Ball in-and-out of Goal

When the ball has entered the goal for a valid score, but rebounds back onto the field of play—or if there is any question about whether it has crossed the goal line—the assistant referee should come square to the field, raise the flag vertically to signal "ball out of play" and make eye contact with the referee. When the referee whistles to stop play, the assistant referee then performs the mechanic for "goal scored," running a short distance upfield, signaling the goal. It is critical, when using this sequence, that the assistant referee stay positioned on the end line until the referee blows the whistle to stop play—not only to ensure the credibility of the call, but to make sure that the referee does not confuse the mechanic for "goal scored" for the assistant referee simply following play back upfield.

Mechanics—Houston, we have a problem....

When the ball enters the goal for an apparent score, but the assistant referee has detected an infraction that may require disallowing it, there are two different mechanics to use, depending upon the nature of the infraction:

3.12 Problem with Goal

- If the player scoring the goal was offside, the assistant referee should use the standard offside mechanic. Raise the flag to signal the infraction and make eye contact with the referee. After the officials are in visual contact, the assistant referee should signal the spot of the infraction, and the referee will give the signal for an indirect free kick.

- If someone other than the shooter was offside—or if there is *any other infraction* by the attacking team that casts the validity of the goal into doubt—the assistant referee should stand stiffly at attention, while attempting to make eye contact with the referee. The referee will either disallow the goal, or consult with the assistant to get the pertinent information.

If the referee misses the signal indicating a potential objection to the goal, it is your responsibility to intervene and bring the matter to light by any means at your disposal *before the ensuing kick-off.* After the restart, the goal will stand as valid, regardless of the offense that called it into question.

Substitutions

A referee should be visually checking with his assistants during each stoppage in play—to see, among other things, whether either team is requesting a substitution.

Rules on substitutions vary from game-to-game. Some competitions permit substitutions to occur at any dead-ball stoppage, while others restrict substitutions to specific events such as goal kicks, injuries, kick-offs, or a team's own throw-in. Whatever rule a particular game may employ, the mechanics remain the same:

Mechanics—Request for Substitution

When a team requests a substitution and an appropriate stoppage occurs, the assistant referee signals the referee by raising the flag horizontally, above his head and holding it between his hands with arms fully extended. After the referee acknowledges the request, the assistant referee should lower the flag. If the referee does not notice the request, the assistant referee on the opposite side of the field should mirror the signal. Nothing prevents either assistant, or any participant, from getting the referee's attention by using the voice.

In some games, a Fourth Official will monitor and control all substitutions. In other games, the official on the sideline with the substituting player will supervise. In either case, the technically correct procedure is to wait until the player is off the field before allowing the substitute to enter. To do this the

3.13   Substitution

assistant referee must usually jog to the half-way line, but in lower-level games with unlimited substitutions this procedure is often overlooked.

In games with limited substitutions, a substitute will need to produce and surrender a player pass before entering the game. The official supervising the substitution is responsible for collecting any such documents.

Fouls

As the name implies, assistant referees are expected to help control the match by calling fouls. Your pre-game instructions should include guidelines about when—and when not—to signal a foul,

3.14 Subsitution: Poor Mechanics

including a penalty kick, and how to communicate a recommendation to issue a misconduct card. As with everything else a referee does, there is a right way for an assistant referee to call a foul, or help place the spot of the restart:

Mechanics—Foul Play Observed

Having observed an act of player misconduct, or a foul that justifies a stoppage of play, the assistant referee first stops moving along the touchline and comes square to the field, attempts to make eye contact with the referee, and signals by raising the flag vertically and waggling it from the wrist:

- If the referee whistles to stop play, the assistant referee signals the direction of the free kick.

- If the referee waves down the flag, the assistant referee lowers the flag and moves to resume a proper position along the touchline.

3.15 Foul Play Observed

By and large, it is better to raise the flag in whichever hand would signal the direction of the ensuing kick. This helps the referee make an intelligent decision on the use of advantage.

Mechanics—Penalty Kick Offense

Having indicated a foul by the defense occurring inside the penalty area, when the referee's whistle sounds to stop play the assistant referee lowers his arm, runs directly to the goal line, and stands in front of the corner flag. When the referee confirms the decision by signaling a penalty kick, the assistant moves to the appropriate position at the juncture of the goal line and penalty area.

3.16 *Foul in Penalty Area*

Mechanics—Spot of Whistled Foul Occurring Inside Penalty Area

Seeing that a foul whistled by the referee occurred within the penalty area, the assistant referee stops and comes square to the field. Making eye contact with the referee, the assistant stands with legs parted, and places the flag in front and between the legs.*

Often, the referee will direct an assistant to include a signal indicating an indirect free kick when it would be the appropriate restart—such as raising the arm vertically after indicating the direction of the kick. Common ways of communicating a recommendation for a misconduct card include tapping your badge—which usually suggests a caution— and tapping your rear pocket, which is often the recommendation for a send-off.

Switching Hands

Given enough time, all assistant referees eventually raise the flag in the wrong hand. Sometimes, the referee will overrule a directional signal; other times, a reflexive signal communicating "ball out of play" or

---

* Considering the consequences of calling a penal foul against the defense inside the penalty area, and as a concession to occasionally ambiguous flag mechanics by some newer officials, many referees will ask their assistants for additional confirmation of the location of the foul. A common, yet discreet practice is to have the assistant—once eye contact is established—take a step toward or away from the goal in order to confirm the location: a step toward the goal confirms that the foul occurred inside the penalty area; a step away from the goal indicates that it did not.

recommending a stoppage may find the flag in a hand other than the direction of the restart. Or, imperfection being part of the human condition, the assistant may simply make a mistake in the initial signal.* When this happens, the proper mechanic sometimes lets the officials cover the error (or the disagreement) by making the correction appear to be part of a sequence of signals.

Mechanics—Oops, Wrong Hand

Having raised the flag in the opposite hand from the appropriate restart, the assistant referee first lowers the flag, then shifts hands to the appropriate hand to identify or confirm the direction.

3.17   *Switching Hands*

Assisting the Referee

Officiating a soccer match is a team enterprise. Each official must do his best to contribute to the performance of the crew. Unlike some sports, however, soccer does not engage in "officiating by committee." Due to the nature of the game, play does not stop to permit routine consultations after every event that occurs on the field, and the fact that the clock does not stop places a premium on quick and firm decision-making.

An assistant referee's job is to *assist* the referee. It is not to second-guess the match official, call the game from the sidelines, or intervene whenever the assistant views the play differently. As the official responsible for controlling the game, the referee is in charge of the officiating crew as well as the match. While you may do things differently when handed the whistle, if assigned to be an assistant referee you should do your best to

---

* This can be a particular problem early in the second half, after the teams switch ends at halftime. Even veteran officials sometimes keep signaling in the same direction for the same team until an obvious blunder serves asa reminder. It can be a particular challenge when doing multiple games in the same day.

carry out your instructions and to help administer and enforce the referee's vision and preferences for the match at hand. The task, after all is to *as*sist, not to *in*sist.

This assistance can take many forms, beginning with the arrival of the officials and ending only when they leave at the end of the game.

PRE-GAME ASSISTANCE

As we saw in Chapter 2, the officials have many administrative duties to fulfill before a match can get under way. The referee may delegate any of these, assigning one or both assistant referees to a variety of tasks. Some of them may include:

- Player check-in and pass cards.
- Collecting the pass cards.
- Collecting the Game Reports.
- Collecting the Game Fee.
- Inspecting the ball.
- Inspecting the field.
- Checking or repairing the nets.
- Clarifying points at the pre-game conference.

To provide help before the game begins, however, you cannot be late arriving at the field.

DURING THE MATCH

During the game, the assistant referee must always be ready to give any assistance needed. This help can take many different forms:

- Timely offside calls—neither late, nor early.

- Help with restarts, including identifying the place of the foul and aid in dealing with encroachments at the restart.

- Help in spotting and dealing with off-the-ball incidents.

- Help with substitutions, and with incidents occurring along the sidelines.

- A back-up clock, in the case the referee's watch fails or he forgets to start the clock.

- Help with record-keeping in general, including duplicate records of goals, misconducts, and injuries.

- Assistance and support in case things get out of hand.

- Another pair of eyes, and a voice of calm reason along the sidelines, to keep the players from fouling with impunity in the corners.

- Assistance with fouls, especially fouls occurring outside the referee's view, or for which the assistant referee has the superior viewing angle.

In some games, the success or failure of the crew's performance often depends upon a critical call, or no-call, by the assistant referee. For the team to functions as a unit, each official has to pitch in to make the whole crew look good.

Following the Referee's Lead

Napoleon once observed that an army is better served by marching into battle led by one bad general than by two good ones. Though strongly preferring excellence, soccer has largely adopted a similar philosophy. Unlike some other sports, our Laws give the responsibility for controlling the match to a single referee, conferring wide-ranging discretion to keep the game flowing while maintaining order on the field. To do this, all officials must view events on the field in the same way, and the viewpoint that they will use on any given day is that of the official assigned as the center referee.

As with all things arising during the course of the match, the referee's preferences determine how the officials perform their duties. It is also the referee's perception of events, and threshold for foul play, that will set the tone of the match. The crucial question for you as the assistant to ask, then, is not "Would I call this?" but "Would the *referee* call this....and would *today's referee* find my flag to be helpful, or a burden?"

If doing so would contribute to the crew's effort, then you should raise your flag. If it would probably hurt, then you should keep it down. Being able to tell the difference can be the assistant referee's major challenge during the game and will remain a lifelong quest. In the meantime, there will be a number of things to ask yourself at every game you do:

Is the action clearly within my responsibilities as outlined in the pregame conference, particularly in the areas of offside or out-of-bounds decisions?

If so, you are the official responsible for making the appropriate call and should not hesitate to do so.

Is the action on the field clearly within the referee's sight?

If so, unless mirroring the referee's call you should probably refrain from signaling, just in case your judgment conflicts with the referee's.

Is the referee looking to me for help?

If the referee is partly screened from the play, or was looking elsewhere when something happened, he may need your recommendation discreetly, and in a hurry.

A benefit of frequent eye-contact is that it helps the officials establish a non-verbal rapport. If something happens, and the referee is looking at you, he is probably asking for help. Often, his body language—pointing at you, perhaps, a look of panic on his face—will be begging you for assistance. If so, you should give it, raising the flag if you think he would have called it, indicating a "no-call" in some way if you do not[*]. The referee will be grateful for the help.

Is a signal from me needed to rescue the referee from a mistake he probably does not realize he is making?

Most referees take pride in their jobs and try their best to keep on top of events on the field. Sometimes, though, things happen that no one expects, and which any sane person would want to deal with. A classic example is a blatantly intentional handball, such as Maradona using the "hand of God" to score—something that everyone on the field has seen, except for the referee.

Almost without exception, referees are grateful when they are rescued, even if they did not know they were in trouble at the time. While a new assistant may have trouble detecting an obvious blunder by a distracted referee, more experienced officials can often spot a colleague in distress. In either case, you should be reluctant to intrude in this manner, and only do so if you are sure that the referee will appreciate the help.

Have I been specifically instructed not to raise my flag in this situation?

Some referees, having been embarrassed by misplaced or unhelpful interventions by colleagues in the past, will specifically instruct their

---

[*] Or, perhaps, simply shrugging your shoulders if you are just clueless as he is. A blank or vacant expression can convey the same message.

Neither is an approved mechanic, of course, and repeated use of either signal may suggest that both of you need to work on improving your level of concentration.

assistant referees not to raise the flag in some circumstances. They may instead give you an alternate mechanic to use—stepping off the pitch rather than raising the flag to indicate encroachment by the keeper at a penalty kick, for example—in order to avoid the needless controversy that a visible flag might cause. In these circumstances, you should follow the referee's directions, using whatever informal signal he wants you to use.

On rare occasions, a referee may order you simply not to make a call when it would otherwise be your responsibility to do so, directing you not to call a foul or penalty kick, perhaps, or in extreme cases to make no signals except for offside and out-of-bounds. If given these instructions, you should try your best to follow them, and to remain loyal to your colleague even if players or spectators start demanding to know why *you* are not calling things that everyone else can plainly see.

Referees who give you these sorts of specific instructions expect you to follow them. They may not understand the problems these limits impose on their assistant referees and are not always there to deal with the reactions that can follow. But for the particular game, those are your instructions and you should follow them. You do not, however, have to refrain from bringing the matter to the attention of your assignor if you prefer not to work with that particular colleague again. And you are under no obligation to make excuses for the referee to any assessor who asks you why you were so passive or unhelpful along the touchline during the game.

Missed Flag Signals

Occasionally, referees become distracted, or their attention is elsewhere when the assistant raises a flag. In the absence of any instructions to the contrary,[*] to avoid disrupting the match needlessly what you do will depend upon the reason for the flag and the subsequent course of action on the field:

If the ball has gone out of play, you should hold your flag until you catch the referee's eye, using your voice if needed to get the referee's attention. If play subsequently stops and restarts despite your best efforts, you may lower the flag and discuss the missed signal at the end of the half. Under the rules, when the ball goes out of bounds play must resume with

---

[*] What to do in the event that the referee appears not to notice a signal from the touchline should be among the topics to discuss at the pre-game conference.

the appropriate restart, but in most cases a restart ends the crew's chance to correct a mistake.

If you raise your flag for an offside infraction and the referee misses your signal, you should keep your flag raised until the defense gains clear possession of the ball, either winning it away from the other team, or gaining it through a goal-kick or throw-in.

If you raise your flag to signal that you have information relating to a misconduct, or indicating information that calls into question the validity of a goal, you should maintain your signal until it is acknowledged, dropping it only if play resumes despite your determined efforts to bring the matter to light. In this case, however, you may need to go beyond a visual flag signal and make a loud verbal stab at getting your colleague's attention. If play resumes despite your best efforts, you need to bring the matter to light at an appropriate time, as discreetly as possible.

If the referee misses a flag on the other side of the field, you should raise your flag as well, to mirror the signal. The referee ought to be making frequent eye contact with each of you, and mirroring one another's signals will help bring the missed flag to his attention.

Avoiding Contradictory Signals

We officiate soccer with a single whistle to minimize dissension and conflict on the field. By making a single referee responsible for all decisions, we can make timely calls and communicate our rulings quickly, letting everyone get on with the game. But crossed or contradictory signals, where the officials seem to disagree over a call, can suggest confusion and undercut the referee's authority.

The referee should indicate any preferences for avoiding these problems at the pre-game conference. Common methods include:

Making eye contact before signaling.

Non-verbal communication is a soccer referee's most important skills. It lets officials relay information at a glance, without the need for an extended discussion.

When the ball goes out of bounds, or you see what looks to be a foul, it is best to make eye contact with the referee before raising your flag. This lets you exchange information before signaling to avoid pointing in different directions. A referee who is certain who last kicked the ball out of bounds, for example, can confidently, and discreetly, indicate the proper direction of the throw-in, preventing the embarrassment of a contradictory signal.

Setting responsibility for different areas of the field.

All three officials need to cooperate to manage a game properly. Each will be in a different place, with varying angles of view for events on the field. This requires a common understanding of which official has primary responsibility for any particular call, and what to do in case of uncertainty.

Ordinarily, each assistant takes primary responsibility for all out-of-bounds calls in his own quadrant of the field, and for fouls occurring near the touchline. The referee usually makes out-of-bounds calls in the opposite quadrants, as well as final decisions on fouls throughout the field. Referees may depart from this convention, however, so allocating these tasks should be part of the pre-game discussions. In addition, all three officials need to have a common understanding about calls inside the penalty area.

No matter who is responsible for making it, officials should freely mirror the signals of whoever makes a given call. Lending visual support to each other's decisions helps promote confidence in the officiating.

Establishing a prescribed signal for "Help!!"

Assigning responsibility for areas of the field is unlikely to work, though, if the official responsible for the call did not see what happened. While no one tries to miss a play, there will be times when the players' bodies are screening the area of play at the critical moment. Rather than simply letting a call go unmade, the crew should have a pre-arranged way of calling for help. A look of panic or confusion usually communicates the need for rescue, though it can easily be mistaken for nausea or constipation. More helpful signals include the referee looking (or, in extreme cases, pointing) at the assistant to indicate uncertainty about a call; the assistant referee keeping an out-of-play flag raised vertically, without indicating direction (perhaps with a pitiable glance at the referee); or any other non-verbal signal that will indicate the need for rescue.

Mirroring the referee's signal at once, if overruled.

To maintain confidence in the officiating, and ensure the officials' cohesiveness as a unit, it is important for all three referees to close ranks immediately, once the center referee announces a decision.

Whether a flag signal is honored or overruled, the final decision on all matters related to play belongs to the referee. If the referee waves down your flag, you should lower it at once, and return to the proper position on the offside line. If the referee indicates a restart different than your recommendation, your signal should immediately change to match the referee. If disagreements continue, this is something you can discuss at the end of the half. On the pitch in the middle of a game is neither the time, nor the place, to air any such differences of opinion.

POST-GAME ASSISTANCE

Your job as an assistant referee does not end when the final whistle sounds. Once the match is over, the assistants traditionally run to join the referee in mid-field and the crew leaves the field the same way that they entered—as a team. There are also things for the crew to do after the game ends, and your help can take a variety of forms:

- Gathering and returning the game ball.

- Consulting with the referee about incidents occurring during the match, especially those involving instances of misconduct.

- Confirming information needed for the game report, such as goals scored, misconducts issued, serious injuries sustained by either team, and, most importantly of all, the final score.

- Obtaining signatures from both sides on the game report, and distributing the final copies to each team.

- Returning any pass cards retained pending the outcome of the match, and helping to see that any pass card retained for submission with the game report is the correct one.

Aside from official tasks, you should also be available to help any crew member who needs it—intervening, for example, to prevent a disgruntled spectator from disturbing a referee who is busy preparing his report, or making sure that no member of the crew is stranded at the field due to car trouble or the lack of a ride home.

Positioning and Movement Along the Touchline

For the crew to function as an effective unit, the referee must be able to locate each assistant at a glance and both assistant referees must be in the proper position. Except in unusual circumstances,[*] an assistant referee's proper position during a game will be along the touchline and at the offside line—or, in other words, even with the ball, the next-to-last defender, or the half-way line. You should also carry your flag in the hand closest to the referee. If your referee is running a standard left diagonal, your flag will usually be in your left hand as you move downfield, and in your right hand as you move back upfield. As play shifts back and forth, you should be switching hands often, to keep it in the proper place.

Once you unfurl your flag to signal that a half is ready to begin, your flag should remain unfurled and in one of two positions— either up and signaling the referee, or down at your side. You should also try to avoid flapping your flag as you run. Though it may take practice to be able to run at a full sprint while holding your flag straight down, it is a skill you need to master in order to look professional on the field.

Along the sideline, you will be moving constantly to maintain your position at the offside line. If play is moving slowly you may simply walk up and down the sideline, but at other times you will have to sprint to keep up with the play. You should also try to stay square to the field whenever possible, so that your field of vision spans the whole field of

3.18   *Moving Along the Touchline*

---

[*]At penalty kicks the proper position for a lead assistant referee will be at the juncture of the end line and the penalty area. Other exceptions will be at the discretion of the referee or dictated by reasons of practicality. At kicks taken by the keeper from deep within the defensive end of the field, for example, it will often be more realistic for the assistant referee to take a position even with where the offside will be once the ball is away, rather than trying to race upfield to get into proper position by the time it lands.

play. To do this, the most useful skill you can develop is the ability to side-step up and down the field. A "cross-over step"—twisting your body to watch the field while your legs cross over as you move downfield—not only looks ungainly, but also makes it likelier that you will stumble. Side-stepping —shuffling your feet together, then apart, then together as you move up or down the field—lets you stay square to the field without tripping over your feet.* While you will never be able to side-step as fast as you can sprint, your speed will increase with practice.

At all levels of play, the job of an assistant referee can be every bit as physically and mentally taxing as that of the center referee. During a competitive match, an assistant may run three miles or more, much of it sprinting at top speed. And new officials are often surprised at the level of concentration it takes to monitor the ever-changing offside line. As a result, you will need to be in good physical shape to do your job well.

Things to Watch

During a match, an assistant referee's attention constantly shifts between any number of tasks. Unfortunately, humans have two eyes and, not having independently controlled ocular senses like our friends the chameleons, both of those eyes are usually focused on the same thing.

With much to watch but only one pair of eyes, you will have an endless string of priorities to set, events to juggle, and decisions to make. Learning where to focus attention during the run of play will help make the job easier. Fortunately, events can take place in one of two places—in the area near the assistant referee...or elsewhere.

WHEN PLAY IS NEAR: Too many players, not enough eyes

A Roman sage once observed that trying to do two things at once is to do neither.** Soccer, apparently believing that adding a third will not make matters appreciably worse, gives its assistant referees three primary tasks: the offside line, out-of-bounds, and fouls. As a result, when play is nearby your job can sometimes seem impossible, and new officials can become frantic trying to juggle all of their responsibilities.

---

* Tripping over equipment bags, chairs, or someone else's feet, is a different matter—and a topic to which we return, shortly.

** Publilius Syrus, Maxim 7.

As you gain experience, it will become easier to shift attention between different parts of your job. Monitoring each assignment will come to take less time as you learn to sense what is important at each given moment. You may even find that you actually *can* do everything at once—glancing to make sure you are still on the offside line, catching a quick look down the touchline to make sure the ball is still in-bounds, watching the players near you to check for fouls—all the while talking to them if things start getting tense to let them know you are watching. Learning to use your peripheral vision, as well as your ears, will also make it easier to monitor your different responsibilities.

It is natural to feel uncomfortable at first, since you are probably not used to splitting your attention quite so much. And if you are simply unable to keep track of all three assignments at the same time, your highest priority will generally be to watch the offside line. The referee will already be looking for fouls and can back you up in case you miss seeing who last touched a ball out-of-bounds, but nobody else will be in the right position to make the offside call.

WHEN PLAY IS FAR: *Watching the referee's back*

It is tempting for an assistant referee to become a spectator when play is on the opposite end of the field. Soccer is an exciting spectacle, and the action can be entrancing for those watching. Soccer is also a game of constant motion, however, and there will always be something happening in all corners of the field.

There are three officials at a soccer game for a reason, and three pairs of eyes should not all be watching the same thing. As an assistant referee you must always guard against the tendency to "ball watch." When play is on the other side of the field, you have more to do than taking a moment to relax and enjoy the show. You should be scanning the rest of the field to watch for players becoming testy or unruly, to maintain your position on the offside line, and to spot any incidents that you may need to bring to the referee's attention.

It is not, however, enough simply to notice an event. You must also be ready to report the incident to the referee, which means identifying any players involved. With a field-full of players to watch there is a great risk that you will not be able to identify the player merely by his appearance, and you do not want the culprit to go unpunished merely because you forgot to note his number.

Spotting Misconduct or other Off-Ball Incidents

An assistant referee who detects misconduct that is part of a play for ball, but out of the referee's view, should raise the flag to indicate an incident of foul play. As part of its pre-game conference, the crew should have agreed upon a pre-arranged signal for the assistant to recommend a card for misconduct. Commonly, tapping the front pocket will advise a caution, while patting the back pocket will suggest the need for a send-off. This corresponds to the pockets where the referee often keeps his own cards—front pocket for a yellow card, back pocket for the red one.

If you spot misconduct occurring away from the ball, your course of action will depend on your pre-game instructions. Many referees prefer to deal with off-ball misconducts at the next stoppage of play. Offenses posing a serious risk to control of the match, however—like violent conduct—usually need be dealt with immediately. In any case, there are ways to call the referee's attention to the right part of the field. But when the event occurs far from play, he will probably not look behind his back until play starts back in the other direction. This means that he is likely to miss a flag signal by the trailing assistant, and both assistant referees must coordinate their signals to bring the incident to light. And when all else fails, nothing prevents assistant referees from communicating necessary information by use of a verbal signal—as loud as needed to deliver the message.

Mechanics—Match-Critical Incident Away from Referee

An assistant referee who detects a misconduct or other event requiring the referee's immediate attention should raise the flag vertically and try to get the referee's attention. Upon seeing this signal, the lead assistant should raise his own flag to mirror the signal from the far side of the field. When the referee stops play, the lead assistant should point to the colleague on the opposite sideline, and the referee will inquire to determine the nature of the incident and decide on the appropriate action to take.

Dealing with the Sidelines

In most amateur games, the field is a simple rectangle with goal posts at each end. There are often no bleachers for the fans, and spectators commonly watch the game from the sidelines. Because an assistant referee's position is along the touchline, this makes contact with spectators, substitutes, and coaches unavoidable.

Practical Problems

Along the sidelines, in addition to coaches and substitutes, you are likely to encounter feet, equipment bags, and chairs, belonging to players and spectators alike. To avoid colliding with anyone during a sprint down the sidelines, or tripping over a misplaced foot or piece of equipment, you will need to make sure that you have a clear area for running. One yard is usually adequate clearance; three yards is better. Most people are not trying to get in the way and will move if you ask them. If they don't, bring the matter to the referee's attention during a stoppage of play.

While you are free to answer polite questions from coaches and spectators, you should avoid extended conversations along the touchline. It is one thing to answer a fan's question about how much time is remaining, or a coach's question about a call that he missed; it is quite another to allow yourself to be drawn into a debate over the referee's style of officiating.

Behavioral Problems

At the typical soccer game, feelings can run the gamut of emotions from elation to despair. Sometimes, emotions turn into complaints, and the sidelines can become an unfriendly place for the officials.

Owing to his position in the middle of the field, the referee can literally run away from trouble. Because the assistant referee is simply stuck in place along the touchline, it is important to be able to keep tempers along the sidelines under control.

When possible, use whatever gifts of tact or diplomacy you may possess to keeping things from boiling over. If this is impractical or unavailing, bring the problem to the referee's attention before things get out of hand.

Complaints about the Referee

By the very nature of the job, the referee cannot avoid provoking grumbling, and murmurs of discontent. Roughly half the players and spectators will disagree with every call, and spirits can run high on and about the pitch. Apparently missed calls, or different lines of sight can produce bad feelings or complaints from those at the field.

As an assistant referee, you must be careful not to contradict any call or action by the referee. This is so even if you personally disagree with a call and think that the complainers have a point. Doing so will only lead to further discontent, and will undermine the credibility of the entire officiating crew.

You do not, however, have to parrot a "party line" and pretend that all calls by all officials are perfect. A referee can, after all, acknowledge human imperfections, even if the call still stands. Acknowledging that "things look different on the field," or "the referee had a different angle on the play," or other vague expressions of sympathy are usually enough to mollify the complainers, while remaining loyal to your teammate.

Helpful Habits to Develop

As with any job, some things make being an assistant referee easier, and other things only get in the way. While it can be easy to develop bad habits, there are many helpful things that new officials can practice:

- Sidestep down the field as often as you can.

- Try to make eye contact with the referee at all stoppages.

- Try to make eye contact with the referee before signaling.

- Learn to use your peripheral vision to monitor some events on the field. With practice, this can help you stay on the offside line while focusing your attention on another part of the field.

- Use your ears as well as your eyes. At most levels of play, you will be able to hear deflections that pass too quickly for you to see. In addition, using your ears may tell you when the ball is kicked, freeing you to watch the players moving near the offside line.

- When signaling for a foul, try to raise the flag in the hand which will indicate the direction of the restart. Assuming that the referee runs a left-diagonal, this means raising the flag in the left hand for a restart favoring the defense and in the right hand for a restart favoring the attackers.

- If you raise a flag in the wrong hand, lower the flag before changing hands.

- Run all balls to the end of the field, and signal all goal kicks and corner kicks from the end line.

- Always stop and come square to the field before signaling.

- Make your flag signals crisp and unambiguous.

- Train yourself to wait for participation before raising an offside flag. It helps you make a correct call and lets you avoid "phantom flags."

- Try to be proactive along the sidelines, using your voice and presence to keep things under control.

Habits to Avoid like the Plague:
- Do not become a ball-watcher.

- Do not turn your back to the field during the game.

- Do not leave your position along the touchline to retrieve a ball.

- Do not change a directional signal with the flag extended.

- Never signal across your body.

- Never signal while still moving up or down the line.

What do I do if the Referee Makes a Mistake?

Your job as an assistant referee is to convey information. It is the referee's responsibility to act on that information in an appropriate manner. You are not there to argue with a decision, and in the vast majority of cases the decision to overrule your signal should not be taken as a sign of disrespect for your abilities.

- A referee who waves down your offside flag may prefer to let the keeper collect the ball, rather than stop play—or, from his own vantage, may have concluded that the offside player did not participate in play.

- A referee who waves down your foul signal may be about to apply advantage, may be waiting to see how the play develops, or, deeming the contact trifling, may simply have a professional disagreement with your decision to call a foul.

- A referee who overrules your restart decision when the ball goes out of bounds may have seen a deflection that was hidden from your point of view.

- A referee who misses your flag signal may not even realize that there is any reason to stop play.

There may be times, though, when the referee is clearly mistaken, and no amount of rationalizing can change things. When this happens, here are some guidelines to consider:

Final decisions on all judgment calls belong to the referee, *but employing the wrong restart after a stoppage of play is misapplication of the Laws, not a judgment call.* If this kind of mistake affects the outcome of the match, it may be the subject of a protest and could result in the game being replayed. If you see that an incorrect restart is about to take place, you need to bring the matter to the referee's attention.

As a general rule, the officials can correct a mistake only until the next restart of play. Once play resumes, the referee cannot go back to correct an error. If you see a mistake about to occur, you must bring the matter to the referee's attention *before the restart.* After that, it will be too late to do anything except hope that the error makes no difference to the outcome.

Your pre-game instructions should include a discussion on what to do if the referee misses a flag signal. If so, you should follow those instructions exactly. If they did not, a good rule of thumb is to hold an offside flag until the defense gains clear possession of the ball. You should feel free to use your voice to catch the referee's attention, and be prepared to mirror a flag signal from the opposite sideline, if it will help catch the referee's attention.

Sometimes, people just insist on digging themselves a hole. Most of us feel a sense of hopelessness when we see a train wreck coming that we are powerless to prevent.

Occasionally, a referee will insist on doing things his own way, even when that way leads to disaster on the field. It is simply a part of life, and you will see it happen from time to time, on the soccer field and elsewhere. In those circumstances, simply do your best, and note the experience as another entry in your list of *Things Not to Do.*

In no case should you let a disagreement with a referee become a matter of public knowledge during the game. Everyone calls a game differently, and most professional disagreements are just that— differences of opinion among people of good will. In a well-called game, the players decide the outcome, not the officials, and minor variations in the way we do things will not matter in the least. Venting your displeasure at a colleague in front of the players or spectators only undercuts the authority of the entire referee crew. You should, therefore, avoid commenting to anyone about the merits of any decision given on the field. If pressed, acknowledging that the referee might have seen things differently from his angle on the field should suffice to satisfy the coaches or spectators.

On the other hand, we are trained as professionals, and all of us should act like professionals. If a referee does something that violates the rules, and you feel strongly enough about the matter to report it, there are channels to bring the matter to the attention of the appropriate authorities. In cases like this, seek the advice of a trusted mentor or senior referee, or contact your State Referee Administrator.

When you have information that affects the validity of a goal or has bearing on an instance of misconduct, it is your duty to bring the matter to the referee's attention before play resumes. Acts of violence, information relating to a caution or send-off, or issues affecting the validity of a goal, are potentially game-changing events that have a significance beyond a mere professional difference of opinion and go to the integrity of the game itself.

As officials, we all do our best to get things right, and there are times when doing the right thing may be embarrassing to ourselves or to those around us. Information on match-critical events like goals and mis-conducts is important enough to override our concerns about maintaining the united front that a crew needs to maintain its credibility with the participants. In these circumstances, our own sense of integrity requires us to take action, since not to do so would undercut our own reason for being there—to act as a fair, impartial arbiter of the match.

Your duty does not, however, include arguing the point with the referee. You only need to report what you know discreetly, and in a way that will not cause further trouble. It then becomes his duty to take the appropriate action. If asked, you should give your colleague your honest opinion and assessment of the appropriate course of action to take. But it is still the referee's job, not that of the assistant, to make the final call.

Chapter 4

Blowing the Whistle

ALTHOUGH ASSISTANT REFEREES ARE VITAL to any competitive match, the official who draws the most attention will be the one in the middle of the field. The center referee is the official who bears the ultimate responsibility for controlling the match, and at all levels of play it is the referee who makes all final decisions about the manner and conduct of play. This responsibility starts upon arrival at the field and does not end until the match is over and the officials leave.

Before the Match Begins—Setting the Tone

As we saw in Chapter 2, there is much to do before a game can start. It is the referee's job to make sure that everything is done properly, promptly, and professionally, so that the match can begin on time. There will be paperwork to collect, players to check in, equipment and grounds to inspect, and the officiating crew to organize. It can be a time-consuming and frustrating job, especially if players or colleagues are late arriving, or if the field or nets are in need of repair. When assigned as the center referee for a match, you can help things go smoothly by setting the right tone for the day by arriving early at the field, and handling all pre-game activities in a thorough and professional manner.

Mental Preparation

A referee's game does not start at the field. It begins in the privacy of home, and in the mental and emotional attitudes the official brings to the game. Like any athlete, a referee who is psychologically unprepared cannot be in top form, particularly if distracted by problems at work or home.

As you prepare for the game, you should take a few moments to relax, focus your mind on the upcoming match, and get your mind and emotions ready for the exertions to follow. Your efforts will not only be more effective, but you will probably find that it makes the game more enjoyable, as well.

Setting the Tone

The heart of a referee's job is managing people—up to twenty-two of them on the field, two colleagues along the sidelines, and whoever else shows up for the game. For the match to go smoothly, you must be able to convince everyone at the field—the coaches, the players, the crowd, and the two assistant referees—to cooperate with you. To accomplish this, the game arms you with only a badge, a whistle, and a set of cards. Each of these is a tool for you to use: the badge representing your authority under the Laws of the Game, the whistle representing your power to stop the game in the name of fair play, and the cards granting the authority to deal with any incidents that exceed the bounds of sportsmanship. None of these tools will be effective, however, without a fourth tool that you must supply for yourself: the force of your own personality.

The Importance of Body Language

People can tell a lot about us simply by watching. The way we walk or shake hands, our facial expressions, our tone of voice—even whether we make eye contact with others—says a lot about our moods, our personalities, and our level of confidence. With the possible exception of our uniform, our body language will be the first thing that people will notice about us when we arrive at the field, and may be the single most important part of our pre-game behavior that people will use to form their first impressions.

Humans instinctively recognize signs of authority. Good posture, a firm voice, crisp body movements, and a calm, even-tempered demeanor all announce to the world that someone is confident in his ability to handle whatever challenges the world has to offer. On the other hand, slumped shoulders, a slow or half-hearted stride, a whispered voice, and eyes that seem haunted by ghosts all convey uncertainty and the presence of stress. Throughout your games, people will be watching and evaluating you based on what they see and hear. If they see decisiveness and strength, they will usually relax. If they see weakness, they often become worried and, on occasion, loudly agitated.

A self-assured demeanor, a strong handshake, a face that radiates good humor and quiet confidence will all contribute to a good first impression. Once the game begins, of course, you still must maintain an air of assurance and authority to retain everyone's confidence in you. All the self-assurance in the world will not help you, if you fail to control the match once the game begins.

While you can only practice foul recognition at the soccer field, you can and should practice your mechanics on your own, in front of a mirror whenever possible. You may be surprised to see yourself as others see you, but at least you will be able to see whether your on-field persona conveys authority or self-doubt. As with everything else, practice may not lead to perfection, but it always leads to improvement. That is all anyone can ask.

Attitudes of the Successful Referee

There is a thin line between confidence and arrogance. All the positive body language in the world will not help the referee who offends people through an air of superiority or indifference. Most successful referees take pains to avoid insulting people needlessly, or conveying the impression that they are doing everyone a favor just by showing up at the field. Though we need confidence and a healthy ego to succeed on the pitch, arrogant or self-centered officials often succeed in doing nothing but digging holes for themselves, and dragging everyone else at the field down with them.

By contrast, most successful referees understand the benefits of a healthy ego as well as the pitfalls of being egotistical, and manage to avoid displays of arrogance or officiousness. They do this by cultivating a healthy perspective about themselves and their duties as officials, and by keeping their focus precisely on what they want the players to concentrate on as well— the game. As you gain experience, you will notice that most successful referees have adopted similar sentiments about the game:

Successful referees recognize that the game is not about the officials. It is about playing soccer.

Successful referees approach the game and their duties with an attitude of cooperation. They always try to nurture the three elements that make for a successful match: safety, equality, and enjoyment for all participants.

Successful referees have and project an attitude of respect for the game, and for the players.

Successful referees avoid taking actions designed to make themselves feel important, preferring to take whatever steps are needed to ensure that the players play fairly.

Successful referees are willing to set aside their own egos for the duration of the match.

Successful referees display patience as well as firmness in dealing with problems that arise during a game.

Successful referees share an appreciation for skill, as well as a determination not to let foul play succeed.

Successful referees hold and project a sense of trust in their own judgment, as well as that of their colleagues.

Unfortunately, these attitudes are easier to describe than to acquire, and even the best referees occasionally forget them during the stress of a difficult match.

Pre-Game Activities

Referees who set a confident, professional tone start the game with a number of advantages. Foremost among them is the confidence, however transitory, of the other people at the game.

A self-assured referee who knows the pre-game routine usually has the benefit of the doubt for much of the first half. When you are in charge of a match, people will notice how you handle checking the players and their equipment, and whether you come across as personable and approachable.

For your assistant referees, a solid pre-game conference helps the whole crew start the match on a note of confidence. Topics for discussion will vary from match to match, and may be more- or less-detailed at various levels of play, but all should touch upon some basic concerns that arise at every game:

- Coverage of fouls, including guidelines for calls and no-calls, particularly in areas of possible disagreement among the officials such as handballs, shirt tugs, foul throw-ins, and the like.

- Communicating in cases of misconducts or other emergencies.

- Any special or non-standard mechanics to aid in relaying information among the officials.

- Any special instructions about positioning during set plays, including penalty kicks and free kicks near the defending goal.

- Discussion of likely playing styles and any anticipated problems with players, coaches, or spectators.

- Any special concerns that the officials will need to monitor carefully.

- Allocating primary responsibility for signaling direction whenever a ball goes out of play.

- Reminders about maintaining good habits on the field, such as frequent eye contact, running balls to the end line, proper positioning on the offside line, and waiting to see participation before flagging a play offside.

- How to handle substitutions.

- Delegating pre- or post-game administrative duties, as well as any other special instructions for the assistants to follow.

Whistling While You Work

Once the match begins a referee's work starts in earnest, and you will come to feel you are earning every penny that the teams are paying you. A good referee will run six miles or more during a competitive match, and you will need every ounce of physical and mental stamina you can muster.

In the real world, there is often no substitute for experience. Experience can teach us what works and what does not, which tactics can lead to disasters and which ones can help us avoid them. In the end, there are some things that we simply must experience in order to understand, but some aspects of officiating can come more quickly through study and reflection. This can shorten our learning curve, and make us more effective on the field.

Using the Whistle

Because of its high pitch, shrill tone, and ear-piercing decibel level, the whistle is the referee's most noticeable way of communicating on the field.

Many varieties of whistles are available, and the choice among them is entirely a matter of personal preference. Even so, there are some rudiments of basic whistling that all referees should know:

Communicating by Whistle

Blowing the whistle communicates two possible messages: "Stop!" or "Start!" Regardless of context, this is the message you convey—simple, direct, and unambiguous. Like Pavlov's dog, players quickly learn how to respond to your whistle. Depending on the circumstances, they know that they should either stop whatever they are doing or resume playing the game. But life is full of pitfalls, and even something as simple as blowing a whistle can lead to complications.

Musicianship and the Referee

Most players and many spectators have met referees whose whistling technique leaves much to be desired. Rather than communicating decisiveness and resolve by a strong, confident blast, some whistlers sound more like a baby robin begging for food, or a wheezing horse on its way to the glue factory. Most of these problems are easily corrected, and stem from improper technique—mostly from using the lips and throat to sound the whistle, rather than the referee's entire body.

Musicians, especially singers and those who play wind instruments, quickly master the fundamentals of breath support. They know that without proper use of their diaphragm the tones they produce will be weak and anemic. The diaphragm—the wall of muscle separating our thoracic and abdominal cavities, located under the front of the rib cage—is what musicians use to give power and substance to their sounds, and actors use to project their voices to the back of the theater. By supporting your tone with your diaphragm, which you do by breathing deeply and expanding your rib cage *downward*, you allow your entire torso to deliver air to your instrument, the whistle. The result is a stronger, more easily controlled sound for referee and musician alike.

A few minutes of practice will have you sounding like the referee's equivalent of Pavarotti, able to split eardrums at will. This does not end the matter, for the whistle is more useful when used in a flexible, controlled manner to convey shadings of meaning beyond the simple commands of "stop" and "go."

Varying the Tone

Some referees use their whistle as if it were a fire alarm; others use it to talk to the players.

A fire alarm has one tone—loud—and one meaning: "Get out of here—NOW!" Some referees use their whistle in the same way. They have a single volume—loud if they feel confident, soft if they do not—which communicates nothing to the players beyond the two basic commands of "stop" and "go."

Veteran referees learn to vary the tone of their whistle and convey a wide range of sentiments and commands, each with a subtle shading of meaning. Some tones share information, some convey displeasure, some call down the Wrath of God from the heavens. As we might expect, the universal rule seems to be that the louder the whistle, the greater the referee's displeasure at whatever just happened. If you experiment with a variety of tones, you will hear the wide range of messages that are possible. With experience, you may come to appreciate the different meanings that you can convey, especially when combined with the appropriate body language or facial expression:

- Game on!

- No, no, no, guys....the throw-in is way back here!

- I saw that....that was a foul.

- Hey! That was nasty!!

- *Come back here...!*

- *Ummm*...guys? You can stop now. The ball went out of bounds.

- Okay...enough of that!

- *Vengeance is mine*, saith the Referee....

- Oh, for crying out loud....

- Don't make me come over there.

- Foolishness, thy name is Sweeper

- Somebody is in *BIG* trouble now!

- Hey!!! Yes, you!

- I'm getting pretty fed up here.

- Okay...half-time!

- Yes, I know everybody's tired. That's still no excuse.

- A minute left and you just had to do that, didn't you?

- All right, everyone....that's it for today.

There is, of course, no secret code or any sort of intricate musical vocabulary for you to use. You just need to be aware that you can actually speak with your whistle, and then simply whistle whatever you mean. You may, however, want to be careful when signaling with a particularly loud shriek. You do not want to blast away the ears of an innocent bystander.

To Pea, or not to Pea

When choosing a whistle from among the many different ones available, there is one distinction among them that every referee comes to know: some whistles have peas, and some of them do not.

A whistle made with a pea produces sound from the flow of the air through the air-chamber and around the pea. Its pitch will vary depending upon the size of the chamber, the flow of the air, and the caliber of the pea. Because the whistler's breath is diverted around the pea, however, the sound produced may not be as loud as that from a pea-less whistle. In addition, the pea itself can clog in cold, wet weather.

A pea-less whistle is often higher-pitched, and its sound can pierce through wind, eardrums, and many surrounding noises. Because of its design, however, it is usually harder to vary the tone of a pea-less whistle.

The Care and Handling of Whistles

Some referees use a lanyard to keep from losing their whistle during a match. Others prefer to carry the whistle loose, allowing easier signaling with either hand. Still others prefer a finger-whistle.

Regardless of your preference, it is a good idea to carry a spare whistle with you on the pitch. And for the day when you discover your whistle to be a perfect match for the one being used on the next field, you may want your spare to carry a different tone than your primary instrument.

It is never a good idea to run around the field with a whistle in your mouth. The time it takes to bring the whistle to your lips after a foul can help you tell if there is an advantage in letting play continue. More importantly, you do not want play to stop if you happen to trip over a soft spot in the turf and blow your whistle by accident.

Using the Voice

In addition to the whistle, referees have a second audible tool to take with them onto the field. Though often overlooked, the voice can be a powerful tool that lets you communicate directly with the players.

During Active Play

A referee must be careful not to distract players or interfere with play when speaking to them. While you may use your voice to coax them out of fouling, you must avoid distracting players during a contest for the ball.

The Discreet Word

Referees and players pass each other constantly on the field, during active play as well as at stoppages. This lets you deliver a private message to any player in a discreet manner—perhaps a reminder to tie his shoelaces or pull up his socks, or a mild admonition to settle down or keep his mind on the game. Used wisely, you can avoid making your admonition public, sparing the player some embarrassment. It also lets you humanize yourself by exchanging pleasantries.

A quiet word to a player can be quite effective in keeping tempers under control on the field. It may help the player calm himself. At other times, merely taking a troublesome player aside discreetly communicates to others—including, perhaps, the player who was just fouled—that the referee is on top of things.

Discretion being in the eye of the beholder, however, you may find it useful to conduct some of these "private" discussions in ways that send messages to others on the field as well. Experienced referees sometimes use others to talk to their real target, and enlisting a troublemaker's teammates to help keep their friend under control has a number of advantages. It avoids confronting a player whose temper is not firmly under control. It lets you develop a rapport with players who are behaving themselves. And it shows that you are doing your best to calm tempers, establishing you as a voice of reason on the field. Though often unnoticed by the enlistees themselves, it also isolates the troublemaker and places the burden for controlling him on those with the greatest stake in getting him to behave—the teammates who will be playing short a man, if their friend insists on getting himself sent off.

Pleasantries aside, if you need to discuss something serious with a coach or player, you should usually conduct the discussion in private. This lets both of you be candid and helps resolve your problems without drawing onlookers into the discussion.

The Public Word

Even so, if your intended message is aimed at a broader audience than just the player you are talking to it can sometimes be more useful for others to overhear what you are saying. An audible word to a player concerned about the other team's substituting near the end of a close match, for example, delivers the message to both sides that you are not fooled by gamesmanship and will be adding time as needed. Or, a voiced comment about "heel nips" at the right time may signal that you are watching to prevent cheap fouls from escalating into major problems.

If you choose to make your comments audibily you should avoid embarrassing or humiliating a particular coach or player. Doing so will only cause tempers to rise. Even worse, it may lead his teammates to feel protective, which could lead them to rash actions in response.

Using Your AR's

While the center referee is the official that most people notice at a soccer game, an officiating crew rises or falls as a team. At any moment, one of the assistant referees may be the only one watching the game's most important event at the time. Given soccer's fast pace and constant motion of play, the performance of the assistants may be every bit as critical as that of the referee. All successful referees not only know how to function as the assistant referee, they also know how to use them when they are in the middle.

Before and After the Game

As the referee, you will have a number of administrative duties in addition to officiating the match itself. You can delegate many of these book-keeping details to your assistant referees, such as checking in the teams, collecting the game reports, pass cards, balls, and fees, overseeing repairs on the nets, and anything else you think would be helpful. After the match, your assistants can help with post-game duties as well, helping you compile the game report, and distributing the reports and pass cards to the respective teams.

As we have already seen, before the match begins you should lead a pre-game conference for the entire crew, going over your expectations for the upcoming game and outlining any special instructions you have. This will help make sure that the whole team is working toward the same end when the whistle sounds and play begins.

During Active Play

Once the game begins, the whole crew must turn its attention to managing things in a professional manner, and you will be responsible for making sure that your own team functions efficiently and well. This means knowing when to look for help, and how to act on the advice of the assistant referees along the sidelines.

Keeping the AR in Sight

Though we will discuss positioning in greater detail below, a referee who cannot see his assistants cannot expect them to provide timely assistance. Whenever possible, you should keep play between yourself and the lead assistant, boxing the action between the two sets of eyes.

In addition, it does little good if you and your assistant each have similar viewing angles, or are both screened from the play. This just increases the chance that the two of you will miss something important. Making sure that you each have a different view of the play minimizes the chance that you will both be blocked from seeing what is happening.

Through Balls and Clearing Kicks

Whenever the attacking team sends a ball past the last defender, you should glance at the lead assistant to see whether the play is offside.

Similarly, players will often make a long clearance during the run of play, kicking the ball from one end of the field to another. It can be a good idea to take this chance to glance at both assistant referees, looking to see if anything needs your attention before turning upfield and focusing your attention on the drop zone for the kick.

Offside Calls

Ordinarily, the lead assistant referee will be the only official in the right position to judge whether a play is offside, and the only one watching the offside line when play is elsewhere on the field. You should generally defer to his advice when determining if a player is in an offside position. This includes some situations that are not obvious at first glance, such as when a player returns to an onside position after the ball is kicked.

Sometimes, the assistant will raise a premature flag, or be unable to detect that the ball was retained by the kicker or collected by an overlapping player. Occasionally, you may be in the right spot to see that the ball was last played by a member of the defensive team. If so, you should thank the assistant for his help by a visual or audible signal, but wave down the flag and let play to continue. You can discuss any questions about the matter at the end of the half, or at an appropriate stoppage of play.

Fouls

Responsibility for calling fouls is among the topics for discussion at the pre-game conference, and is usually the most important facet of the game for the referees to handle properly. There are many styles and philosophies of officiating. All of them work best when there are three sets of eyes watching play rather than one, and when there are three officials prepared to deal with foul play.

Depending upon the age and experience of the assistant, it is usually best to trust the assistant referees to signal fouls observed along the sidelines. This not only fosters cooperation and teamwork, but since the assistant will be closer to the play she will often have the superior angle of sight on what is happening. As we saw in Chapter 3, the waggling flag is the appropriate signal from the assistant who is recommending that the referee call a foul. If you want, you may also choose to have another discreet signal for a recommended "no-call," in addition to the unraised flag. A referee unsure of a call and deferring to an assistant's proximity to play gets no help if the assistant, reasoning that everything is within the referee's sight, keeps his flag down out of deference to the referee, despite his own judgment that the play was a foul. A silent signal, such as a shaking head for a recommended "no-call," is one way to communicate the information without calling attention to the consultation between the officials.

At times, you may want to use your own non-verbal "no-call" signal communicating the other way as well. If you have decided not to call a foul—viewing a contact either as fair, or too trifling to warrant a stoppage—it will not be helpful for your assistant to raise a flag to announce a different opinion. A shaking head, or a discreet "no-call" sign (like a modified baseball umpire's "safe" sign), can communicate the to an assistant referee looking to make eye contact before signaling. Though not an officially sanctioned signal, similar conventions are common and can be quite helpful in keeping the match flowing smoothly.

When signaling a foul, experienced assistants usually try to raise the flag in the hand that would signal the direction of any ensuing restart. This, in turn, permits an intelligent use of advantage if events look promising for the fouled team. If you want to use this convention, you should discuss it during your pre-game. Regardless of your preferences, however, you should recognize the flag in one of three ways—whistling for the foul; acknowledging the foul but awarding advantage; or thanking the assistant and waving down the flag.

Acknowledging Flag Signals

Though the referee makes all final decisions on the field, each flag signal by the assistant referee communicates information. Sometimes, the message is ball out-of-play. Sometimes it signals an infraction of some sort. Occasionally, it is meant to alert the referee to a misconduct or other emergency that requires attention. In all cases, as the referee you should make a point of acknowledging every signal by one of your assistants. You are still free to overrule any recommendation if you take a different view of the play, but recognizing the flag confirms your receipt of the signal and, as a common courtesy to your colleague, it is only polite to thank him for his help.

If you choose to honor the flag, simply blow your whistle to stop play and proceed with the appropriate restart. If you decide to overrule it, you should have identified your return signal at your pre-game conference. Customarily, it is a visible wave of the hand. In either case, a discreet "thumbs-up" sign is an easily understood way to express your thanks, and encourage your colleague to keep up the good work.

Teamwork

Like any team, a crew of officials must function as a unit in order to succeed. This means that each official not only must perform professionally and well, but must also be ready to back up a teammate who has missed a play or is temporarily out of position. Communication will be critical to success, and everyone should be alert for signs that indicate a need for help.

Encouraging your assistants and complimenting them when they perform well promotes cohesiveness and camaraderie. Honest feedback, if done in a helpful, constructive manner, can also help referees learn the craft of officiating and promote competence and professionalism in all referees.

On the other hand, harsh criticisms of your fellow officials in public, even if you are voicing your opinions at a game you are watching as a spectator, tends to promote misunderstanding and cynicism by other spectators and undermines the authority of all officials. Although explaining a rule, or the likely reason for a call, may further other spectators' understanding of the game, things always look different from the sidelines, and a professional difference of opinion is no reason for you to impugn the competence of a colleague. If necessary, there are other avenues for you to bring matters to the attention of the authorities, and if you have critical opinions to express it is better to do them "within the family."

Dead Ball Stoppages

At each stoppage of play you should make a habit of glancing at both assistant referees to see if they have any information to convey. Doing so has the added benefit of developing a sense of fellowship among the officials, and providing the chance for some non-verbal communication about the course of events on the game.

Foul Recognition

Probably the most important challenge for a referee is learning to recognize and deal with foul play in its various forms on the soccer field. Because a good referee will never stop learning, it is an undertaking that will never end.

Beginning referees often discover that they are tentative and unsure of themselves. This happens for a very good reason. It is easy to officiate from the sidelines, where nobody is responsible for making decisions and the "right" call is largely a matter of partisan opinion. But things look completely different in the middle of the field, where play races by without waiting for the referee. Events often seem to blur together, and it can take quite a while to get used to the pace of the action on a field, let alone learn what to watch and where the dangers may lie.

Referees who play the game have an initial advantage, since they come to the field knowing what fouls feel like. But for all referees, there is no substitute for watching as much soccer as possible—whether live, on film, or on television. We can, after all, practice mechanics in the mirror, but we cannot learn to recognize a foul by studying a picture, or reading a description in print. Fouls always involve movement and real-time motion, and getting a sense of what is, and is not acceptable on the field takes time, practice, and a lot of trial and error. It does, however, get easier with experience.

In the meantime, there are some basic fouls that all referees must master, and a few fundamental points about them that we can watch for.

Learning to Focus

Spectators usually follow the ball as it bounces or sails across the field. Referees soon learn that the ball will never commit a foul, and that they need to watch the players, instead.

Whether working in the middle or on the line, it can be tempting for a referee to turn into a spectator. The participants are not paying us simply to watch the match, however. They are paying us to officiate it. And as the center referee you must learn to focus your attention on the area around the ball.

There is a saying among some referees that good officials "referee the defense," and concentrate on judging what the defenders are doing to take the ball away from whoever has it. Concentrating your attention on the defenders lets you focus on the players who will be taking the most aggressive action at any given moment. By doing, so you can still notice anything out of the ordinary that an attacker may do, but since he already has the ball he usually has no reason to foul. It is, rather, the defenders who may be feeling the need for a bit of extra self-help.

All parts of the field will need your attention during the game, however, and you must also begin to develop habits and instincts that will let you monitor off-ball incidents and sense when to watch behind the play for late contact. But for the beginning referee, the most critical skill to develop is learning to sense the kind of challenge that is likely, and focusing on the areas of the body that will be coming into contact. The rest will come, over time.

Points of Contact

A beginning referee can feel overwhelmed by the sheer volume of things going on during the course of a game. People are shouting and screaming, (either at the players or the officials), the players are all running about in different directions, and play can rush along in a seamless blur. This can make the new official start questioning his own senses, and wondering how the other referees can keep track of it all.

The answer is that nobody can keep track of everything. Experienced referees have simply learned to filter out much of what is going on around them in order to concentrate on what is important. The challenge for the newcomer is discovering what to watch, and learning to anticipate the play while keeping an open mind about the call. To do this, we first need to know the likely points on the body where fouls generally occur. This will vary, depending upon the type of contact each play is likely to generate.

Feet and Ankles

Soccer—called "football" in many parts of the world—is generally played with the ball at the players' feet. Since most fouls occur in the immediate vicinity of the ball, it follows that most fouls involve a careless knock on the feet, shins, ankles, or calves of a player trying to keep or win the ball. This is best detected by concentrating on the movement of the feet near and around the ball. If you see no contact, or contact is with the ball before a player falls as a result of the play for the ball, the challenge is "fair" and should be allowed. If the challenge results in tackling the foot or leg instead of the ball, then it is "foul" and may warrant stopping play. In either case, the challenge may be very quick, and you can miss it entirely if you are watching something else.

Shoulders and Bodies

Sometimes players use their bodies, instead of their feet, to win the ball. Though this can happen anywhere on the field, it is typical of challenges occurring along the touchlines, when two players are racing headlong after the ball, or when one player is shielding the ball from an opponent. Unlike tackles with the feet, contact can extend from the shoulder to the hip, and you will need to watch for attempts to use the arms or hips to push the opponent off the ball. The contact may take place over a relatively longer period of time than a tackle, however, and you will need to watch the whole play unfold in order to judge the fairness of the challenge. Often, particularly at higher levels of play, the players will be grappling with each other trying to win the ball and it would be unfair to penalize one for conduct that is indistinguishable from that of his opponent. The solution would be either to penalize the initiator by calling the "first foul," or to allow the contact on grounds that with a fifty-fifty ball, and "fifty-fifty" contact, there is simply no reason to stop play. The choice between the two will depend upon the temper of the game, the level of play, and the level of contact that you are willing to permit.

Airballs

Crosses, long-distance goal kicks, long passes or clearances, and long-range shots on goal all have one thing in common. All of them involve a ball, launched into the air, that must eventually come back to Earth. When it does, the ball will attract a crowd of players, leading to a host of problems for all concerned.

For a player, fielding a ball in the air requires a number of quick decisions. The player must decide whether to settle it or attempt a one-touch pass, and whether to play the ball with his foot, body, or head. To win the ball, players must try to out-jump their opponents who will, in turn, be faced with the same array of choices. For the referee, players aloft pose two main concerns, one relating to safety, the other to fairness.

A player who has left the ground is, in many respects, at the mercy of others. Having set his course by leaping, the player is bound to fall in accordance with the laws of gravity, and if concentrating on the ball he will be helpless if bumped or upended by another. On the other hand, a player electing to receive the ball while remaining on the ground may well be at risk of injury himself, if crashed into by a player hurtling wildly through the air. Leaping players can, in fact, be the source of some of the worst injuries in soccer through mistimed leaps, ill-chosen landings, or deliberate bumps intended to cause a leaping player to lose his balance.

When dealing with a long ball in the air, you cannot concern yourself with the ball. You must instead focus on the players in the drop zone. Watching their eyes can indicate whether they are more concerned with the ball or the player beside them. Watching their movements will give important clues about what they are trying to do. Important points to watch will be the players eyes, their hands and shoulders, and the angle of any leap they make into the air:

- A player who places his hands on his opponent's shoulders before leaping to head the ball may be intent on playing the ball, but is still holding his opponent down and using the other player to gain additional height, as well.

- A player who backs up while concentrating on the ball is probably concentrating on trapping or settling the ball. A player who does the same thing while looking back at his leaping opponent may be (a) trying to draw a foul by fooling the referee into believing that the opponent is jumping carelessly, or (b) sending the opponent a grim message that jumping will be dangerous.

- A player who leaps at an oblique angle is trying to make up in enthusiasm what he lacks in positioning, and is likely to crash into players who are already in place to receive the ball.

- Two players who are both intent on winning the ball may well crash into each other in mid-flight, perhaps with dire consequences for one or both of them, but without anyone being at fault.

Challenges in the air can bring about some of the most exciting moments in soccer, as well as some of the worst injuries. You must be ready to view the entire play in order to judge it accurately.

The Benefits of Patience: *Weighing the Consequences*

Just as a hunter cannot un-shoot a gun, a soccer referee cannot un-blow a whistle. Once the whistle sounds to stop play, nothing that happens afterwards matters so far as the flow of the game is concerned. The whistle that sounds just before a score disallows the goal just as surely as if the shot had never taken place.

For this reason, it can be useful to wait and see the consequence of an event before deciding on a course of action. Waiting a moment before blowing the whistle gives you a better sense of how play will develop, and helps you decide whether it would be better to award advantage and let play continue, or halt play and award a kick. It may also spare you the embarrassment of having to dig the ball out of the back of the net and explain to the team that just scored that their goal does not count after all—but that to punish the other team for its foul play a free kick is awarded, instead...and best of luck trying to score.

Under the Laws, you can change an advantage call if the advantage does not come about after a couple of seconds. This gives you more time than you may realize to make up your mind. Developing the habit of waiting to see the result of a foul before blowing your whistle is just an extension of the same principle and leads to the same result: better match flow and the appreciation of the players.

This does not, however, mean that you should judge a foul merely by the result of the contact. A player can trip over an outstretched leg following a fair tackle, just as a player may fall following a fair shoulder charge, or injure himself when he loses his balance after attempting a header. You must evaluate each challenge on its own, to decide if it is fair or unfair—that is, whether undertaken with due care, or done carelessly, recklessly, or with excessive force. But just concluding that a challenge is unfair does not force you to blow the whistle. Soccer instructs its referees not to stop play for "doubtful" or "trifling" breaches of the laws, and proper application of the advantage clause will keep us from whistling even clear fouls if the fouling team would benefit from the stoppage. By waiting to see the disadvantage to the fouled team you will help each team in turn, for every foul you whistle will benefit the victim, rather than the offender.

Some fouls, of course, require stern and immediate action. Others so clearly disadvantage the victim's team that a delayed whistle is unnecessary. As always, experience is the best teacher, and new referees must be careful not to wait too long before making up their minds and seeing the play race on without them.

Basic Fouls

A foul in any sport is a violation of that sport's code of conduct in some form, and each sport punishes foul play in its own unique way. In soccer, we define a foul as an unfair action a player commits against an opposing player, or the opposing team, during the course of a match[*]. The punishment will depend upon the infraction, but will be either a direct or indirect free kick. To be a foul, the act must occur on the field, while the ball is in play. Otherwise, it may constitute a misconduct, and may even warrant a caution or send-off, but it will not be a foul.

While some fouls occur mostly at higher levels of play, the fouls described in the Laws of the Game are all basic infractions that can occur at any game. While you must see an entire incident to make a final judgment on any particular act, there are some attributes of each particular foul that all referees must watch for, in determining whether the play is a fair one, or an act of foul play.

Penal Fouls

Under Law 12, there are ten offenses for which the punishment is a

---

[*] USSF, *Advice to Referees on the Laws of the Game*, §12.1 (2006).

direct free kick, from which the fouled team may score directly. If committed by a defender inside his own penalty area, this direct free kick becomes a penalty kick. Though described in broad, general terms, these fouls seek to punish those actions that soccer deems to be playing in an unfair or unsafe manner.

Most acts are fouls only if committed carelessly, recklessly, or with excessive force.

Some acts on the field are fouls only by degree. In other words, many actions occur routinely during the course of play which are harmless in themselves, and become fouls only if done in a manner which unfairly places an opponent at a disadvantage. Players may bump into each other while running, or push past each other while trying to avoid a collision. They may struggle with other players over the ball, or leap to head a long pass and collide with an opponent attempting to do the same. They may kick at the ball and narrowly miss kicking their opponent's shin. All of these actions are simply part of soccer, where most bodily contact is quite incidental to the players' efforts to win the ball and passes quite uneventfully during the course of the game.

At other times, a player will mistime a kick, misjudge a jump, or overestimate the body's ability to follow whatever instructions are coming from the brain, and those actions will exceed the bounds of fair play. When it does, you must be able to spot the infraction and unafraid to take appropriate action. But first you must be able to distinguish fair from foul contact. While this is impossible to do from a cold narrative, or even a picture frozen in time, there are some elements of each foul that can help determine the result in a particular case:

Kicking

While kicking the ball is an objective of every player, kicking an opponent is a foul, and deliberately trying to kick an opponent may be an act of misconduct, as well.

There may be times when a player's foot will come in contact with an opponent through an otherwise fair play. Contact may be minimal or superficial, or a players's foot may strike an opponent as one or both are falling to the ground. On the other hand, kicks can be quite painful, which is why a player who does not exercise due care to avoid kicking his opponent commits a foul. A referee watching two players contesting for a ball on the ground should pay careful attention to the likely point of contact involved in this sort of play— the feet.

Tripping

Players often trip on a soccer field, many times without the help of foul play. They trip over the ball, over uneven ground, and, on occasion, over the outstretched foot of an opponent who is making a play for the ball. In these circumstances, there is no foul to call, since it is the player himself who is tripping, through no fault of an opponent. Tripping (or attempting to trip) an opponent is the foul; tripping by oneself is just being clumsy.

Where, however, a player fails to exercise due care—by raising a foot during a tackle, for example; or extending a leg as an opponent is running by—then it is not a case of someone stumbling during the natural course of play, but tripping through the careless actions of someone else. In these circumstances, the trip is the fault of the player who is being careless, and the proper response is to call the foul. In either case, the referee sensing a play for the ball with the feet should be watching the legs and lower body to judge the fairness of the challenge.

There is another form of tripping which can be quite dangerous. Also called "bridging" or "making a back," this foul occurs when one player jumps to head the ball while an opponent moves to undercut the airborne player, often by backing into him. Referees sometimes mistake the nature of the action and call the leaping player for a "jumping" foul when it is really the fault of the player on the ground. Even if done inadvertently, this action can result in serious injury if the player aloft lands off-balance. If done deliberately, it may be an act of misconduct. Experienced referees will be watching the eyes of the players involved in order to judge their actions. Players intent on playing the ball will be focused on the ball; players who focus on their opponents are usually bent on foul play.

Striking

If a player is struck by an opponent's foot, we call the act "kicking." If done with any other part of the body, or with the ball or any hurled object, it will be a form of "striking." Like kicking and tripping, the foul of "striking" includes attempts to commit the offense, and if done deliberately will constitute a form of misconduct. Commonly associated with violent conduct, striking may also occur carelessly through ordinary contact during the run of play. The important thing for the referee to judge will be whether the contact was superficial (in which case there would be no foul since it will have no effect on play) or whether it injured or placed the opponent at a disadvantage. If done carelessly, it will warrant a direct kick; if done deliberately, it may warrant a caution or send-off, as well.

Aside from incidental contacts, or careless actions arising from clumsy play, many striking incidents take place very quickly and can turn a game from sportsmanlike to nasty in a heartbeat. Deliberate elbows to the face, elbows dug into the ribs of players leaping to head the ball, and blows delivered with a balled fist can all escalate into a game-ending melee. You will need to distinguish careless arm motions which carry no malice from deliberate attempts to do violence. Deliberate violence has no place on the soccer field, and neither do those who commit it. Violent conduct is a red-card offense, and for the good of the game offenders should be sent off the field as soon as possible.

Jumping

Players jumping *to play the ball* can be among the most exciting parts of a soccer game. Players jumping *at their opponents* are engaging in foul play and can cause serious injuries. As with most other fouls, jumping during the course of play is a neutral act by itself. It only becomes a foul if done carelessly, recklessly, or with excessive force.

The referee has three principle ways of judging players going airborne: watching their eyes, their arms, and their angle of flight. Noting the details of each area should tell whether the jumping player is exercising due care in executing a leap.

Charging

Soccer is a contact sport in which players can use their bodies and muscles while challenging for the ball. On the other hand, soccer is not ice hockey, and soccer players do not crash into each other to body-check their opponents. The important thing for the referee will be the force of the contact, as well as the targeted area of the opponent's body. In addition, once a keeper collects the ball and assumes possession by controlling it with any part of his hands or arms, opposing players may not lawfully try to play it and trying to do so by way of physical contact will probably be a charging foul.

We often hear about "shoulder-to-shoulder" charges, but this is not, strictly speaking, a requirement of a fair charge. Owing to human anatomy, though, fair charges will be in the general direction of the shoulder area and not directed toward the spine or the hips. If performed with clearly undue force, particularly toward the small of the back, a charge may be deemed reckless or worse, and sanctioned as a misconduct.

Pushing

Players often tussle after the ball at a soccer match. Most of this contact is quite fair and, if qualifying as a "fair charge," would be well within the normal range of fair play. Occasionally, a player will go beyond the customary challenges and shove an opposing player out of the way, either to clear a path to the ball or to ensure that the opponent is in no position to contest for possession.

To determine when an action crosses the line from fair contact to an unfair push, the referee should look to judge the force of the contact, and whether it stemmed from an unnatural movement of the arms or body to stop or alter the opponent's momentum. A referee sensing a physical challenge for position with the upper body should be monitoring the players' use of their arms and hips, in addition to watching their feet.

Some actions are fouls if the referee determines the fact of occurrence, regardless of how they are committed.

A few acts on the field are considered fouls whenever they occur, regardless of how they occur. Even so, saying that the referee must make a simple factual determination on these fouls oversimplifies things, for we must still make a judgment about both the nature of an act and its effect.

Tackling the opponent instead of the ball

Because soccer involves a struggle for the ball, players are constantly challenging each other for custody, and a player trying to dispossess the other side will often tackle for possession with his feet. Since cleats are hard, and the ball is soft and filled with air, the ball acts as a natural cushion during these contests and helps keep everyone safe and uninjured. As a result, "fair tackles" are those in which a player contacts the ball first, before making any contact with the opponent. By contrast, a tackle which first makes contact with the opponent before touching the ball is a foul tackle and penalized by a direct free kick.

Though a common excuse among players is that they "got the ball," the mere fact that they did, in fact, contact the ball first does not end the matter. While perhaps not a "tackling" foul, tackles committed carelessly, recklessly, or with excessive force may still constitute the separate fouls of kicking, tripping, charging, or striking.

Holding

The dictionary tells us that to hold means to hinder or restrain,[*] and in the context of soccer it means restraining an opponent by use of the hands, arms, or body. It can also mean, within the context of the game, stretching the arms out wide to prevent or impede an opponent from moving laterally. The foul involves holding an opponent, however. It does not mean catching hold of the opponent's shirt, socks, or other apparel, unless it hinders his freedom of motion and keeps him from moving into a desired position. Simply put, grabbing a fistful of shirt may be offensive to the player, but need not be whistled as a holding foul. On the other hand, holding onto a fistful of shirt to slow the player down, win possession of the ball, or gain any other tactical advantage would warrant punishment as a foul.

While holding usually consists of the use of the hands or arms, it can also include the use of other portions of the body. Struggling to remain atop a fallen player, or using the legs to keep an opponent from moving, would both be instances of holding even though neither involves use of the arms. And sometimes players hold onto opponents to keep them from rejoining play after the ball is cleared out of the immediate area. This is among the many reasons to watch behind the play after the ball is away.

Spitting

Spitting, though always vulgar, is regarded in some cultures as a particularly vile and offensive insult. For this reason, spitting at an opponent during play is a foul as well as a misconduct, punished by a direct kick as well as a send-off.

Referees must, however, take care to punish the misconduct, and not

---

[*] *Random House Webster's College Dictionary*, 628 (2001).

simply the vulgar. Like many athletes, soccer players have an unfortunate tendency to spit quite innocently, occasionally on indoor carpets as well as natural grass. Despite what their mothers might have to say about the matter, on a soccer field only spitting at another person is a misconduct.

Deliberately handling the ball

Among all fouls arising during the course of the game, handballs—or deliberately handling the ball, in the terminology of the Laws—may well cause the most trouble, especially for beginning referees.

Handling is the only foul not committed against an opposing player, but against the opposing team. It is also the only penal foul that requires deliberate intent by the player committing the foul. The foul is not, after all, "letting the ball touch the hand" but "deliberately handling the ball." As a result, it is often said that if the ball plays the hand it is not a foul, but if the hand plays the ball, then it is.

Unfortunately, this rule of thumb is more easily stated than put into practice. It also conflicts with the more conventional rule applied by players, coaches, and spectators around the world: if it hits the hand of an opposing player, it is a handball. As a result, applying the Laws properly may lead to sharp comments by participants and spectators alike, but they are usually comments born of misunderstanding and should not be taken to heart. It would be unfair to penalize a player for an accidental touch which is neither intended nor avoidable, and a few moments of thought should be enough to grasp the basic concepts involved.

Handling fouls require deliberate contact between the ball and a player's hand or arm. This, in turn, means that the player either chose not to avoid touching the ball, placed his arms in an unnatural playing position to make it likely that he would touch the ball, or that he chose to continue playing a ball after an initial, accidental contact. Perhaps this is best illustrated by studying examples of what handling is *not*:

- Using the arms instinctively to protect a sensitive area of the body from the sudden approach of the ball is not a foul.

- A ball deflecting off a player's hand or arm from a shot or pass taken a few feet away is not a foul—unless the player deliberately placed his arm in an unnatural position to block the pass. (And placing the arms or hands over a sensitive area of the body while standing in the wall at a free kick is not, by any stretch of the imagination, unnatural).

- A ball striking the arm of a player who is looking the other way is not a foul.

- A ball innocently striking the arm of a player does not magically turn the play into a foul by falling in a place that happens to benefit that player.

- On the other hand....a player who continues to control the ball with his arm after an initial, innocent touch is committing a handling foul.

- And a referee may have cause to wonder just how innocent a hand-ball contact is, if the ball just keeps happening to fall in a convenient place for the same player in the same game.

There are many aspects of hand-to-ball contact to note and consider when deciding whether a handball is deliberate or inadvertent. Uneven playing surfaces often causes the ball to deflect at odd angles, making it hard for players to know how it will bounce. Players who are unchallenged in the open field have no incentive to handle the ball, since it will be easily detected. Often, this suggests an unintentional handling, especially on the many fields where the playing surface itself is less than putting-green smooth. On the other hand, since players intending to commit a foul may want to hide their actions from the officials, many intentional handballs will occur just out of sight of the referee, or when the referee is screened from the play, making cooperation between all three officials essential.

Technical Fouls

For some infractions the punishment is an indirect kick, meaning that the ball must be touched by a second player before the attacking team can score. These fouls are often called "technical fouls" because most are not the direct result of foul play, but are violations of one of soccer's procedural rules, which are generally designed to keep play flowing or prevent penal fouls from happening.

Playing in a dangerous manner

Among a referee's chief concerns is the safety of the players. As a result, the Laws authorize the referee to penalize dangerous play by awarding an indirect kick to the other side.

The rules do not define precisely what is meant by "playing in a dangerous manner," except to defer to the opinion of the referee. Commonly accepted notions of "dangerous play" include high kicking near other players, kicking wildly on the ground with players nearby, tackling for the ball with the cleats exposed or when it is in the keeper's possession—even, on occasion, exposing oneself to the risk of harm, if it causes someone to refrain from playing the ball for fear of injuring his overly adventuresome opponent. It is only a foul if it places an opponent at risk, however. A high kick alone in mid-field endangers no one, while the same kick in a crowded penalty area very well may.

At higher levels of play, where gifted players are used to taking greater chances during the course of a match, this infraction is usually called only if it causes the opponent to react by trying to avoid the contact. At most youth games, and many amateur adult games, everyone expects the referee to impose a greater level of sanity on the players than their enthusiasm might otherwise suggest is present.

Impeding an opponent

Though players often get in each other's way during the normal run of play, players sometimes deliberately block their opponents from running after the ball or moving into tactically important space on the field. Impeding an opponent—or "obstructing," as most of the soccer world calls it—involves the deliberate use of the body to interfere with an opponent's movement in order to delay his progress, and is punished with an indirect kick. Often, this foul occurs when a player senses that a speeding opponent will beat him to the ball, or anticipates a potentially troublesome pass into open space. By stepping in front of the opponent and blocking his progress, the player hopes to slow down the opponent and let a teammate collect the ball. If the action causes more than incidental physical contact caused by the momentum of the blocked player, it may constitute a "charging" or "holding" foul, rather than "impeding."

A player within "playing distance" of the ball may legally block his opponent's pathway to it without being guilty of a foul. This is known as "shielding," and involves the use of the body to keep possession. Playing distance will vary depending on the speed of the players and the ball, and ultimately rests with the referee's judgment, but the shielding player need not actually touch the ball to shield it legally from the other side.

Shepherding the ball out of bounds or towards the keeper is a recognized and quite legitimate tactic, as long as the player guarding the ball stays within playing distance.

Interfering with the Keeper's Release

Once the keeper takes possession of the ball with his hands, the opponents' ability to challenge directly for the ball ends and does not resume until it is released back into play. To keep the match safe, and ensure that balls collected by a goalkeeper are promptly returned to play, the Laws punish players who interfere with an opposing keeper's attempt to release the ball by awarding an indirect kick.

This does not mean that players must move out of the keeper's way, or refrain from exploiting any blunders in releasing the ball unwisely or prematurely. But even though the players need not get out of the way, they cannot move to hinder or block the keeper's movements, or do anything to prevent the keeper from hurling or punting it downfield.

Goalkeeper offenses

Due to the keeper's unique authority to handle the ball, the Laws also place limits on a goalkeeper's uncontested possession. This keeps the game flowing by preventing keepers from wasting excessive amounts of time before releasing the ball back into play, where it is free for anyone to claim.

Failing to release the ball

Because opponents cannot challenge a keeper's possession of the ball, soccer places a time limit of six seconds to return the ball into play. Violations of this rule are punished by an indirect kick. A keeper need not punt or hurl the ball downfield to do so. Laying the ball on the ground at his feet is sufficient, since this eliminates the privilege of handling the ball and lets anyone try to win it. The time limit does not begin until the keeper has uncontested control of the ball, and any time taken in collecting it is excluded.

The reason for the rule is to keep play flowing; it is not to give one team or the other a chance at an easy goal. As a result, you should never make any signal, verbal or visual, to count down the time, and you should not penalize the keeper for this infraction without giving a clear warning. Keepers making a good-faith effort to release the ball into play are complying with the rule, and referees who are overly fastidious about time limits risk losing the respect of the players.

Backpasses

Before 1992, at a time when the Laws still allowed the goalkeeper to be charged, they also permitted a team trying to run out the clock to pass the ball back it its own keeper. The keeper could then pick it up and, if he stood very still, wait. When an opposing player came to challenge for the ball, he would release it to a teammate who, if the chance came again, could kick it back to the keeper to pick up...and wait some more. In theory, this cycle could repeat indefinitely, until time expired or the players became bored.

This thrilling tactic came to an end with the advent of the new "back-pass" rule in 1992. To promote attacking soccer, and remove a technically lawful and universally despised means of wasting time, the Laws were changed to withdraw the keeper's authority to handle the ball when kicked directly to him by a teammate. Keepers can still play the ball, but unable to handle it they now face the same restrictions as any field player—except that, to guard against the prospect of a cheap goal caused by an inattentive keeper or a differing view of the play by the referee, a keeper handling a backpass inside his own penalty area does not risk a penalty kick for handling. The offense is, instead, punished by an indirect kick for the technical offense of handling the backpass. In its present form, the rule also includes throw-ins to the keeper from his own team, as well as backpasses.

Though the cause of considerable on-field debate at many soccer games, the rule is limited in scope and not terribly difficult to understand. To prevent time-wasting, a keeper cannot handle a ball deliberately kicked to him—or in his direction, enabling him to collect it—by a teammate. If the ball is deflected or misdirected, or the pass comes from the chest, head, or other body part not commonly used for kicking, the rule does not apply. And if there is any doubt about the matter, then there is no reason to make the call.

Second Touches and other Technical Offenses

There are a number of Laws relating to "second touches" by a player who has put the ball into play. By and large, players who initiate a restart may not play the ball a second time until someone else has touched it, and the keeper, having released the ball into play from his hands, may not handle it again until some other player has gotten a touch on the ball. As with other "technical offenses," including offside infractions, penalty kick encroachments by the attacking team, or cautionable offenses coming to light during the run of play which are not themselves fouls, these infractions are punished by an indirect kick.

The Geography of Restarts

The basic rule of thumb on a soccer field is that play resumes wherever it stopped. Free kicks take place from the spot of the infraction; a throw-in occurs where the ball went out-of-bounds; and with modifications to accommodate restarts within the goal area, a dropped ball takes place wherever the ball was when play stopped. As with any rule of thumb, there are, of course, exceptions:

Designated Points of Restarting Play

There are a few places on the field where particular restarts occur, regardless of where the ball went out of play:

- Kick-offs will always take place in the middle of the center circle.

- Penalty kicks will always take place at the penalty spot—or, on fields that are not fully marked, at the spot mid-way between the goal posts, and half-way between the six-yard line defining the goal area and the eighteen-yard line defining the penalty area.

- Corner kicks will always take place at one of the corner arcs.

- Goal kicks can take place anywhere inside the goal area. However, as with any defensive kick taken from inside the penalty area, the ball is not in play until it clears the area.

Mechanics

Even recognizing what a foul is, you still need to communicate the decision and "sell" the call. For this, knowing and using the proper mechanics is crucial, demonstrating that you are on top of things on the pitch.

The mechanics themselves are simple, designed to look sharp and professional. Soccer keeps referee mechanics simple for a number of reasons. The game extends across nations and cultures, and the signals chosen must be readily understood and inoffensive to everyone. Simplicity also minimizes the chance of confusion and lets the game resume quickly, without fuss, and with fewer chances for the players to complain. Except for those associated with misconducts, most signals by the referee do no more than announce the restart for play to resume. When combined with cooperation by the entire officiating crew, proper mechanics can enhance match control by coordinating all of the officials' signals to reinforce each other.

Goals and Kick-offs

Oddly enough, there is no single, approved mechanic for the ceremonial restart that begins each half, or restarts play after a goal—the kick-off.[*] Law 8 requires only that "the referee gives a signal," which it does not specify. This means that the signal for a kick-off can be anything, as long as the players understand it to be the signal to start playing.

The customary signal for a kick-off is a blast of the referee's whistle, often accompanied by an arm gesture in the direction of the kick. The signal for the event that often precedes a kick-off—a goal—is equally understated. The referee just points in the direction of the center circle, indicating the next restart of play.

Ball Out-of-Bounds

There are three different mechanics to signal when the ball completely crosses a boundary line, each denoting the appropriate restart:

---

[*] Law 8.

Other governing bodies have adopted different mechanics for many signals by the referee. In high school soccer, for example, the official will give a signal to the time-keeper to start the on-field clock—a circular motion with his arm—which is, by default, the signal for the kick-off.

For purposes of this book, we will concentrate on standard FIFA mechanics. Referees working games under the rules or procedures of other associations or groups should check to make sure that they are aware of any differences, and to apply the mechanic appropriate for the competition.

Mechanics—Throw-in

When an assistant referee signals that a ball has crossed the touch line, or the referee observes it himself, the referee indicates the direction of the throw by raising his arm at a 45-degree angle toward the goal defended by the team that kicked the ball out of bounds (or, toward the goal being attacked by the team entitled to the throw-in—whichever is easier to remember). Signaling direction even if the assistant referee has already done so confirms the assistant's decision and may help avoid controversy or dissent by the participants. In addition, the referee should be prepared to help players uncertain about the proper place of the restart to find the right spot for the throw-in.

4.1　　　*Throw-in*

4.2　　　*Goal Kick*

Mechanics—Goal Kick

To signal a goal kick, the referee points at the goal area, extending his arm downward.

Mechanics—Corner Kick

To signal a corner kick, the referee points upward at a 45-degree angle, toward the corner flag closest to where the ball left the field, which will be the place of the restart.

When the ball is clearly out of play, there is no need for a routine whistle to confirm what everyone can plainly see. Doing so just draws attention to yourself for no useful purpose. When there may be doubt about the matter, a short blast of the whistle will announce the stoppage, and you can then signal for the appropriate restart.

4.3　　　*Corner Kick*

Though not required, when overruling a directional signal by the assistant referee it often helps to indicate that you saw a deflection. A brushing motion against the arm or hand will suggest a last-second deflection visible from your own line of sight, and is a commonly used, if unofficial signal. Doing so explains the reason for the decision not only to the assistant, but also to any spectators who happened to notice the disagreement. This not only fosters a spirit of cooperation among the crew, but also helps retain the confidence of the participants by showing that the officials are helping each other to make the right call.

Fouls and Misconduct

Stopping play to deal with acts of misbehavior on the field will lead to one of three restarts, in addition to the appropriate display of any misconduct card:

Mechanics—Direct Free Kick

Having determined to stop the match for a penal foul, the referee sounds the whistle to announce the stoppage of play. He then indicates the direction of the restart by extending a fully extended arm toward the goal defended by the team that committed the foul (and toward the goal being attacked by the victim's team).

4.4   Direct Free Kick

Ordinarily, you should run toward the spot of the foul, both to deter any incidents and to make sure that the ball is placed properly for the re-start. You do not, however, want to linger in the vicinity of a restart longer than necessary. As always, you should be moving toward the next area of play.

Mechanics—Indirect Free Kick

Having stopped the match for a non-penal infraction, for which the restart is an indirect free kick, the referee first signals the appropriate direction for the restart. Having done so, the referee raises an arm vertically, fully extending it above the head, to indicate the indirect nature of the restart, maintaining the signal until a second player touches the ball, or it goes directly out of play.

Occasionally, the ball will go directly into the goal from an indirect kick. If it does, being able to point to your raised arm squelches any dissent. When this happens the restart would be a goal kick, and the sooner it is signaled and taken the quicker the attacking team will forget about their mistake and return their attention to the game. Failing to raise your arm does not change the nature of the restart, though, and you will need to award a goal kick to the defending team. You may also need to use your common sense in handling complaints from the attacking team, and an apology for your poor mechanics will probably do more to calm tempers than a quick caution for dissent.

When there is an indirect kick for the defense from deep inside its own defensive end, you should keep your arm raised until the next touch by a player, no matter how long that may take or how

4.5   *Indirect Kick*

far you run while chasing after play. Even so, no one will notice if you lower your arm after the ball is away, so long as the chance of a direct score seems non-existent. Days with gale-force winds blowing in the direction of the restart will, however, pose practical problems if you get into the habit of lowering your arm prematurely.

Mechanics—Penalty Kick

Having stopped play for a defensive penal foul inside the defending team's penalty area, the referee signals a penalty kick by delivering a loud blast on the whistle to communicate a stoppage of play and pointing downward directly toward the penalty spot to indicate that the restart will be a penalty kick.

4.6   *Penalty Kick*

Before letting a penalty kick take place, you must make sure that all players except the kicker and the defending keeper are outside the penalty area, upfield from the penalty spot and at least ten yards away from the ball. Once keeper and kicker both indicate that they are ready, you blow the whistle to let play resume. The ball is put in play as soon as it is struck by the kicker and moves forward, and the keeper must remain on the goal line until the kick.

A penalty kick is often a controversial call. Upset players may accost you to complain, or with pleas to reconsider. Moving past the penalty spot toward the end line can be an effective way of coping with the emotions of the defensive team. Moving off the field, while pointing to the boundary line and motioning for them to stay back, can help restore order while the attackers are retrieving the ball and getting ready for the ensuing kick. Players who follow you off the field to continue protesting the call are clearly guilty of dissent, making the reason for a caution apparent to all.

Mechanics—Player Misconduct

Having determined that a player is guilty of misconduct, and after identifying and isolating the player, the referee raises the appropriate-colored card high over the head to signal either a caution (a yellow card) or a send-off (a red card). If a player is receiving a second caution in

4.7   *Card for Player Misconduct*

the match, after signaling the caution the referee should raise a red card high over the head, indicating that the player is being sent off for a second cautionable offense.

Misconducts are stressful times for players and referees alike. You need to remain calm and do nothing to provoke or embarrass the player further. You should also remain at least an arm's length away from the player involved, discreetly beyond "lunging distance" in case he suffers a loss of temper.

Ideally, you should talk to the player involved, not only to help him regain control of his emotions but also to explain the reason for the caution or send-off. Sometimes—particularly if you sense growing tensions by the player or team that was just fouled—you may want to display your card quickly, to head off any attempt at retaliation.

When a player is sent off, or a team official is dismissed for "irresponsible behavior," play should not resume until the offender has left the field. Under Law 12, only players and substitutes are shown cards for misconduct. Unless league rules provide otherwise, coaches, trainers, and other team officials may be dismissed under Law 5 without the display of a card. You will, however, need to include a full report of the incident on your game report. If events lead to a dismissal or send-off, the competition authorities will need the information to determine the appropriate disciplinary action.

Mechanics—Advantage

Having observed a foul, but concluding that the fouled team is better off continuing with the run of play, the referee swings her arms forward and calls "Advantage" or "Play on!", acknowledging the foul and indicating a decision to allow play to continue, nevertheless.

4.8   *Advantage—Play On!*

The artful use of advantage is one of the hallmarks of a skillful referee. You must be careful not to invoke it carelessly, and should reserve it only to signal real fouls, and not trifling or doubtful offenses. If the advantage proves nonexistent, and does not materialize within a moment or two, the Laws now permit you to stop play and award the free kick. In this case, you may want to let everyone know what you are doing. It shows that you are not trying to protect them, but also attempting to let both teams play without unnecessary interruptions.

Dropped Balls

Of the eight restarts, the dropped ball is the only one directly set in motion by the referee, and the only one that can place him at some risk of peril.[*] Owing to the need for flexibility, there is no precisely defined mechanic for conducting a dropped ball. There are, however, many practical constraints on your options, leading to a variety of approaches for keeping your arms and legs out of harm's way, most of them the result of our instinct for self-preservation. Common methods include darting, flinching, and backing up very quickly.

Proper Form

Having determined that no other restart is appropriate, the referee restarts play with a dropped ball. Holding the ball in the palm of one hand at waist level, with his other hand over the top of the ball, the referee removes the lower hand from beneath the ball, letting gravity bring the ball to the ground, restarting play.

Dropped balls are not "thrown balls." You should let the ball fall, rather than tossing it to the ground. If a player touches the ball before it hits the ground, the restart is aborted and must be repeated until the players get it right—no matter how many times it takes, and no matter how impatient it makes you. And if the ball goes out of bounds before anyone touches it, it must be dropped again, though for this you probably have nobody but yourself to blame.

Keepers, being players, may participate at a dropped ball. If the drop is within the keeper's own penalty area, he is not forbidden from using his hands to pick it up. There is no also requirement that both teams

---

[*]In some respects, *all* of the restarts can place the referee in peril—though in the others it is the *call leading to the restart* that actually causes the danger, rather than the restart itself. By contrast, in the dropped ball setting it is the referee's proximity to the players' feet and other limbs that poses the direct potential for misadventure, if not handled properly.

participate in the restart, a fact that experienced referees often use to restore the status quo when play is stopped for an injury.

A Few Words of Caution

At higher levels of play, most dropped balls are uncontested. They usually arise from injuries or other unforeseen events, and the players generally decide among themselves which team is entitled to the ball. Skilled players tend to be well-schooled in soccer etiquette and it is understood that the team with the ball when the game is stopped is entitled to it when play resumes. This is so whether they put it out into touch themselves, or whether the referee halted play before they could do so. A lower levels of play, however, the participants are often ignorant of etiquette and tradition, and in the United States, some players and coaches view a dropped ball much like a face-off in hockey: two players get an equal chance at the ball and everyone gathers round. In this situation, with the ball free for all comers as soon as it hits the ground, you may find yourself in dicey circumstances. You need to remind the players not to play the ball before it hits the ground, and do your best to step away, well beyond the reach of anyone's cleats, before the ball lands.

Experienced referees try to avoid needless dropped balls, and often tell players to tap the ball out of bounds before tending to an injured player. If this advice proves unavailing, you may be able to convince someone to send the ball sailing toward midfield where a drop will not disadvantage either team. Particularly in recreational games, but also in some higher-level matches where temptation threatens to get the better of sportsman-ship, you should try to avoid dropped balls near either team's goal area by delaying the whistle to let players send the ball to a less dangerous part of the field. If this proves impractical, simply remind the players of proper etiquette—or, if the players seem determined to contest the drop, you may carelessly drop the ball to the keeper. The ensuing squawks by one side or the other usually fade quickly. The Laws do not, however, require both teams to participate at a dropped-ball restart, and nothing requires you to give anyone "fair warning" that you are about to drop the ball.

Common Supplementary Signals

Compared to many other sports, soccer has very few official signals. This is a deliberate choice, made for a very good reason. Each culture has its own unique mannerisms and expressions, and because soccer is an international game we do not want to use gestures or signs that some nations or cultures may find offensive.

All referees need to know and use the officially sanctioned signals and mechanics for soccer. These signals convey specific information in a form easily understood by anyone familiar with the game. There are, however, other bits of information that may be useful, helping to foster cooperation and communication between officials at the field. Knowing whether a colleague responsible for a call has a good view of an important play, for example, can be critical in making the correct call. While not actively encouraged, most governing bodies let officials at the field devise their own methods of communicating with each other. The only requirement is that any "non-official" signal be well-understood by the whole crew, and not so intrusive as to call attention to the officials.

There is no set of approved supplementary signals, and custom will vary from place to place. Some will be artificial, while others may be quite intuitive—if not, at times, little more than involuntary reflexes. And though the potential list is endless, a few common situations arise often enough during the course of a game to warrant discussion during the pre-game conference. Possible ways to communicate about them include:

"I know it's my call...but I didn't see who kicked it out of bounds."
Referee: Looks at assistant.
AR: Holds flag straight up in air, no direction given.

"Nothing here, in my opinion."
Referee: Eyes keep following play, or makes discreet "safe sign" with arms.
AR: Eyes keep following play, or shakes head to signal "no-call."

"Great call!" or *"Thanks for the help!"*
Either: Thumbs-up sign.

"That sure looked like a card from this angle...what do you think?"
Either: Taps badge (caution) or back pocket (send-off).

"We need to talk."
Referee: Goes and talks to AR.
AR: Holds flag across body, or hand over badge.

"Time remaining."

Referee: (Informing AR)   Holds appropriate number of fingers over black shorts.

AR: (Inquiring) Taps or points at watch.

"Offside player was 'over-and-back.'"

AR: Indicates with non-flag hand pivoting over elbow, from defensive toward offensive end of field.

"Crikey! I didn't see what just happened. I sure hope you aren't clueless, as well."

Referee: Points at assistant, hopeful look in eyes.

AR: Looks at referee...and shrugs sheepishly.

Chapter 5

Elements of Match Control

IT IS SOMETIMES SAID THAT A soccer referee spends the first season or two learning when to blow the whistle, and the rest of his career learning when *not* to blow the whistle. The realization that there are alternate ways of dealing with minor infractions other than by stopping play— such as a quiet word, or a carefully time reminder at an appropriate time—is a major step forward for the new referee. But because each game is different, each game will present unique challenges. The problems likely at an adult men's game will not the be same as those at a U-8 match, and a women's recreational match will differ markedly from a women's premier-league game. Before the game starts, you should know the level of play you will encounter, and have some idea of the likely sources of trouble for each match. After the kick-off, you will need to adjust to the temper of the game and the expectations of the players. Having some idea of what awaits you will help you prepare, mentally and emotionally.

Before the Match

While some youth games can be challenging, most of those challenges will come from outside the field of play. Adult games pose separate problems which vary depending on the level of play. Generalizations, though inaccurate, can give you an idea of some of the concerns you may face at any given match:

Youth Games

Although individual players develop at different paces, some common characteristics of each age group may be useful to remember:

U-8:   At this instructional level, most players are beginners with no tactical awareness about the game. They play for pure enjoyment, even if that enjoyment comes from playing in the dirt rather than kicking the ball. Players obey adults at the game instinctively, whether referee, coach, or parent, and are usually unaware of any rules other than the one about not using their hands. Aside from skinned knees or other minor injuries, trouble at this age level will come exclusively from the sidelines, where most parents and many coaches are as ignorant about the game as the players. Because the games are generally non-competitive, however, problems tend to be few.

U-10: While most players are still playing for fun, some players are starting to develop technical skills and a competitive desire to win. As a result, a single skilled player can sometimes dominate an individual match, and games can become quite lop-sided. Players still offer no dissent and cause no problems on the field. Spectators and coaches, however, often have enough partial knowledge of the game to exhibit profound misconceptions about many of the rules, occasionally leading to significant problems along the sidelines.

U-12: Players are beginning to stratify according to skill and desire, with most of the better players moving to more competitive teams. Boys and girls teams are starting to show marked differences in playing styles, with the boys engaging in more roughhousing on the field. Recreational games generally exhibit the same level of fun, sportsmanship, and ignorance along the sidelines as before. Competitive games now pose the risk of substantial dissension by spectators and coaches. Players, especially competitive players who are learning tactics, may start questioning calls by the officials.

U-14: Male players will show considerable disparity in size and skill, as some enter puberty. Female players at upper levels are beginning to demonstrate considerable intensity, often adopting a more physical style of play. Sporadic dissent and displays of temper are now seen on the field at all levels as the players enter adolescence.

Recreational players and spectators remain generally clueless, although rec-level boys may cause trouble through rougher play. Competitive matches, for both boys and girls, are starting to exhibit skillful play, and competitive players, coaches, and spectators are becoming more sophisticated in their appreciation of the game. For the officials, match control is becoming more difficult at all levels of play.

U-16:   Most boys, having grown considerably faster and stronger, are now testing their newly formed muscles through rough-and-tumble play at all levels. Girls' play, though continuing to improve, is starting to seem slow by comparison but may be significantly more sportsman-like. Players at all levels can be contemptuous of authority, making match control by the referee both more essential and harder to achieve. Although decreasing involvement by the parents is making sidelines problems less pronounced, the on-field problems in boys' matches are starting to assume critical proportions.

U-19:   Competitive players now fancy themselves experts on all facets of the game, while many recreational-level players have dropped out of the sport. Girls' games are becoming more physical and emo-tionally intense, but tend to remain significantly more sportsmanlike than those of the boys. Boys' games are fast and intensely physical, and the field may seem filled with barbarians. Retaliation is common, and players frequently test the referee by challenging decisions and committing pointless infractions. Encroachment at free kicks is common. At the highest levels of play, however, play can be surprisingly clean, as the superior players are starting to develop a dislike for unskilled play and focusing on winning through skill rather than brute force.

Adult Games

As we saw in Chapter 2, adult games will vary from division to division. Premier-level matches will often be intensely competitive, while recreational-league matches tend to pose fewer problems of match control. You should, however, know which kind of game you are officiating, so that you come to the field prepared:

Over-20: Games with college-age players can be fast and quite competitive. Players continuing to play at this age tend to take the game seriously, and are often quite knowledgeable about the sport. Match control problems abound, for both men and women.

Over-30: Premier teams are still quite good, though the pace is slightly slower. Men's games, particularly upper-division matches, may be a bit less troublesome, as players start calming down with the approach of middle age. Recreational players, including new soccer moms and dads, are returning to the game.

Over-40: Men are beginning to slow down considerably, causing some frustration-related problems in upper-division matches. Players' expectations are changing considerably, as the roughhousing of past years gives way to aching muscles, and players often prefer less physical contact.

Over-50: Play is often slow-paced, but considerably more relaxed. Brittle bones are now overcoming the competitive instincts of most players, who are just as concerned about self-preservation as playing soccer.

You can tell much about a team by watching its warm-ups. A well-drilled team often plays with discipline during the match, while one that looks disheveled may well play in a chaotic, disorganized manner on the field. But neither style of warming up will tell you much about how they will react to the frustrations they encounter during the game. For that, you have to learn how to read the temper of the match—which can change in a heartbeat, depending on events happening on the field.

During the Game

In many respects, a referee controls a soccer game much like a conductor leads a symphony. The maestro can wave his baton as much as he likes, but if the musicians ignore him there is little to do but follow along. On the field, a referee can bring his own preferences about soccer to the game, but without understanding what the players want and need it will be hard to avoid getting in the way. Whistling a tight game, for example, can make players angry if everyone prefers a bit of roughhousing, while allowing generous contact can be lethal if the players come to believe that the referee is letting the other team hack them to bits.

Reading the changing moods of a soccer game is an art, and one that can be described, although not readily taught. It takes experience to develop a sense of how players are reacting, and experience can only come with time. But there are many things that even beginning referees can use to anticipate what to do on the field, and what everyone there is likely to expect.

Consider the Level of Play

Soccer is a sport designed for everybody and can accommodate a wide range of abilities. The needs of the game will vary considerably, though, depending on the skill, intensity, and competitiveness of the players. It is important to understand this, and to adjust your calls to the actual match before you. Calling a competitive adult game the same way as a U-8 instructional match will satisfy nobody, and only make everybody at both fields question your judgment. While precise guidelines are impossible, imprecise generalizations are not:

- The lower the level of play, the less reason there is to apply "advantage."

- The lower the level of play, the greater the likelihood that a foul is due to clumsiness rather than malice.

- The lower the level of play, the more appropriate it is for the referee to help teach the players about the rules.

- The lower the level of play, the easier it is to bend a rule to help it accomplish its intended purpose.

Regardless of the abilities of the players, of course, there is no substitute for common sense and an instinct of fair play. And at any level, you should not be afraid to offer a quiet word of encouragement to a team that is getting thrashed. Younger players will value the kind words of any adult. Older players may need a gentle reminder not to let the score become an excuse for letting things get out of hand.

Consider the Time in the Match

It can be surprisingly tough for a referee to maintain full concentration for a whole game, particularly if all is going well. If things seem firmly in hand, we may be tempted to coast along, expecting everything to continue smoothly. This is, of course, a dangerous mind set for anyone—from sentries, to truck drivers, to fighter pilots—and is potentially disastrous for soccer officials, as well. You will probably be on your guard after an act of misconduct or a hard foul, anticipating some bad feeling on the part of some of the players. But just as lightning can strike even if the skies above are clear, melees can arise from nothing.

Trouble can come at any time, but there are particular times of danger when, due to fatigue or a lack of mental energy, you may have a tendency to get careless. Unfortunately, it is precisely at these times in the match that incidents can be quickest to arise, for you may not be expecting problems and can overlook the warning signs that might help you prevent them. As a result, sometimes you need to be on your guard even if your senses and instincts are assuring you that you have no cause for concern:

> *First five minutes:* Because nobody is expecting trouble, an incident early in the match can poison the entire game. Until you get a sense of the mood of the players, you will need to be extra vigilant during the opening minutes.

> *After goals:* Goals can energize both teams. The attackers are thrilled to have beaten the defense, while the defenders may be determined to even the score. Occasionally, one or two players become so intent on playing as hard as they can, or so angry at having been beaten, that they lose their perspective and take out their frustrations on the opposition. In addition, confrontations can occur near the goal mouth if one team begins to taunt their opponents. It is a good idea to keep a careful watch on things in the aftermath of a goal.

> *First ten minutes after half-time:* Referees are often surprised that two halves of the same soccer game can be so completely different. The teams that take the field after halftime can sometimes resemble the ones from the first half only by the color of their uniforms. The reasons are many, but foremost among them is the influence of the coach on a team's performance. Coaches always try to motivate their teams at halftime, and a team getting beaten consistently to the ball will probably have their coach trying to get them to be more aggressive. Sometimes this has the desired effect, and the team improves its performance. Occasionally, the effect is to send them onto the field angry, and eager to take the play to—or through—the other team. Do not expect an easy second half simply because the first half went so smoothly; and be particularly alert if the tempo of play picks up noticeably after half-time.

Last ten minutes of each half: Players, like referees, can get tired. When they do, they may lose their concentration, focus, and occasionally their tempers. Each team also knows that rest is just a few minutes away, letting them push themselves as hard as they can until the whistle sounds to end the half. Near the end of a close match, the players may become frenzied and desperate as they try to win the game. You may be tired yourself—your legs may be aching, your lungs are desperate for air, your brain may be counting down the seconds until your body can relax—but the closing minutes of a half are not the time to relax. Whether due to fatigue or raging emotions, many misconducts and fights occur in the closing minutes. The time to start relaxing is after you blow the whistle to end play—and not one second before.

Consider Whether Stopping Play Helps or Hurts

Under Law 12, the referee can stop play as needed to enforce fair play on the field, and for any infringement of the Laws of the Game. The "Spirit of the Game," however, grants considerable leeway in enforcing the rules, directing us to interfere as little as possible in order to let players spend their time playing the game, rather than exchanging free kicks:

> The Laws of the Game are intended to provide that games should be played with as little interference as possible, and in this view it is the duty of referees to penalize only deliberate breaches of the Law. Constant whistling for trifling and doubtful breaches produces bad feeling and loss of temper on the part of the players and spoils the pleasure of spectators.[*]

The traditions of the game do not make us stop the match just because we witness an act of imperfect soccer. Rather, we need to distinguish between fouls that matter and those that do not—between those that have a substantial effect on play and those that have no real consequence—and to overlook the imperfections that are too trivial to justify interrupting the game. This lets the match flow freely and generally leads to a better, more exciting contest.

---

[*] IFAB Decision 8, Law V. As defined by one authority, a "trifling" offense is one which "has no significant impact upon play," while a "doubtful" breach of the law would be one that none of the officials "can attest to" with any degree of reasonable certainty. *USSF Advice to Referees on the Laws of the Game*, §5.5 (2006).

Still, what is trifling at one level may not be trifling at another, and you will have to sense the different needs of the players at each level of play. Competitive players often prefer to play through contact that does not place them at a disadvantage, while recreational players may find that even minor fouls interfere with their ability to play the ball. And while many harmless scrapes and bumps occur in the scrums of the youngest players, you still need to watch for the occasional push in the middle of the swarm.

Common to all levels of play is the need to prevent unfair tactics from hampering either team. Regardless of the age or division, a team that thinks itself consistently on the receiving end of unpunished foul play will react in one of two ways: they will complain, or they will respond in kind. Both responses undermine the authority of the officials, and either can lead to the game getting out of hand. The trick for the referee will be discovering how to balance everyone's desire for an exciting, free-flowing match with the need to keep the game under control.

Reasons for Stopping Play

Officials in many sports view themselves largely as enforcers of the rules. They see an infraction, they whistle the infraction, and they impose whatever sanction the sport requires. As soccer officials, we have a wider range of discretion on the field than officials in most sports, and can avoid intruding needlessly into the game. In many instances, stopping play for a foul is discretionary with the referee, and examining the reasons why we blow the whistle may teach us when to intervene and when to stand aside and let the players play.

When a foul occurs, a soccer referee has four basic reasons for stopping play: to restore fairness to the match by preventing a team from gaining an advantage through foul play; to send a message to the players that they will be protected, or punished, as the case may be; to prevent a recurrence, by demonstrating that crime on the field will not pay; and to keep the match under control, by setting the limits for acceptable conduct on the field. The reason for allowing play to continue will be twofold. Either stopping play will help the foul work by benefitting the fouling player's team, in which case the appropriate call would be to award the advantage and "play on!" Or else the foul is so minor and of such little consequence that it results in no effect on play, in which case the appropriate conclusion is "no harm, no foul," and the best response is no whistle.

In games played in good spirits by players who prefer to keep playing rather than exchanging kicks, you can allow much to pass without stopping play. So long as the players understand that they will get the ball back if they have it stolen from them, they are usually willing to play through minor contact. If you reinforce this notion by a timely word or two during the match, you may find yourself able to control some matches largely by the use of your voice.

Sometimes, however, this approach is simply unworkable. At lower levels of play, for instance, the players may be too clumsy, out-of-shape, or unsophisticated to appreciate a free-flowing match, and may simply blast the ball downfield rather than working it down the pitch. And a field filled with hotheads, or players who keep escalating their fouls, will need to be watched carefully and kept under tight control. In these games, minor fouls can have a major effect on play, either because they keep recurring or because ignoring them will undermine your match control and lead to a breakdown of discipline on the field.

As we have seen before, every game will be different. With experience, you will be able to sense what each game needs from you, and adjust accordingly.

The Referee's Leash

As a referee, you will often hear cries for "consistency" on the soccer field. Players and coaches will be watching the fouls you call, and choose not to call, and can be quick to complain if they perceive an inconsistency between fouls you have called earlier in the match, and calls (or no-calls) you are making later in the game. Some officials pride themselves on their own internal consistency, taking pains to call fouls at the end of the game exactly the way they were calling them at the beginning. As Emerson once noted, however, a "foolish consistency is the hobgoblin of little minds,"[*] and it will not help the players, or ourselves, if we sacrifice control over the match just to congratulate ourselves for our inflexibility. If we become obsessed with consistency, we risk losing the ability to adapt to the changing conditions that arise during a game. In the end, what matters most is not whether you call the game exactly the same from minute one through the end of stoppage time, but whether you are calling things exactly the same for both teams at all times.

A concept many experienced officials use to help maintain control on

---

[*] Emerson, *Self-Reliance* (1841).

the soccer field comes from common experience with other forms of animal life—namely, the family dog. A dog owner will know and understand his pet's natural temperament and can usually keep the animal well behaved. At times, however—particularly in close quarters with other animals, or while taking a walk to the park—there is a need for tighter control. This is one reason why dogs in the city are walked on a leash: the tether gives the owner the ability to control the animal at times when misbehavior could lead to serious trouble.

On a soccer field, the referee's leash is the whistle. We use it to maintain order on the field and announce when play has crossed the line from "fair" to "unfair." In a well-played game exhibiting abundant good sportsmanship we can use the whistle sparingly, letting more "trifling" fouls go unpunished and allowing the players greater freedom to display their skills. But in a match filled with anger and frustration, we can use a frequent whistle to keep tempers from rising and rough play from getting out of hand. In a typical game, where the players moods change several times during each half, this lets us tighten or loosen the leash to accommodate the current temperature of the match, as long as we are willing to adjust our calls during the course of each half.

You will find that it is usually easier to loosen your standards as the players relax than it is to tighten the leash when things start getting ugly. Many experienced referees like to begin each game calling things very tightly, easing up only when certain that the players want to play soccer, rather than hockey.

"Real Fouls" and "Match Control Fouls"

In an ideal universe, the only fouls a referee would ever need to call would be the hard, deliberate fouls that would, in a perfect world, never occur. Players would all play in a sportsmanlike manner and never be careless in their challenges—and, even if they were, none of the fouls would affect play, letting the game continue with no need for officials. In the real world, of course, we need to balance the need for order with the players' desire to play without unnecessary interruptions. And since nothing is ever ideal, we will be making constant adjustments to accommodate the changing conditions on the field.

Between the obviously "hard" fouls that a referee will call in every game and every corner of the field, and the common "trifling" infractions which will never have an impact on play, there is a substantial "gray" area where officiating is more art than science. A forceful shoulder charge that seems fair in an older boys game, for example, may seem entirely out of place at the U-10 level. Or a hard tackle that might warrant no more than a free kick in a game filled with good spirits may need a caution to keep things under control in a match where tempers are rising.

Because each game is unique, your foul threshold will be different for every match you officiate. The calls you make for purposes of match control may be quite different from those you would make in an ideal setting, and you should not avoid making them simply because you might allow a similar play under other circumstances.

Players will understand and accept some weak or questionable fouls called to keep things under control, and usually appreciate the fact that you are trying to protect them. They will not, however, appreciate those kinds of calls inside the penalty area. Match-critical calls like penalty kicks should never result from "doubtful" or "trifling" fouls.

Avoiding the Extremes

Regardless of their playing styles, all players want at least two things from the officials. They want to be protected from fouls, and they want to be able to play the game. Each team and every player may have preferences about how they like games called, some preferring a tightly controlled match favoring speed and ball-handling abilities, others preferring a looser, more rough-and-tumble style of play. But regardless of playing styles, nearly everyone understands that you have to draw a line somewhere. As long as you seem to be trying to be fair to both sides, most will view your own personal style as a condition of the match and muddle through as best they can.

Problems can arise if the referee imposes his own personal preferences on the match and is perceived as not even attempting to accommodate the teams on the field. This will become noticeable, however, only if you ascribe to one of two extreme philosophies about soccer—either the "Soccer as Basketball" school of thought, or the "No Autopsy–No Foul" brigade.

Some officials, though acknowledging that soccer is a contact sport, seem uncomfortable with most physical contact on the field. All touches become pushes; charging is deemed either dangerous or excessive; and a foul is judged not by the unfairness of the contact, but by whether contact caused someone to fall down. Games called this way tend to be choppy and slow, and often resemble the closing minutes of a basketball game, with free kicks rather than free throws being exchanged throughout the game. Play will tend to favor teams with superior ball skills—though barely, given the number of stoppages that keep interrupting the match—but will seem unsatisfactory to all concerned.

At the other extreme are officials who are entirely comfortable with physical contact, so much so that bumping and crashing bodies are no cause for concern to the referee, no matter how much commotion they cause along the sidelines. This kind of game favors strong, physical teams who can bully their opponents, but games involving two very physical teams can easily turn ugly as tempers rise on both sides due to the rugged play— and the referee, seeing nothing to alarm him, remains blissfully unaware of any problems.

Fortunately, most officials manage to avoid either extreme. New referees, who often fluctuate between the two while learning the craft of officiating, usually find that calling things too tightly will pose fewer risks of a game-ending riot than ignoring overly physical play.

Fifty-Fifty Balls

Many new referees instinctively blow the whistle whenever a player falls as the result of contact. One reason for this is simple self-preservation. Many spectators are parents who become upset if their child, or their child's teammate, falls down after being bumped by someone from the other team, and will yell at the referee if they do not hear a whistle. The other reason is a logical fallacy that seems unique to humans— the belief that whatever happens, somebody must have caused it and, therefore, someone is at fault.

Many things in life, however, are nobody's fault. Accidents sometimes just happen, the result of unforeseen events or acts of nature. On the soccer field, everyone is supposed to exercise due care when playing or challenging for the ball. Even so, whenever players are competing with each other for an often-bouncing ball, they can trip or bounce off each other without anyone being to blame, simply because the act of competition itself means that each player is trying to push his own limits while at the same time seeking to thwart whatever his opponent is trying to do. A player does not, however, lose the right to play at his best just because he is stronger than his opponent. Whether the opponent can fight off the challenge or falls to the ground, a player who has done nothing wrong should not be punished simply for trying to play the ball.

Rather than merely noting that someone has tripped or fallen, or two players have kicked each other's boots or stumbled after tangling their legs together, you need to evaluate the entire play to decide whether anyone really is "at fault" for whatever happened. There are many factors to consider in making your decision—none of them conclusive, but all of them helpful in judging what you have seen:

- Was the ball in anybody's possession at the outset, or was it a free ball?

- Did both players have an equal chance to win the ball?

- Did either or both players do anything careless to cause whatever happened?

- If both players were being careless, was one player primarily at fault?

If neither player did anything wrong, then there is no reason to call a foul no matter which of them fell or stumbled, and regardless of whether they did so in mid-field, or in the penalty area. On the other hand, if one player's carelessness caused the mischief, then he is "at fault" for the mishap and his opponent is entitled to a free kick.

If both of them were equally "at fault" for what happened, of course, then you have a decision to make. You may allow play to continue, reasoning that any fouls cancelled each other out, and tell both players to be more careful next time; or you may blow the whistle and point in whichever direction seems most appropriate. The former course will likely be more popular with the players, while the latter course may be more popular with half of the parents. But the choice is up to you.

Using Advantage

Soccer's advantage rule gives us a wonderful tool to keep play flowing. It can, however, be misused and, when invoked carelessly, can lead to confusion and turmoil on the field.

Advantage calls can be among the most exciting parts of a soccer game (at least for any referees in attendance), letting us intervene in the game in a positive way by ensuring that neither team benefits from breaking the rules. Advantage must be used carefully, however. It is used only to call actual fouls—those for which the referee would actually be stopping play if doing so would not help the wrong team. Neither the terms "advantage" or "play on,"nor use of the sweeping arm motion that gives a visual signal to the call, are appropriate indicators of a "no-call." Misusing the signal confuses everyone, and its careless use can lead to dissension on the field if habit leads the referee to award an apparent advantage for a dubious offense inside the penalty area.

As with all tools, the principle of "advantage" has a proper time and place. Just as we would not think to use a hammer to change a light bulb, there are other circumstances in which using advantage would be a bad idea:

A Good Use of Advantage:

- Attackers are near the goal with reasonable chance to score.

- Attackers near the goal have open space ahead of them.

- Attackers near the goal have numbers, and the defense is lagging well behind the play.

- The attacker with ball is their best player, and looks to have a good chance to close on goal.

A Reasonable Use of Advantage:

- Attackers at midfield have momentum.

- Attackers at midfield have open space ahead of them.

- Attackers are on a counterattack, and most of the defenders are trailing the play.

A Less-Than-Optimal Use of Advantage:

- The foul was committed deep in the defensive third.

- The fouled player is heading right for trouble, even if he recovers the ball.

- The fouled player's body language suggests anger, rather than pleasant surprise at the fact that he kept the ball.

- The fouling player has just committed his third foul in the last ten minutes.

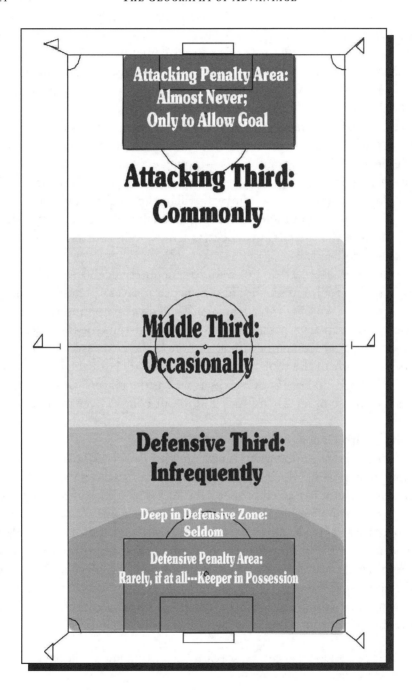

By and large, it is often a good idea to award "advantage" in the attacking third of the field. At midfield, it is often a good risk for the referee to take, especially if the match is going smoothly. In the defensive end, however, "advantage" is unlikely to end well. Unless the ball comes to a defender with forty yards of open space before him, the defense is probably better off with the free kick. And in either penalty area, it is usually a mistake to award advantage, except in very limited circumstances. In the defensive end, it often helps the defense to let a keeper in possession of the ball maintain it, giving the defense more options for releasing the ball into play. In the attacking end, by contrast, a penalty kick is usually all the advantage that a team needs—though even there, however, a slow whistle can be useful, since it lets you see what happens in the aftermath of the foul. A team that scores anyway will not appreciate having you take the ball out of the net merely to award a penalty kick, especially if they muff the kick. In both circumstances, you must train yourself not to blow the whistle too early.

By the same token, we do not want to sanction or enable foul play. The play was still a foul, and we should not excuse a player's persistent fouling merely because we award an advantage. The Laws do not put us in a bind, however. We can always issue a misconduct card at the next stoppage of play, as long as we remember to do so before the next restart.

As with many of the tools at our disposal, the trick for the referee is to use "advantage" to benefit ourselves as well as the players, and to reserve its use for those times when it will add to our control over the match.

Dealing with Garbage

A recurring chore on the pitch is coping with the occasional displays of temper that pop up during the match. While usually meaningless by themselves, if not managed properly these episodes can set the game on a downward spiral and lead to trouble later in the game.

Often, these episodes arise at stoppages, and are common on set plays in and around the goal area. Even in games that are otherwise going smoothly, kicks near the goal can cause problems as the players crowd into a confined space, and tempers start rising as they jostle for position. Knowing that these are "danger zones," experienced referees often prevent trouble from happening by taking a few precautions:

- Taking a position that gives you a clear line of sight into the likely trouble spots can keep players honest.

- Moving closer to the goal can deter nonsense in the goalmouth, and a loud warning at close range to all players can surprise them into behaving.

- A simple admonition to the keeper—assuring him that he does not need to do anything rash, since you are watching out for any funny business by the other team—often makes players on both sides settle down.

- While you cannot whistle a foul until the ball is put into play, calling an outgoing foul at the first sign of trouble often prevents further shenanigans for the rest of the game. Teams do not like to waste corner kicks, or any free kicks near the opposing goal, and communicating to both sides that you will deal quickly with any nonsense in the goal area usually convinces everyone to behave themselves.

Unfortunately, minor displays of temper are not confined to particular places on the field. They can arise anywhere, at any time of the match. Sometimes they will occur in plain sight of everyone, other times they will be well away from the play and visible only to an alert assistant referee. The problem in dealing with temperamental players is to avoid overreacting, or under-reacting. You do not want to turn a minor problem into a major one by dealing with the players too harshly. At the same time you do not want to seem to be sanctioning inappropriate conduct by treating it too lightly.

If faced with two players who are getting on each other's nerves, it is often helpful to speak to them privately—together if you deem it best, or separately, if you would rather separate them. You may do so publicly, at the time of a flare-up, or discreetly, during a subsequent break in the action or while moving past them during the run of play. Getting them to talk to you can be a useful way of easing tensions, since it gives them an outlet for their frustrations that does not involve confronting their opponent. What you say to them, of course, is up to you, but it is usually helpful to get them to tell you, as calmly as they can, what is bothering them, and then to assure them that you will keep an eye on things in the future. This often solves the problem, even if you promptly forget about it. The players will feel that you have listened to their concerns and will keep watch for the rest of the game.

Of course, if this does not resolve things you may have to deal with it later, most likely through the use of a card for misconduct. But even if subsequent events lead you to sterner measures, trying to solve it first through the force of personality will enhance your credibility on the field. It also gives you a wider range of options throughout the match.

Watching for Trouble

The nature of your job will keep you very busy during a match, often leaving little time to notice the subtle clues that can give insight into the mood of the players.

It is impossible to tell what everyone on the field is thinking or feeling at any given moment. There are, however, some common indications that trouble is brewing. A referee who detects them in time can often ease tensions before they cause problems.

- A growing chorus of complaints by both sides often means that the players are angry, or getting tired.

- A series of cheap fouls against players who are racing past the defense often means that the defenders are tired or over-matched.

- A player rising quickly after a foul is often angry, particularly if he turns to face the player who fouled him.

- Players who glare at each other are probably not admiring one another's physique.

- Players who make tackles that are clearly more vigorous than needed can be venting frustrations or sending a message to the other side. A series of tackles that are each more vigorous than the last is usually a sign of growing tension on the field.

- Players who scream at their own teammates may simply be blaming them for their team's difficulties. Players who scream at opponents are often on the verge of doing something rash.

- A player who is screaming at you for not carding an opponent following a hard tackle may simply be blowing off some steam. A player who screams at you after a routine foul called in his own favor may be an omen of serious trouble brewing on the field.

No list of "warning signs" can be exhaustive, since the variety of temperaments and personalities on the pitch is infinite. But you should try to monitor the players' changing moods, looking for signs of growing tension. Noticing the players' body language can give you clues about their emotions. You should also develop the habit of watching behind the play when the ball is cleared forward. Players often make late contact after the ball is away, and many of the ugliest incidents arise from a late tackle behind the play. You will be wise to trust your instincts when a voice in your head is telling you that all is not well on the field. The worst that will happen is that you will be on your toes and at a higher level of alertness than would otherwise be the case. On the other hand, being prepared may help you keep an incident from escalating into a major confrontation.

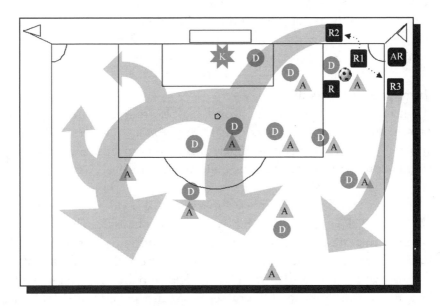

5.2

KEEPING THE PLAYERS IN VIEW—DROPPED BALL

While it is usually best to keep the lead assistant referee in view, there are times when this is counterproductive. When conducting a dropped ball in the AR's corner, for example, keeping the AR in view leaves the Referee (Position R) with his back to the field. Dropping the ball from position R1, on the other hand, permits a view of the entire field, and lets the Referee move as needed (R2 or R3) to avoid getting in the way.

Keeping the Players in View

You will soon realize that there is no perfect position on the field. Your best position will always be a compromise between the best place to view what is happening now, and the spot on the field which will best enable you to see what will be happening next. Experienced referees learn to make intelligent choices about positioning by balancing the need to monitor the active play with the need to keep an eye on potential trouble spots—all the while taking into account tactics and personalities, and trying not to occupy space that the players need.

Among the skills you need to develop is a sense for where you will best be able to monitor active play while keeping watch on as much of the field as possible. In many cases, simply changing your angle of view by turning to face toward the largest part of the pitch, rather than away from it, will help you keep tabs on the entire pitch. The more players you can see, the less chance there is that something bad will happen.

Humanizing Yourself

In our modern, impersonalized world, people are bombarded with cold statistics every day and often come to view others as faceless bodies in a crowd. Yet even a statistic as impersonal as the government's monthly unemployment report can become quite meaningful if we, or someone we know, is out of work.

On the soccer field, players develop a personal bond with members of their team, and occasionally with players on the other side. They share the joys and frustrations of their games, which are soon part of their weekly routine. Referees, on the other hand, simply come and go. Officials often tend to pass as unnoticed as the playing field, and are memorable only if the cause of some disaster. Otherwise, we are just a condition of play that nobody will remember once the game is over.

Part of the reason players and spectators feel so free to vent their frustrations at us is that we are often faceless and anonymous. It is easier for them to say something cruel or thoughtless to someone they do not know. And when things are going badly on the field, it can be more gratifying for them to lash out at the first available target than to confront the mistakes and misplays that are causing their poor performance.

Taking a few moments to introduce yourself to the coaches or captains, or smiling and exchanging mild pleasantries with the players during the game, costs us nothing and will hardly jeopardize our integrity as officials. It may, however, do much to make the participants come to see us as people, rather than uniforms. And it may even make them think twice about taking their disappointments out on us when they meet with setbacks on the field.

Of course they may still yell at us, and many of them probably will. But at least some of them will feel guilty about it.

Punishing the First Foul
Any run of play carries endless possibilities. A wing moving downfield may cross the ball to the middle. A give-and-go pass may move the ball past the defenders. A tussle for the ball may result in a clearance or a goal, all within a few heartbeats. But as players contest for the ball, contact often escalates, and what starts as an inconsequential bump can become a minor push which turns into a wrestling match ended by a hard tackle. Everything happens so quickly and seamlessly that it can be hard to tell when the fair challenge ended, and the foul began. Missing one unfair contact may lead to others later in the run of play, as players try to recover from the initial challenge. An official who is out of position, or who lets his concentration lapse, risks missing the critical part of any play.

As a referee, it is your job to determine which charges are fair and which ones are fouls. Just as crucial will be deciding which foul started the sequence. Punishing the last foul you see, rather than the first, only rewards the fouler and teaches the players that it is better to get their foul in early, because if they can provoke a response by the other team, then their team will get the ball while the other team will get into trouble.

An inexperienced referee may see Red shove Blue out of the way to run toward the ball, and award Blue a direct kick to punish the push. A more experienced referee, however, might see the act of impeding that preceded the push, and award an indirect kick going the other way. Being able to recognize and identify fouls is essential to any referee. Identifying the first foul in a sequence of play is one of the things that distinguishes the veteran referee from the beginner.

Avoid Cutting Your Own Throat
We all have friends who are constantly meeting one disaster or another. Some people cannot do anything on the computer without getting the machine to freeze, others are always knocking dishes off counters, or getting into trouble on the job because they cannot solve one problem without creating at least two more. As with any group of people, there are referees who are always in trouble at the field, calling games that seem to explode into anger and are marred by frequent and numerous mis-conducts. At times, this is more a matter of approach and temperament

than experience. Some referees avoid self-destruction instinctively from the outset. Others keep having the same problems year after year and are almost immune to learning from past mistakes. These officials may have been referees for ten years, but really have only a year's experience, repeated ten times.

Most people do not set out to do things the hard way. For referees, there are many holes that we can dig for ourselves. Those who do well usually learn to avoid them.

Exact Blade of Grass Syndrome

All beginning referees take their new jobs seriously. Having studied the rules, and sporting a new badge and uniform, we believe ourselves to be experts on all facets of the game and are determined to enforce the Laws fairly and impartially.

Unfortunately, some of us come to view the rules as ends in themselves, rather than the means to let everyone enjoy the game of soccer. Rather than following the advice to avoid calling "trifling" infractions, some view it as their duty to be meticulous in detecting and punishing any deviation from the Laws, no matter how minute or inconsequential. Occasionally tolerated, and often otherwise quite talented officials, these referees have an affliction common to beginners and one from which some officials never recover. They all have "exact blade of grass syndrome."

The disease itself comes in various forms and is usually curable. However, as the name suggests, it comes from taking literally some things that most soccer players take for granted. The Laws, for example, specify that most restarts take place at the place where the ball went out of play. In the case of a foul, this will be from the spot of the foul. Some officials, taking this rule to heart, expend large amounts of time and attention to make sure that the restart takes place from precisely the right spot—on the exactly correct blade of grass—to ensure that the Laws are obeyed. If applied throughout the entire game, this approach fixates on the rules rather than the players, with predictable results. Players take a dim view of the referee who makes a great fuss to move a restart two yards laterally deep in the defensive end, but misses calling a hard tackle because he is busy noticing someone's untucked jersey. They much prefer officials who can tell the difference between big problems and little ones, and can handle each appropriately.

There is, of course, a time and place to enforce rules strictly. The entire notion of "trifling offenses" recognizes that while some departures from the Laws simply do not matter, others are very important. Soccer trusts the referee to know the difference:

- A defensive free kick taken five yards from the spot of a foul just outside the defensive penalty area is not a cause for concern. If the call was in favor of the attacking team, however, it would be within easy shooting distance of the other team's goal and moving the kick five yards in any direction could affect the likelihood of a score. A good referee often ignores the imprecise placement in the first restart because it does not matter, but will be fastidious about placing the ball properly in the second, because it would give one team an unfair advantage.

- A keeper who takes an extra step and crosses just outside the line while punting the ball downfield has technically handled the ball outside his penalty area. So does a keeper who comes over the line to punch the ball away from an attacker closing on goal during a breakaway. A wise referee will recognize that the first incident has no significant effect on play since the extra step gives the keeper no real advantage in punting the ball, and will usually handle the matter by discreetly reminding the keeper to be more careful next time. The same referee will deal quite sternly with the second keeper, whose actions seriously affected the run of play, and will probably resolve the matter with a red card and send-off for denying an obvious goal-scoring opportunity.

- A coach running onto the field at a youth game, worried when one of the players goes down with an injury, has technically entered the field without the referee's permission. An experienced referee will do one of two things. Depending on the seriousness of the injury, he will either beckon the coach who is already half-way to the site of the injury onto the field, or find a discreet time to remind the coach to wait until the referee calls him onto the field before rushing to tend to a player. The same referee will deal harshly with a coach who uses the injury as an excuse to harass the referee about some perceived defect in the officiating.

The ability to sense the difference between these and similar situations is largely a function of experience, but what all good referees come to realize is that while rules may not be broken, they may be bent from time to time. The concept of the "trifling offense" lets us keep the game flowing without interrupting the match for things that are meaningless to the players, and avoid doing things that are counterproductive for ourselves.

The cure for "exact blade of grass syndrome" is really quite simple, though more easily stated than put into practice: *"Don't sweat the small stuff."* We must recognize that while the referee controls the match, the game itself belongs to the players. We should not be eager to impress people with our mastery of the rules, and guard against the temptation to assert our powers and authority needlessly. We must also realize that simply because the Laws let us take a particular action usually does not make doing so mandatory. What matters is whether an action on our part is an appropriate response to an event on the field. This awareness cannot take place without first realizing that the rules are simply part of the game, and not the game itself.

Getting "Cute" or Playing "Gotcha!"

Some people are just too ingenious for their own good. Armed with enough knowledge to get themselves into trouble, they insist on overextending some common-sense rule or other, leading to predictable and entirely avoidable disasters.

Referees are not immune from the pitfalls of cleverness, and a few officials take perverse delight in playing "gotcha" at the field. Usually, though, overly clever interpretations of the rules are simply wrong. The Laws are designed to be simple, not complex, and any complicated interpretation leading to a result that is unfair or counterintuitive is probably wrong.

Referees should spend most of the energies on understanding how the game itself is played, not on devising intricate variations of the Laws that few will understand, and even fewer will appreciate.

Taking Things Personally

We may be tempted to take affront at events arising at the soccer field. We are, after all, charged with controlling the game, and when people violate the rules or ignore our instructions it can be easy to take it as a personal insult.

There may indeed be times when a player or coach will make personal comments, or say deliberately cruel things during a game. Most of the time, these remarks are calculated to distract us from doing our job on the pitch. Occasionally, they are the result of frustration or disappointment. In any case, they are directed at the match official on the field, and not against the referee as a human being. Becoming angry or upset at these comments will not help you function as a referee. They will only lead you to respond emotionally, sometimes in ways that are inappropriate. While this will not excuse the provocation, lashing out in retaliation may make it harder for you, or the league, to deal with it.

Whatever happens on the field—whether it is a player kicking the ball away in dissent; one team's insistence on harassing the keeper at all corner kicks; another team's habit of moving the ball forward ten yards at all throw-ins; or a coach's constant monologue of complaints—remember that nothing occurring on the field is directed against you, personally. Staying calm and under control will help you deal firmly with any challenges arising at the game, and keep you from reacting with your emotions instead of using the tools that the Laws give you.

Suggested Defaults

There may be times when play moves so quickly that you cannot get a good look at what happened, and sometimes your assistant referee will not get a good look at things, either. The ball goes out of bounds after what looks to be a simultaneous touch by two players, for example; or two players get into a wrestling match over the ball in or near the penalty area, and you could not tell how it started. In these situations, it helps to have thought about things ahead of time, and to decide on a course of action in the event that you need to make a decision...despite having no real idea what actually happened.

Ball Out-of-Play

Under the rules, when one team plays or deflects the ball out of bounds, the other team controls the restart, whether it be a throw-in, a goal kick, or a corner kick. Ordinarily, deciding which team gets the restart is not a problem, since the player last touching the ball is easy to spot, or there is an audible "thud" from a deflection or clearly visible change of trajectory to confirm the last touch by a particular player. If you are lucky, the players may even make the call for you. If one team runs after the ball while the other team falls back to get into position for the restart, you know that the players have gotten the call right all by themselves. When this happens, simply indicate the proper restart, and play will resume accordingly.

On occasion, events will happen too quickly to follow with your eyes and there will be no clues to help you make up your mind. Since you cannot use a dropped ball to avoid making a decision, you will have to choose one side or the other.[*] Aside from using the "eeney-meeney" method of decision making, two possibilities suggest themselves— favoring the attacking team, or favoring the defense.

Default: Offense

Because modern soccer is trying to encourage goal scoring, structuring a default in favor of the offense has much to commend it. Doing so keeps play flowing in the direction of the team with the ball and gives an advantage to aggressive, attacking play. This default makes particular sense when awarding a throw-in, since it keeps play moving in favor of the team that already has the ball. If applied to balls over the end line, however, this approach carries the risk of affecting play by giving one team an unearned chance to score, since many goals come in the immediate aftermath of a corner kick. As a result, many officials shy away from awarding corner kicks by default.

Default: Defense

Some officials prefer to favor the defense whenever there is a question about the direction of a restart. This default eliminates the possibility that a referee error will result in a goal, which justifies its application in cases of uncertainty when the ball crosses the end line. Such discretion is usually unnecessary when the ball goes into touch, however, since it is impossible to score directly from a throw-in.

Mutual Fouls

While the Laws permit a restart by dropped ball in cases of simultaneous fouls, this option suggests the same indecision that precludes its use for throw-ins. For this reason, referees should not to use it as a crutch to avoid making a difficult decision.[**] The realities of play suggest that "simultaneous" fouls will be rare events, since the dynamics of action on the field ensure that second fouls typically take place as a reaction or response to the first, whether or not we pretend that they are "simultaneous."

---

[*] *See*, USSF, *Advice to Referees on the Laws of the Game*, §9.3 (2006).

Under Law 15, the restart for a ball over the touch line is a throw-in, not a dropped ball. In addition, a dropped ball under these circumstances suggests a referee unsure of himself, which not only undercuts his authority on the field, but tends to invite the players to exploit this indecisiveness to their advantage.

[**] USSF, *Advice to Referees on the Laws of the Game*, §8.5 (2006).

When dealing with foul play, the Laws make some defaults dangerous to use on the field. Since a defensive foul inside the penalty area will result in a penalty kick, a default carrying the risk of undeserved goal cannot help but have a direct impact on play, and may well change the outcome of the match. For this reason, most referees unsure which player began a run of foul play will award a kick coming out of the defensive end.

The Moment of Truth

While many games pass uneventfully, sometimes the success or failure of a referee crew to control events on the field can be traced to a single incident:

> 2nd minute: Red defender slides in hard with cleats exposed well after the ball is away, barely missing Blue's star player near midfield.

> 25th Minute: Coach loudly complains about a no-call in the opponent's penalty area, and his continuing complaints are heard around field. Five minutes earlier, the referee had admonished the coach to keep his voice down.

> 53rd Minute: Blue having scored in Minute 50 to extend their lead to 3–1, the referee calls a foul against Red in 53rd Minute for a routine trip. This leads a Red player to kick the ball twenty yards downfield, well after the whistle.

> 79th Minute: With the score tied, 2–2, Black #10, while racing down the midfield sideline past the entire Yellow defense, is held back from the ball by Yellow #2, who was cautioned for dissent in Minute 40.

> 89th Minute: With the score still tied, Black #6 goes down inside the Yellow penalty area after what looks to be superficial contact.

What all these events have in common is that each one can determine whether the officials will succeed in keeping the match under control. If handled wisely, timely action can assert firm control over the rest of the game and keep other problems from arising. If handled poorly, these incidents can lead to an escalation of misbehavior on and around the pitch, and to ugliness later in the match.

Every game carries a potential "moment of truth," one that will challenge your courage and judgment. Often, these moments beg for misconduct cards. Other times a stern, public word will suffice. These critical moments can occur at any time in the match—from Minute 1 through the end of stoppage time—but observers can usually detect them when they happen. They are a time of tension on the field, when everyone is looking to you for firmness and decisiveness. If you meet the challenge, tensions ease and the game settles down. If you do not, the tension just keeps mounting.

Expect a "moment of truth" at each of your games, and do your best to rise to the occasion.

Dealing with Misconduct

Some acts on the soccer field go beyond carelessness and past any reasonable notions of fair play. Law 12 specifies seven misconducts that warrant cautions, and seven others that justify send-offs. Some involve excessively rough or violent play, others involve gamesmanship or the cynical use of foul play, and still others involve technical offenses for which no other punishment is practical. All violate the spirit of sportsmanship that is at the heart of soccer, and each referee must be able to recognize and deal with all of them.

Misconducts Involving Rough Play

Under Law 12, most acts are punished as fouls only if done "in a manner considered by the referee to be careless, reckless, or using excessive force." We can see the relation of fouls to misconduct by using the concepts of negligence, recklessness, or violence:

Negligence: An act done "carelessly," undertaken without due care and caution and involving a player's mistake or misjudgment during the run of play, is a routine foul.

Recklessness: An act done "recklessly" is one well outside the bounds of fair play, committed by using unnatural or deliberate actions to intimidate an opponent or gain an unfair tactical advantage. This sort of action warrants a caution and yellow card.

Violence: An act done "using excessive force" is one far exceeding the physical force needed for any legitimate play for the ball, and places the opponent in considerable danger of bodily harm. This act is intended to do physical harm and requires a red card and send-off.

Acts that are fouls if done carelessly—such as tripping, kicking, striking, charging, jumping, or pushing—can become misconducts if done in a manner that goes beyond mere negligence. For the referee, the deciding factor can be one of practicality as well as degree. There are infinite gradations of physical contact, and many fouls may seem to warrant more than a mere free kick, even though describing them as "reckless" would be something of a stretch. In addition, a referee who is perceived as too quick to rely on cards may well diminish their value, as players cautioned for what they perceive to be insignificant fouls come to mistrust his judgment. In many cases, a stern word to the offending player is sufficient to maintain order, without the need of a yellow card. Referees must always calibrate their use of cards to the match and level of play, for what is well-intentioned clumsiness at one level may well be a premeditated action at another, even if the fouled player's ankle or shin is just as sore in either case.

In determining whether to issue a misconduct for a particularly rough foul, you should consider whether doing so would have a beneficial effect on the game—or, put another way, whether failing to issue the misconduct would hurt the game, or your ability to manage the players. Among the factors to consider are whether the player had any real chance to play the ball, whether the act contained an obvious element of retaliation, and whether the act carried a risk of serious physical harm. If the nastiness of the foul, or the circumstances in the game, support issuing a card, you have three basic options:

Caution for Unsporting Behavior

Because send-offs are rare events, the likeliest course of action for you will be to issue a yellow card for unsporting behavior. This is the most common misconduct issued because it covers a wide range of misbehavior,[*] and will often be the least controversial response to an action for which a mere free kick seems inadequate. This caution would be appropriate for any foul committed in a reckless manner which results in a direct free kick, including tackles from behind which do not endanger the opponent's safety.

---

[*] As we shall see, cautions for unsporting behavior are not limited to instances of rough or nasty fouls, and can include many other offenses, including behavior on and off the field, and incidents occurring before, during, and after the ball is in play.

Send-off for Serious Foul Play

A player making a violent challenge for the ball, on the field and against an opponent, is guilty of serious foul play, punishable by a red card and an immediate send-off. Examples of this misconduct include two-footed or cleats-exposed tackles aimed at the leg, ankles, or knee; violent challenges directed against the small of the back or the Achilles tendon; and tackles from behind which place the opponent at risk of physical harm.

While virtually unseen among young children, competitive play can get quite intense among older players and may lead them to lash out at each other out of anger, frustration, or an eagerness to retaliate. The higher the level of play, the likelier it is that the player committing the foul is fully aware of the dangerous nature of the play, and that the resulting harm was intentional. Failing to issue an appropriate send-off for a violent tackle or other challenge can lead to a breakdown of match control with astonishing speed, and referees witnessing such contact must take care to rush to the scene immediately, to prevent players from taking matters into their own hands.

Send-off for Violent Conduct

If play is stopped, or violence is shown outside the context of a play for the ball, then the offender cannot be dismissed for serious foul play. The appropriate misconduct in this case—whether on or off the field, and directed at an opponent, teammate, referee, spectator, or anyone else—would be a red card for violent conduct. As with serious foul play, failing to take appropriate action against a player guilty of violent conduct can lead to events quickly swirling out of control.

Violent conduct can result from the use of any part of the body, or a projectile such as a rock, shoe, hand grenade, or in some cases, the ball. As with the misconduct of unsporting behavior, violent conduct can occur while the ball is out of play and may take place on or off the field. If the conduct results in a separate foul, then the restart would be a direct free kick. If the conduct occurred off the field, then the restart would be a dropped ball at the appropriate place on the field.* If the ball was out of

---

* *See*, Law 8 and USSF, *Advice to Referees on the Laws of the Game*, §12.35 (2006). Ordinarily, the "appropriate spot" would be wherever the ball was at the time play stopped. Inside the goal area, of course, the drop would occur on the six-yard line, at the point parallel to the goal line nearest to where the ball was when the stoppage occurred.

play at the time, the restart would be dictated by the reason for the stoppage.

Misconducts Affecting the Integrity of the Game

Some acts are misconducts because they have a direct impact on the integrity of the game. These actions either cast the game into disrepute, or threaten the referee's ability to control the match.

Caution for Dissent

To maintain order on the field, and keep the match from degenerating into a festival of oratory, everyone must accept and obey the referee's decisions on all aspects of the game. This helps both sides focus on playing, rather than constantly debating the merits of any particular call.[*]

To protect the referee's ability to control the game, the offense of dissent is a cautionable offense warranting a yellow card. The misconduct of "dissent" goes beyond mere disagreement with the referee's opinion, however, and requires verbal or physical expressions overtly rejecting a call or decision. When deciding if a reaction to a call is merely an expression of momentary frustration, or cautionable dissent, you should consider not only what was said or done, but whether it was directed at a particular official, whether it was done in a loud or public manner, and whether it was part of a persistent pattern of complaining calculated to affect the referee's future judgment. These "Three P's"—Personal, Public, and Persistent—are not firm rules, but guidelines to help you evaluate the nature of the action confronting you.

Send-off for Denying an Obvious Goal-scoring Opportunity

Because scoring goals is the climax of play on the soccer field, the use of foul play to deny the other team a goal affects the heart of the game and is among the most serious misconducts under the Laws.

Handling the Ball to Deny a Goal or Goal-Scoring Opportunity

In soccer, only the goalkeeper may handle the ball and even then, only within his own penalty area. Yet a player using his hands to block a shot

---

[**] At least it does in theory. In practice, of course, there will be the usual diversity of opinion on the soccer field, and the yellow card is merely a means to ensure that the debate eventually comes to an end.

that would otherwise score can be just as effective at keeping the ball out of the net. Without some incentive not to do so, even the sanction of a penalty kick would make this course of action a wise tactic in most circumstances, since it would trade a certain goal for the chance that the other team would miss the ensuing kick. To cure this disparity, the Laws make the deliberate use of the hands to deny a goal (or an obvious goal-scoring opportunity) a misconduct punished by a red card and a send-off.

As with all rules, there are a number of fine points and exceptions that you must know and be able to apply. While this misconduct does not apply to the keeper within his own penalty area, for instance, it may apply to instances where a keeper comes outside of the area to deny a goal-scoring opportunity. As with all handling offenses, an unintentional handball is not even a foul, let alone a misconduct.

Use of Foul Play to Deny an Obvious Goal-Scoring Opportunity

To protect the attackers' ability to use their skill to score, and to keep the defense from using cynical fouls to destroy their opponents' most dangerous opportunities, the Laws make denying an "obvious goal-scoring opportunity" a serious misconduct as well, punished by a red card and a send-off.

This misconduct does not, however, depend upon the referee's subjective opinion that the attackers had a good chance to score. There are four required elements for an "obvious goal-scoring opportunity" before the play will warrant a send-off, often described as the "Four D's":

Defenders: Not counting the defender committing the foul, there cannot be more than one opponent between the foul and the goal.

Distance to the ball: The attacker must be close enough to the ball to continue playing it at the time of the foul.

Distance to the goal: The most subjective aspect of the misconduct, the attacker must be close enough to the goal to have a legitimate chance to score. The closer to the goal she is at the time of the foul, the likelier it will be that she has a "goal-scoring opportunity."

Direction: The attacker must be moving toward the opponent's goal at the time of the foul.

If any element is missing, then the play may still constitute another form of misconduct, but it will not be denying an obvious goal-scoring opportunity and the player need not be sent off for this particular offense.*

Misconducts Involving Offensive Acts

Because soccer is an intense, emotional game, players sometimes lose their tempers as well as their sense of perspective. To help keep emotions at the field directed toward the game of soccer, several misconducts punish acts which most reasonable people find offensive.

Caution for Taunting or Excessive Celebrations

Goals are exciting but stressful times at a soccer game. While one team is celebrating its good fortune, the other team is coping with disappointment or, perhaps, blaming the officials or each other for the change of circumstances on the field.

Players who use the occasion of a goal or any other turn of events to taunt their opponents are turning the game from a sporting event into an exhibition of self, and risk causing a breakdown of order on the field. Under the Laws this constitutes unsporting behavior, and is punished by a caution and a yellow card.

Send-off for Spitting

In many cultures, one of the vilest insults people can hurl at each other comes not from words but from actions. Spitting, in addition to being vulgar and unhealthy, is an act that risks creating a major confrontation at any soccer match. For this reason, the offense of spitting at an opponent is a penal foul, and the misconduct of spitting—whether at an opponent or anyone else at the field—is punished by a red card and send-off.

Send-off for Offensive or Abusive Conduct

Players show aggression in a variety of ways: constructively, by channeling their energies into their game; or destructively, by unleashing their frustrations on others.

Physical aggression is punished in ways ranging from free kicks to misconduct. Verbal aggression that becomes offensive or abusive may result in a red card.

---

* USSF, *Advice to Referees on the Laws of the Game*, §12.37 (2006).

Abusive conduct can involve more than words. Obscene or offensive gestures are also misconduct. But in determining the nature of any act, you must be careful to distinguish between actions that offend your own personal standards of behavior and actions which any reasonable person would find offensive. You must also take into account not only the words used, but also the context in which they arise and are received. Good-natured but colorful language, or an outburst that is largely self-directed out of momentary frustration, may offend your own personal sensibilities, but it would hardly be within the spirit of the game to dismiss a player for a poor vocabulary when nobody else is taking offense. The core of this misconduct is abuse, not esthetics, and if what is said in disappointment is accepted by everyone on the field then there is no reason to intrude upon the game merely to enforce your own sense of proper manners.

As with everything else, context determines conduct, and common sense should dictate your choice of actions. Language that may be forgiven at an adult game may be highly offensive at youth games with small children present. At any level of play, outbursts that threaten to heighten tensions or provoke others will clearly meet the threshold for a caution. And threats or abusive actions directed at you, your colleagues, or anyone present at the field, will easily justify a red card. On the other hand, a momentary lapse that is clearly within the range of acceptable conduct among those present is better handled by other means, such as a quiet word to the player.

Technical Misconducts

Several misconducts relate not to how the game is played, but to how it is administered. These "technical misconducts" are punished not because they are inherently dangerous, but because without the sanction of a yellow card the rules they reflect are likely to be unenforceable. These offenses include:

- Entering or re-entering the field without the referee's permission.

- Leaving the field without the referee's permission, other than during the ordinary run of play.

- Changing the keeper without the referee's permission.

The reason for these misconducts is that the participants must notify the referee of some events to ensure that the game proceeds smoothly.

Substitutes dashing onto the field, for example, may interfere with play that has resumed because the referee had no idea that new players were coming into the game. Even so, experienced referees know that some of these offenses can occur through oversight or an excess of enthusiasm. Since trifling offenses need not be cautioned, you should use your common sense in dealing with them. If they are attempts to cheat, then the appropriate action is a caution; if they stem from an innocent oversight or ignorance, then a word of reminder should correct the problem.

Misconducts Involving Cynical or Continuing Misbehavior

Yet another category of misconducts involves players who do not commit reckless or violent acts, but rather seek to use unfair play for tactical reasons. To punish these cynical attempts to violate the rules, the Laws give you tools to keep them from working.

Persistent Infringement

We punish fouls by awarding a free kick, hoping to restore justice on the field by giving the ball to the fouled team. This will not deter players who persist in fouling, however, since this tactic not only shows a disrespect for the game but is often used to compensate for a lack of skill. Beyond this, players who constantly commit fouls will anger opponents who are trying to play by the rules, which can lead to an escalation of foul play by both sides.

Under Law 12, persistent infringement is a separate category of misconduct, punishable by a caution and a yellow card. You may consider all fouls, even those to which you have applied advantage, in determining if a player is guilty of this offense. Although you should ordinarily warn a player that he is at risk for a yellow card for this offense, a quickly established, blatant pattern of fouling will also justify a caution, and in this case there is no need for a warning. While the Laws do not specify a minimum number of fouls needed for this offense, the nature of the misconduct requires that it be at least two: a "persistent" pattern cannot, after all, involve a single act. Because issuing the card is discretionary, you may consider not only the number, but also the nature of the foul play observed. You may, for example, want to give a verbal warning following two hard fouls in quick succession to prepare for a card on the third occurrence. On the other hand, four minor fouls, spread over the course of the entire match, will probably cause no particular trouble, and may pass without notice by most referees.

A particularly troublesome kind of persistent infringement involves several players fouling a single opponent, usually the other team's star. In these cases, the fouled player will feel unprotected if you do not take action and he—or his teammates—may simply take matters into their own hands if you do not intervene. When you observe the pattern, the proper course to take is to warn the offending team that you have noticed the tactic and will caution anyone who continues it. If it persists, you may caution the next player who appears to be following the plan, whether or not the player in question has committed an earlier foul.[*]

Detecting persistent infringement is a challenge even for experienced referees. Events pass quickly on the soccer field, and it is easy to overlook which player is committing a foul and which player is the victim. It may help if you start saying the numbers of the players involved whenever you whistle a foul, either out loud or to yourself. You will probably not remember the players's faces for more than a few moments, but you may be able to recall fouls called against "Blue 6 " if you keep repeating that number to yourself during the game.

In addition, you may want to write a note to yourself in your notebook whenever a player commits a hard foul that is just short of a caution. It can help you remember those who are engaging in borderline play, and seeing you write something in your little black book often has a civilizing effect on a player's behavior.

Caution for Delaying the Restart of Play

Under the Laws, play must be restarted within a reasonable period of time after the ball goes out of play. Occasionally, one team or the other—typically, the team that would be thrilled if the game ended at once—will try to run out the clock by wasting time, and dawdle when it is their turn to put the ball back into play. At other times, one of the teams may have its players caught well behind the play and want to keep the game from restarting until they can arrive on the scene. Common examples of time-wasting are keepers who take forever to take a goal kick, players who keep repositioning the ball at free kicks, or players who take

---

[*] USSF, *Advice to Referees on the Laws of the Game*, §12.28.3 (2006). You should, of course, use your common sense in determining if the foul actually fits the pattern. Another push or trip as Red's star striker moves to collect the ball in midfield may well fit the pattern, while a minor foul committed amid a tangle of bodies while jossling for position during a corner kick in the Red penalty area may not.

the ball away from the spot of a restart (possibly risking a confrontation with their opponents), all of whom may have tactical or practical reasons for dawdling.

A strong word from the referee usually stops such tactics in their tracks. If that does not work, a yellow card will usually do so.

Caution for Failing to Respect the Distance at a Free Kick

Under the Laws, each team is entitled to a zone of ten yards around any free kick or corner kick. This distance was chosen carefully by the lawmakers. It is the same "free-fire" distance we see at a kick-off, and permits a fouled team to begin play without interference by the other side. Often, a team with insufficient numbers to defend will try to delay a kick by standing in front of the ball, preventing their opponents from resuming play quickly. This, in turn, can help foul play succeed by preventing the attackers from capitalizing on their free kick by hustling.

To keep this tactic from working, Law 12 makes failing to respect the required distance at a free kick a misconduct, punishable by a yellow card. You must be careful to distinguish this misconduct from ordinary confusion on the part of the players, since players fully intending to obey the rules can innocently misjudge the distance required. When this happens, you need to intervene to enforce the ten-yard separation. Often, a quick reminder as you whistle the foul will suffice. At other times, you will have to move to the appropriate spot and summon the defenders to retreat. You must, however, keep from distracting the defenders as they move into position to defend against the kick, and will need to indicate clearly whenever you are intervening. This will delay the kick until you finish moving the defenders back, and you will need to make everyone wait for your signal to resume play.

Protecting the ten-yard "free-fire" zone at all free kicks is a challenge even for experienced officials, and you may want to enlist your assistant referee to help guard against encroachment. Recurring cases of encroachment are probably not innocent misjudgments by the players, and are often coached tactics to help the defense set itself before play resumes. In addition, players who deliberately stand directly in front of the ball are doing so to make it impossible for the attackers to take a quick kick. In any case, you should be alert to warn or caution as appropriate, to guarantee a retreat to the proper distance.

Unsporting Behavior—Tactical Fouls

Sometimes players find themselves outplayed, or poorly positioned to stop a dangerous attack. If a defender is clearly beaten, with an opponent about to move into dangerous space, a foul can bring the other team's attack to a crashing halt. Intended more to rescue their team from disaster than to intimidate their opponents, these fouls do not need to be rough or violent to achieve their purpose. A simple trip or push can easily disrupt an attack when the attackers have numbers charging toward goal, the defense is trailing the play, and the player with the ball is about to race past the defenders.

Few things are more infuriating to players than to see their opponents disrupt a dangerous attack through the well-timed use of a tactical foul. One of the things that will upset players even more is watching the referee award a direct kick, without issuing a caution for unsporting behavior.

Unsporting Behavior—Diving

An unfortunate development in recent years has been the growing number of players who will simulate the reaction to a foul, hoping to trick the referee into awarding a free kick. Commonly known as "diving," this tactic stems from the benefits gained from fouls called in and around the penalty area, which can lead to set plays in favorable spots on the field or, for a lucky attacker, a goal from an undeserved penalty kick.[*] Diving—or "simulating a foul" in the language of Law 12—can be a troublesome problem for the referee, warranting a yellow card and a caution for unsporting behavior.

While often apparent on slow-motion replays, diving can be hard to detect on the field in real time, when the action is quick and play is getting intense. There are some common traits of many dives, however, that suggest an attacker may be trying to draw a call for an imaginary foul. You may want to watch for them, to keep from being fooled:

---

[*] At some levels of play, players may also simulate being struck or injured, hoping to draw a misconduct for their opponent and, perhaps, the advantage of seeing their opponents reduced in numbers on the field.

This kind of simulation, though rare, tends to occur in higher-level matches where the stakes are particularly high, and where a one-man advantage may well determine the outcome of the game. Referees suspecting that they are being duped may need to consult their assistant referees, to make sure that any blows leading to a send-off were genuine, and not simulated.

Anatomy of a Dive

- Play is in or near the penalty area.

- Attacker has lost or is about to lose the ball.

- It is near the end of a close game and the attackers are desperate for a goal.

- The defender seems to have the play under control and has no incentive to commit a foul.

- The attacker's fall looks graceful rather than awkward, as if choreographed or pre-planned.

- The attacker's fall is unusually spectacular, or his arm motions seem exaggerated, suggesting the need to draw the referee's attention.

- The attacker's feet come together just before he stumbles.

- The defender makes what appears to be superficial contact with the attacker, leading to a reaction that seems highly convenient.

None of these indicators is foolproof, and there is no substitute for being in position to see the play unfold exactly as it happens. You may want to give your assistant referee a signal to communicate the opinion that the attacker is simulating a foul, since the lack of contact is sometimes easier to see from the side. Detecting and punishing dives can be critical for match control, for if you seem easily fooled you are likely to see players from both sides exchanging belly flops in the penalty areas, and hearing loud complaints whenever you fail to call them.

Of course, not every player who stumbles from a non-foul is guilty of misconduct, and before issuing a caution you should be just as certain that a player is simulating the foul as you would be in awarding a penalty kick. Players trip often on the soccer field—from bad footing, from being off-balance, or simply from trying to run or turn too quickly. And the mere fact that you do not call a foul when someone falls in the penalty area does not mean that you must issue a caution for diving. It just means that you were not sure that the action was a foul. If you are also unsure that it was a deliberate attempt to deceive you, then simply let play continue.*

---

* Occasionally, however, you may want to say something to the players, to let them know your suspicions. An angry, indignant tone of voice seems to work best.

Other Forms of Unsporting Behavior

The term "unsporting" is open-ended and general, and the misconduct of "unsporting behavior" covers a variety of actions that are seriously unfair, but which do not fit easily into other categories of offenses. There is no exhaustive list of possibilities, but there are many common examples:

A player who deliberately handles the ball to score a goal is guilty of unsporting behavior.

A player who intentionally distracts an opponent verbally during the run of play is guilty of unsporting behavior.

A player, including a goalkeeper, who puts unauthorized marks on the field is guilty of unsporting behavior.

Players who change jerseys with the goalkeeper during active play are guilty of unsporting behavior.

A player who keeps interfering with a goalkeeper's release of the ball into play is guilty of unsporting behavior.

Players engaging in "trickery" to avoid the backpass rule are guilty of unsporting behavior.

Players using inappropriate but not abusive language may be guilty of unsporting behavior.

Send-off for Second Cautionable Offense

As conceived and implemented in 1970, the yellow card was intended to function as a warning, much like the amber light on a traffic signal. Players committing acts of misconduct are warned by the yellow card, and any ensuing words of caution, to correct their behavior. That warning would be meaningless if the sanction for a second yellow card was the threat of getting a third.

Receiving a second caution in a match results in a red card and dismissal from the game. A player cautioned for the second time in a match is first shown the yellow card for the second offense, then shown a red card and sent off the field.

Timing Can Be Everything

Like your whistle and your voice, your red and yellow cards are tools of your trade as a referee. But while your cards can assist you in controlling a game, they are no substitute for real match control, which comes from your strength of character and knowledge of the game. A referee can sometimes lose control of the match despite issuing a half-dozen or more cards even if he could have maintained control, and had a much more enjoyable game, by issuing one or two cards in a more timely manner.

Some new referees hesitate to use their cards for fear of provoking dissent on the field. This reluctance is misplaced. Since you are the authority on the field, confrontation is nothing you need to fear. You have the entire community of organized soccer backing you up in any dispute, and even a mistaken application of the rules is insufficient grounds for dissent or abuse. What can be tricky, though, is using your cards to maximum advantage to calm tempers and keep things under control, rather than struggling to return civility to the game after the players are already angry.

Many games, especially those at the recreational level, will pass uneventfully, without the need for misconduct cards of any color. In competitive matches, however, the intensity of play often puts players on edge and can lead to trouble if they direct their energies at their opponents rather than toward playing the game. Experienced officials often use the early fouls to set the tone for the entire match.

It is often better to issue a quick early card to set the limits of acceptable play at the outset, and avoid having to issue a host of them later in the match. Just as it is easier to stay in shape than to get into shape, you will find it easier to maintain order than it will be to restore order on the field when things get out of hand.

Taking Care of the Paperwork

To be useful, your game report must accurately recount the nature and circumstances of any misconduct you issue. This is particularly important for red cards, which carry serious disciplinary consequences for the players. Some leagues require explanations only for red cards, while others want you to describe cautions as well as send-offs. Regardless of the competition, the requirements of a game report will be the same. You need to specify the misconduct, describe the action, document the actions taken, and note any effect the incident had on the game:

An Inadequate Report
I issued a red card to Red #17 for a brutal foul.

This type of report says nothing about the incident, and does not even inform the league of the nature of the misconduct. The foul described could be anything from a beating to a mistimed slide tackle. It provides no facts to let the League understand what happened, and nothing to help them decide what sanctions to impose.

A Helpful Report

In Minute 73, I observed Red #17, John Maxwell, execute a violent tackle from behind that placed Blue #12, Cedric Hartwhistle, in considerable danger of bodily harm. I issued a red card for serious foul play and sent Maxwell from the field. Hartwhistle had to be helped from the field and did not return to the game. Play restarted with a direct kick in favor of Blue.

Other details might be pertinent to providing a context, such as the score at the time, the area on the field, earlier admonitions to one or both players, or displays of bad blood between them. They should not, however, be included if the only purpose is to provide a more dramatic narrative. You only need to include those facts necessary for the reader to understand what happened. Here, the referee reported a violent and dangerous tackle committed during a contest for the ball that resulted in the fouled player having to leave the match. It helps the league take the appropriate action—issuing a suspension for serious foul play—and alerts them to the possibility that the injury was severe. If it was, then there should be another account of the matter in the injury section of the report:

Injuries

Following a tackle that resulted in a send-off for serious foul play in Minute 73, Blue #12, Cedrick Hartwhistle, left the match with what appeared to be a serious injury to his left knee. He was taken from the field for medical treatment and did not return.

Inadequate explanations or sloppy attention to details may result in offenders going unpunished and lower your reputation as a referee. On the other hand, accurate and factual reports will help the league understand any unusual incidents that arose during the game, and let them take any appropriate remedial action.

Positioning and Movement

The most astute referee, able to deal with any form of mischief on the field, will still founder on the pitch if out of position and unable to detect foul play.

Being in the right place at the right time is a skill that comes with experience. It also requires the ability to read the game and the players. It all begins, however, with fundamentals—knowing how to move about the field, and where to go to keep up with the play.

The Diagonal System of Control

As you learned in your basic referee classes, the standard system of officiating soccer matches is the "diagonal system of control." This approach calls for three officials—a referee who patrols the entire field, and two assistant referees who each patrol half of a sideline—who combine to monitor play on the field and decide any contested points arising during the game. By running a diagonal line across the field, from corner-flag to corner-flag, the referee can stay close to play and, in theory, keep the play between himself and one of the assistant referees. To work, this system needs cooperation and a high level of fitness, as well as intelligent positioning choices by all three officials.

Dynamic Play

During active play, both assistant referees will be located on the offside line along their respective touchline. The referee, by contrast, has no fixed position. He must adjust his movements according to events on the field, while trying to be in position to see everything—and, at the same time, trying not to interfere with the players or get hit by the ball. It is a job helped immensely by developing an instinct for positioning. This, in turn, means viewing the diagonal not as a barrier to movement, but as a way of sensing what is happening on the field.

Not All Diagonals are Created Equal

Most referees run a left-diagonal. This means that their path trends along a line extending toward the left wing on each half of the field, with the assistant referee off to right along the touchline. As most people are right-handed and right-footed, this has the practical advantage of keeping the referee away from the side favored by the dominant foot of most players. But your choice of one diagonal or the other is not as important as recognizing that the diagonal is not a parade route. It is, instead, a point of departure for the referee.

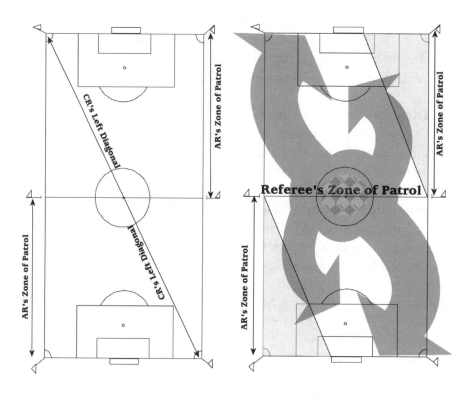

5.3

DIAGONALS

In theory, the "diagonal system of control" places the referee on a diagonal line running between the two corner flags.

In practice, a referee wanting to stay near the play will find himself running a path more closely resembling an open-ended Figure-8 than a diagonal line.

Soccer is played on a large field where the players roam about freely. As the match referee you must be prepared to patrol the entire width and breadth of the field to monitor the game. Inexperienced referees sometimes become "slaves to the diagonal," fearing that departing from the corner-to-corner axis will invite disaster. In reality, adhering to a rigid diagonal can lead to problems by keeping even the fittest referee far from play for a large portion of the match. Staying close to play is more important than an imaginary line on a diagonal, and you should get into the habit of moving as needed to remain within 10-20 yards of the action. Aside from keeping you in position to judge fouls, staying close gives you a better feel for the temper of the match.

Other practical advantages come from learning to depart from a strict diagonal. A referee worried about maintaining a constant route through the middle of the field will be predictable, and often in the way. Players seeking revenge can count on this predictable routine to plan their misdeeds. And players hoping to pass the ball at midfield may be annoyed to find the referee tripping over their passes, or getting in their teammate's way.

Keeping the AR's in Sight

The theory behind the diagonal system of control is that it is better to have more than one line of sight on the play, and that the officials will have better success at controlling the game by keeping play boxed in between them. This will only work, however, if the referee moves quickly and intelligently enough to take positions giving the assistant a different view of the play. The way to do this is for the referee to keep at least one assistant referee in sight at all times, and to maneuver so as to avoid "flatlining" the officials.

Ordinarily, a referee taking a position on the offside line gains little. He has the same viewpoint as his assistant, the only difference being that he is on the opposite end of the players. Anything happening in the line of play between them will likely be screened by bodies, and except for players at either end of the line, any acts of foul play missed by one will probably be missed by both. By contrast, moving the referee from the offside line to an angle giving an oblique view of the players lets the referee catch shirt tugs that are screened from the sideline, while the assistant can spot handballs hidden from the referee by a player's body.

Viewing the Game from the Players' Perspective

Unlike officials in some other sports, a soccer referee moves up and down the field with the players. This offers not only the chance to interact

---

5.4

BEHIND & WIDE

The reason for preferring a position "behind and wide" of the active play is often clearer in a diagram than on the field. Here, referee R1 is likely to find himself in the way in short order. No matter what the attacker with the ball tries to do—whether dribbling, passing, or yelling for help—both sides will find the referee in the way. In addition, R1 will be unable to see whether the assistant referee has raised an offside flag. By contrast, R2 is well wide of the likely action, and can retreat in the event that play comes directly toward the sidelines. He is in a good position to view any challenge for the ball, and has the AR within his line of sight.

Unfortunately, some referees prefer to maintain a position closer to R3...some thirty or forty yards away from the active play. While permitting a good view of the center circle, it is unlikely to be helpful in the event of trouble—and a referee in that position will probably be unable to distinguish between a dive and a foul as play intensifies near the penalty area.

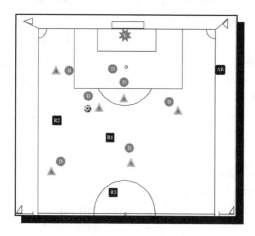

with other participants, but also to share the players' sense of the game. Staying close to the action lets you feel the fouls as they occur, helping you sense when a contact is too superficial to have an impact on play, or when tempers are rising on the pitch. It also gives you a more intimate understanding of conditions on the field—physically, emotionally, and tactically.

You will often hear it said that a referee should stay "behind and wide," meaning that your proper position should be behind the ball, and toward the outside of the play. This gives both the referee and the assistant distinct viewpoints of whatever is happening, while keeping each within sight of the other. As with many truisms, this can lead to disaster if followed blindly or unthinkingly, but understanding the reasoning behind the adage we see that it gives us a good rule of thumb when trying to find an unobtrusive place to be.

Staying wide of the play offers two main advantages. It lets you maintain your lead assistant referee within your field of view while keeping the play between the two of you, and it gives you a wider angle of vision. Staying behind the play not only keeps you out of the way, but offers the added benefit of letting you see the play unfold the same way the player with the ball sees it—helping you sense the options open to him so you can anticipate the best avenues of attack for the next phase of play.

Static or Set Plays

A disproportionate number of goals are scored from set plays near the goals. One authority notes that about forty percent of goals come from kicks taking place near the penalty area,[*] and many teams practice taking and defending free kicks in a wide variety of situations. Knowing what to watch for will help you decide where to be when the action resumes. A willingness to shift positions while the ball is in flight can let you keep the best vantage on whatever will be happening next.

Because each free kick is different, there will never be a single, definitive position to take at any restart anywhere on the field. But since some kicks have a greater chance of scoring than others, you need to be aware of the tactical situation on the field at all times. As always, there are a variety of factors to consider—some counseling a position near the goal, some suggesting a more distant vantage point:

- What are the attackers doing? What about the defenders?

- Are the attackers setting up for a long kick, or a shorter one?

- What is the current temper of the match...and of the players?

- Are the players near the goal grappling for position, or behaving themselves?

- How stiff is the wind...and is it blowing toward, or away from goal?

- Is this a kick on the near side of the field, or the far side?

---

[*] Lover, *Soccer Match Control*, 169 (1986).

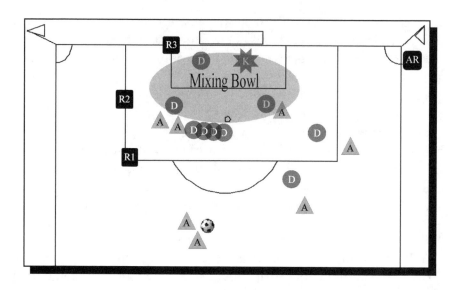

5.5

FREE KICK NEAR GOAL

Free kicks near the goal always present a challenge. Two officials (AR and Referee) must watch a number of things at the same time—including the offside line, encroachment, fouls and misconducts in and hear the wall, off-ball misconducts...and, of course, the goal line, in case the attackers get lucky.

Here, position R1 allows the referee to spot misbehavior in the wall, but will screen him from any activity occurring in the "mixing bowl" area around the goal. Position R2 is wide of the players and offers a better view of the area around the goal, but is useless to spot any mischief in the wall and screens the referee from anything happening on the far side of the penalty area. By contrast, position R3 lets the referee see the back of the wall without letting the players know exactly where he is watching. This position also gives a good view of the "mixing bowl" and a potentially critical view of the goal line...but may see the referee out of position on a quick counterattack, or if the ball is deflected off the wall, and screens the referee from the far end of the penalty area.

All positions involve trade-offs, and compromises between the ideal and the practical. Instinct and experience can help you sense where the best spot will be for any particular play.

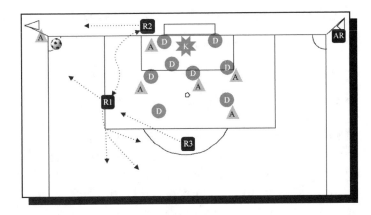

5.6

CORNER KICKS

No matter which side of the field it comes from, a corner kick's target will be somewhere in the middle of the penalty area. There will be problems abounding, as players jostle for positioning. A particular areas of concern will be the immediate vicinity of the Keeper, who may be struggling to maintain his position against a forward determined to block his path to the ball.

Though the conventional position is usually in the vicinity of R1, the referee should vary the position taken on corner kicks, particularly the position taken before the kick is away. As the kicker is getting ready, the players will be concentrating on the ball, and you can move wherever you choose...usually to wherever will give you the best view of where the ball will drop.

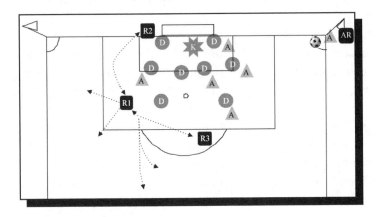

- Will this be a quick kick, or a ceremonial kick?

- Is it early in the game, or late?

- What is the score...and how critical would a goal be at this time?

- Does this look to be an in-swinging kick, or an out-swinger?

Experience will help you sense where to be at set plays, and you will find that varying your position to make yourself less predictable carries advantages, as well. To start, you may do well simply to ask yourself whether there seem to be any potential problem spots at this particular kick. If so, your two best choices for positioning will be the place where you can best prevent any trouble, and the spot where you will best be able to see trouble as it happens. You may be surprised to discover how often those two positions will be the same.

Anticipating Play

Asked to explain his remarkable ability to score goals, hockey legend Wayne Gretzky once observed that the trick was learning not to skate to where the puck was, but to where the puck was going to be. On the soccer field, the referee's challenge is similar. To be in the right spot to judge the what is happening on the field you cannot simply chase after the ball and hope for the best. Your job is not simply to run about the field, but to be in position to judge the most significant event occurring on the field at any given moment. To do this, you must always be moving *toward the next phase of play*. Doing so will help keep you in the proper position, since you will always be arriving at the critical point on the field in time to see and judge whatever is happening.

Needless to say, all of this is easier to say than to do. To make an educated guess about which spot on the field will give you the best view of what will be happening you must first understand what the players are trying to accomplish. Even experienced referees, who have spent years of watching and studying soccer, need lots of hustle and a fair amount of luck to be at the right place at the right time. Educating yourself about the game, learning the common tactics teams employ, and observing as much soccer as you can, will help you develop the instincts needed to position yourself intelligently as play moves around you.

Understanding Tactics on the Pitch

Tactics are different from team to team and vary with the level of play. Some teams rely on physical strength, others on speed and finesse, still others on kicking the ball as far as they can and sending a mob of players after it. Being able to evaluate the skill of the players and the tactics of the opposing teams is critical if you hope to anticipate the flow of play and move to where you need to be. But before you can predict what they are likely to do, you need to determine whether a team is a "physical" team, a "finesse" team, or a "kick-ball" team:

Physical teams often challenge directly, using their bodies to muscle after the ball, and relying on the superior strength of their players. By and large, these teams are used to a high level of contact during their games. They will usually not complain about losing the ball when an opponent wrests it away physically, so long as the challenge is fair. They may, however, push the envelope with the referee early in the match to see just how much rough-housing the referee will permit. And some physical teams may resort to deliberate fouling if the other side proves to be faster, or more skillful at dribbling and passing.

Finesse teams usually rely on quick passing and counterattacks, working the ball around field to set up an opening for a quick strike on goal. These teams often work the ball up and down the entire field, switching the play from side-to-side and probing for an opening. They may disdain rough, physical play, preferring to rely upon their speed and skill with the ball. As a result, they may get testy if the referee permits too much physical contact to suit them. In addition, their own physical challenges are sometimes clumsier and less skilled than those of a team used to using its muscles to win the ball.

Most teams combine aspects of both finesse and muscle, since this approach allows more flexibility to adapt to different opponents and field conditions. Games that pit an exclusively physical team against one that relies entirely on finesse often leads to trouble, since the conflicting playing styles can lead to contradictory expectations from referee.

Kick-ball teams generally inhabit recreational level soccer. Often, God-only-knows where the ball is going when the players kick it. Teams engaging in this style of play also tend to "swing-and-miss" randomly, sending everyone, including the referee, scurrying back and forth around the field. In this style of game, considering the irregular nature of the tactics, positioning is likely to be highly random, and being in the right place will often be a matter of blind luck.

By and large, soccer teams often attack down the wings, before bringing the ball to the middle of field near the opposing goal. A ball sent back to a midfielder or defender is often switched to the opposite side of field, while a ball sent back to the keeper is often blasted far upfield. Often, the referee can use an interior line to go from side-to-side in midfield, conserving energy and making repositioning easier. However, attacks down the wing usually require the referee to get very wide to monitor contact as the players contest for the ball along the sidelines. In all cases, however, the attackers will eventually want to send balls toward the middle of the penalty area. This often forces the referee to choose between following play down the touchline to monitor challenges near the flags, or fading to the middle to set up a good view of the goal area in the event of a cross. As the referee, your positioning will be a series of ever-changing compromises as you determine which facets of play are more critical, all the while taking into account how quickly you may need to recover if the defense wins the ball and races back upfield on a quick counterattack.

The best way of learning to anticipate tactics is to watch as much soccer as possible. While skilled players are often quite unpredictable as individuals, tactics on the pitch tend to follow common patterns of play. Knowing those patterns will be invaluable to you as a referee.

Passing Lanes

Soccer is a fluid game, and action switches quickly from place to place around the field. At each phase of play, however, the ball will either be up for grabs, or in the possession of one team or the other. When the ball is free to whoever claims it, deciding where to be is relatively easy, for you will need to be in place to see the upcoming contest for the ball. When someone actually has possession, however, things can be a bit trickier. Players can dribble or pass; the defense can contain or challenge; and everyone on the field will be moving to get into position for whatever happens next.[*]

As play develops, clear areas will form and shift, giving players the chance to move the ball past their opponents. These moments of

---

[*] Well, they will all be moving in theory. That is what their coach will be telling them to do, and what all of them probably intend. Their legs, however, may have other ideas.

opportunity can pass in a heartbeat, and a misplaced referee can disrupt an attack as effectively as the best defender. In all areas of the field, you must try to avoid interfering with the game. We are, after all, there to help them play, and getting in their way is not very helpful. As a result, there are several areas of the field that you may wish to avoid:

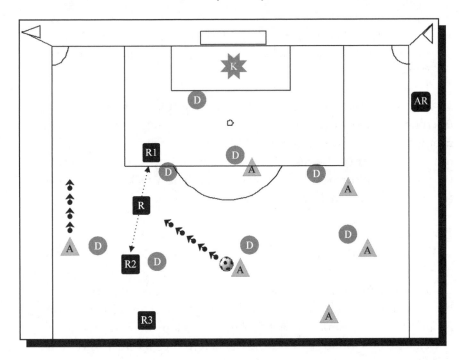

5.7

HIDING THE REF

Though often hard to do, accomplished referees try to avoid taking up space that the players may need.

Here, the Referee is in a passing lane, preventing the player with the ball from dribbling into open space along the wing, or passing the ball to a player running into the same space. By moving behind a nearby defensive player (R1 or R2), the Referee can keep from interfering...though starting in a position behind and wide of the play (R3) will let him avoid being a bother altogether.

- Play flows freely through the middle of the field. Therefore, the referee should navigate around the center circle, whenever possible.

- Play tends to flow from the middle to the wings and back again. Therefore, the referee should try to avoid the clear lanes between areas of the field.

- The players will be trying to pass the ball to whoever is open. Therefore, the referee should avoid taking a position between the ball and open space.

Of course, this is all easier said than done. Open space is constantly opening and closing, and passing lanes will change from moment to moment as play moves about the field. With practice, you can avoid being in the way most of the time. And when in doubt, you can always take a position behind or near a defensive player. The attackers will usually be trying to avoid them, rather than passing them the ball.

Drop Zones

An experienced referee can often predict where play is going and begin moving into position even before the players realize what they are about to do. A beginning referee may not have such well-developed instincts, but can still be ready for many shifts in play just by reflecting on the geography of the game, as well as a study of elementary physics.

When a ball is lofted skyward, gravity determines where it will fall. When anticipating a long kick, therefore, you should take a position near the likely landing zone for the ball, making adjustments as needed to get a good view of the contest for the ball as it drops.

Most goals scored from active play will come from the middle of the penalty area. This means that play along the wings will eventually come to the middle to permit a direct shot on goal, and a referee who is tracking wide to monitor play along the sidelines should anticipate a cross toward the middle of the field. For the referee moving into position for the next phase of play, it is often a good idea to "fade" to the middle, toward the vicinity of the penalty arc, as the ball nears the corner of the field, to be in position to see the action near the goal once the cross is away. This is easier to do when play is along the assistant referee's sideline, since having a nearby official on hand to watch for fouls frees the referee to move further into the middle of the field. Unless play is hotly contested on the referee's sideline, a compromise you may want to make is "cheating" slightly toward the middle to anticipate what is coming next.

As always, when monitoring a "drop zone" you should be watching the players, rather than following the flight of the ball. While the ball will not tell you what the players are doing, the players' eyes will tell you all you need to know about the location of the approaching ball. Besides, the ball will never commit a foul.

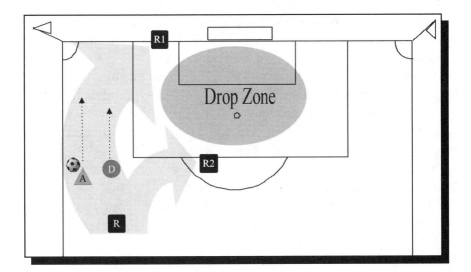

5.8

ANTICIPATING CROSSES

When the ball goes toward the corner flag, the Referee must decide whether to follow the players with the ball, or fade to the middle of the field in order to be in position to watch action in the penalty area following a cross.

The decision is easier on the AR's side of the field, since the assistant referee will be moving toward the corner along with the players.

Free Kicks

You should try to get into the habit of moving quickly toward the spot of any foul. You never know when tempers will flare, and it is better to be on hand to prevent trouble than having to deal with the consequences. In fact, if the players' body language suggests a loss of temper, you may wish to continue the blast on your whistle as you run. Appearing on the scene as your whistle falls silent not only loudly announces your presence, it also makes people think you were always there, right from the start. In addition, being at the spot of a foul lets you set the proper place of the restart before moving off toward the next area of play.

At any free kick restart, the team taking the kick is entitled to a ten-yard zone around the ball that is free of all defenders. Ordinarily, the team taking the kick may put the ball into play as soon as they are wish, and do not need to wait for the other team to get ready. Occasionally, however, a delayed or "ceremonial" kick is needed, perhaps owing to confusion among the defensive players over precisely how long ten yards happens to be. If you need to intervene to set the proper distance, you should first tell the attackers that play will resume on your whistle, and only then should you move the defenders back to the right spot. In these circumstances, play cannot resume until you signal for the restart.

Once having set the place for the restart you should move into position for the next phase of play. You cannot outrun a kicked ball, but you can watch the attackers take their kick from afar. Unless you anticipate trouble, the trailing assistant referee can supervise the restart, freeing you to move to the drop zone for the kick.

You should be alert to defenders who try to delay the kick for their own tactical advantage. This is done most often to prevent a quick kick while setting up a defense that is badly out of position. As we have already seen, delaying the restart is a cautionable form of gamesmanship and can impose a second hardship on the team that has already been fouled. While you should do nothing to distract the defenders, you cannot let this tactic succeed. Using your card, becoming the "first brick in the wall," or conveying a well-timed if stern reminder to the defenders immediately after blowing your whistle can keep small problems from becoming bigger ones later in the game.

Adjustments for Games with Less than Three Officials

Ideally, all soccer games will have three officials: a referee, and two assistant referees. In the real world, many soccer matches must make do with less. The shortage of available officials, last-minute emergencies, faulty communications, and an occasional lack of professionalism can all result in a particular match having less than a full crew. When this happens, you must adapt to the circumstances and change your plans accordingly.

Two Officials

Some governing bodies permit a "dual referee" system, in which the two officials appearing for the match share responsibilities—each with a whistle, and each authorized to call any and all infractions. For a variety of reasons, this system leads to problems and is not authorized for USSF-sanctioned matches. At the very least, splitting responsibilities leads to confusion on the field and may result in conflicting calls and signals.

The standard way of coping in a match with two officials is for one to patrol the middle of the field with a whistle, while the other takes a position along one of the touchlines with a flag. A club linesman is used to call balls out of bounds on the opposite side of the field.* Depending upon the level of play and the experience of the neutral assistant, you will probably choose to alter your zone of patrol in this situation. This lets you rely upon the assistant referee to call fouls more aggressively in his own quadrant of the field, enabling you to move wider and nearer to the opposite sideline. By deferring to your assistant's judgment on most fouls in the appropriate quadrant, you can usually provide adequate coverage for a typical match, as long as you are fit enough to cover the rest of the field.

In these games, offside calls are often a problem. The assistant referee will be properly positioned to make the appropriate call on one side of the field, but you will have to take responsibility for the other side. In one-sided or "half-field" games, you may wish to have the assistant switch ends of the field to monitor whichever defensive zone will see the bulk of the

---

* Club linesmen are not authorized to call fouls, or make offside decisions. In addition, not all club linesmen are created equal. There is a wide range of ability and attentiveness along the sidelines, and referees should take care not to rely too heavily upon volunteers who are neither certified nor neutral.

Before using a club linesman, you will need to explain the rules relating to "out-of-bounds," to make sure that the volunteer understands that the entire ball must cross a boundary line before it is out of bounds. You will also need to make sure that the volunteer recognizes the need not to raise the flag for anything else—including fouls and offside calls. A raised flag may compromise your credibility with the other side, if you make a call that seems to honor the flag, or with the team that provided the volunteer if you do not.

It never hurts to reassure the club linesman that things often look different from the touchline than from a chair along the sidelines...and to provide a hearty "thumbs-up" whenever a raised flag signals that the ball is out of play.

action. Regardless of any squawks from the dominating team, this is well within your prerogatives and a better use of your available resources. In games that are more-or-less evenly matched, however, it will be fairer to give each side a turn on the end with the assistant referee.

5.9

ADJUSTMENTS FOR TWO OFFICIALS

When a game has only two officials, the "diagonal" changes to reflect the Referee's expanded zone of patrol. Rather than a Figure-8, the patrol zone may appear more like an extinct, flightless bird.

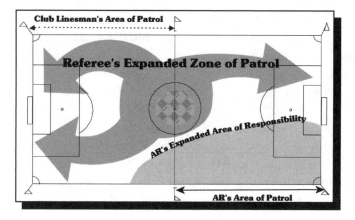

Your choice of positioning in games with a single assistant will be at your discretion. In a recreational match, you may prefer to stay close to the offside line on your end of the field. In a more competitive game, you will need to stay closer to play, and will simply have to do your best to cover the offside line from a less-than-optimal position.

One Official

In much of the world, games with a single referee are the norm, rather than the exception. These games can pose physical and practical challenges, and must be approached with care.

At lower levels of play, and particularly in matches involving very young children, a single official is often all that is needed. Most of these games involve no offside calls, and the field is small enough for a single official to cover with little difficulty. Instructional games, in particular, usually have a single official, and can be ideal matches for a beginning official to learn the art of officiating.

At intermediate or higher levels of play, and particularly in competitive matches, a lone official will have his hands full. Play will be fast-paced and may be physically intense. The need to watch both the active play and the offside line often means that off-ball activities, or incidents occurring behind the play, can go undetected and unpunished, with potentially dangerous consequences. Beginning referees should be careful accepting matches under these condition—and, if suddenly faced with the prospect of handling a match more advanced than they feel comfortable doing alone, should not allow themselves to be pressured or bullied into working a game. The bullying will, in all likelihood, continue after the opening whistle.

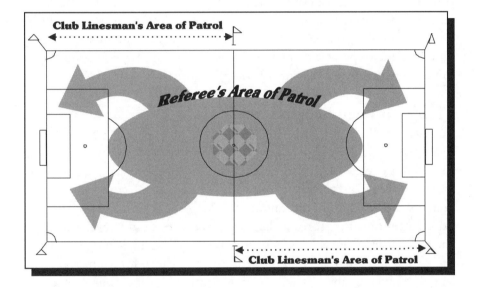

5.10

ADJUSTMENTS FOR A SINGLE REFEREE
When you are by yourself, you will be responsible for covering the entire field. Your zone of patrol is likely to change to something resembling a squashed toad.

When doing a game by yourself, you may want to modify your zone of patrol to stay closer to the middle of the field, rather than running a normal diagonal. The reason for the diagonal—the assistant referee's presence on opposing sidelines—no longer exists, and maintaining a diagonal will keep you a half-field away from most of the action on the field. By trending toward the middle and departing toward each side to stay near play, with a little luck you will maintain enough of an on-field presence to deter most acts of misconduct, while staying near enough to the play to be able to call most fouls.

Making offside calls in games with a single official is, unfortunately, highly problematic. Trying to maintain the offside line on both ends of the field will only exhaust you without accomplishing anything helpful. You will be out of position most of the time. And by spending most of your energy trying to be in place to make a half-dozen debatable offside calls, you will find yourself out of position to make the hundreds of other "foul-no foul" decisions that arise in every game. In most cases, you will be better off advising the teams that this is not the day to run their exquisitely timed offside traps, and that while you will try your best, you do not want to hear any complaints about offside calls during the game.[*]

Things to Keep in Mind

Each of us is different, and everyone brings a unique set of personal tools to the soccer field. But every approach will not work for all of us, and you should not expect that the style of any particular referee, even one you admire, will work for you in quite the same way. By the same token, humans are unique in the animal world for our ability to share the experiences of others through language, and you should never spurn the chance to learn from others. We would, after all, still be living in caves if each of us insisted upon re-inventing the wheel for ourselves, and language gives us the chance to learn from the mistakes as well as the successes of others.

Tips and Suggestions for the Referee

- *Referee the defense*. Since the attacker already has the ball and will be trying to keep it, you usually gain more by concentrating on what the defenders are doing to take it away than you will lose by dividing your attention.

---

[*] You will, of course, still get complaints, but at least the teams will be forewarned. And in any event, the offside rule is designed to prevent cherry-picking...and those who chose to live by the offside trap should expect to die by it, as well.

- *Anticipate the play, but not the call.* Anticipation can get you into position, but you must keep an open mind about what you are seeing. Otherwise, you may be fooled when events do not turn out the way you expect.

- *Respect begets respect.* Officials who are overbearing and officious should not be surprised if the players show them resentment instead of respect. While you should always take your duties seriously, among those responsibilities is showing respect for the players, as well as toward the game itself. You should not, however, take yourself too seriously.

- *Do not be a slave to your diagonal.* The diagonal is a point of reference, not a designated flight plan. You must be prepared to move with the play as it flows between areas on the field.

- *Try to avoid the center circle.* Because of its position in the middle of the field, play is always flowing around and through the center circle. Conceding that bit of ground to the players—and moving through it quickly and only when play is elsewhere—will help you avoid interfering with play.

- *Remember that the game is about the players—and not about you.* As a result, your actions should not be designed to make yourself feel important, but to get the players to behave themselves and play fairly.

- *Patience is a virtue.* Delaying your whistle for a moment lets you see the consequence of a foul before determining whether to stop play. More importantly, calmness and patience in dealing with excited players will improve your rapport with everyone on the field, and lead to a more enjoyable match for all.

- *Never get "cute."* The game of soccer is about athleticism and sportsmanship; it is not a game of "gotcha!" Referees who are open about their expectations give everyone a chance to play by the rules and can usually keep everyone focused on the game. Those who delight in springing traps on unwary players, especially for inconsequential matters, are only digging holes for themselves.

- *Eye contact with the assistant referees* not only alerts you to developments on the field, but also helps build a sense of teamwork and camaraderie.

- *A good official* is fair without being soft, firm without being officious, and impartial without being rigid. A *great* official will also know the reason for every rule, and can use Law 18—the Rule of Common Sense—to bend a rule when needed to achieve its intended purpose within the spirit of the game.

- *Do not turn your back on an angry player*, and never come withing lunging distance when issuing a card for misconduct.

- *Learn where the likely points of contact are for each play*...and when it will be helpful to watch the players' eyes.

- *Remember to swing wide*...and fade to the middle.

- *Players and spectators will be watching the ball.* You should be watching the players.

- *A quiet word at the right time* can work wonders on the field.

- *Calmness can soothe tempers*; agitation will tend to inflame them. There will be times when you need to maintain a stern and unyielding visage, when you are confronting rough play or calculated dissent. But becoming agitated and upset when the players are simply reacting to the emotion of the moment will do nothing to help them calm down, and may actually make things worse. Being firm in your decisions does not mean that you cannot also be calm and polite.

- *Try to isolate troublemakers* on the field if you can, by enlisting their teammates to help convince them to behave.

- *Continue running toward the spot of the restart* as you blow the whistle. It makes it seem like you were there, even if you weren't.

- *Practice judging the ten-yard distance* required for free kicks. It will help you set the defensive "wall" at free kicks with a minimum of delay. You will be surprised to discover just how far it is. For purposes of comparison, it is the exact radius of the center circle.

- *To prevent encroachment* at free kicks, you can become the first brick in the wall.

- ***Don't linger in the vicinity of a restart*** longer than necessary. You should always be moving toward the next area of play.

- ***Be approachable***, but do not appear too familiar with either side.

- ***Admitting mistakes*** can shock people into silence. It will not save you if it becomes your primary method of dealing with dissent, but acknowledging a clear mistake—or even acknowledging the possibility that you are not perfect—often satisfies the participants and returns their focus to the game. Nobody expects you to change your decision, but many times they only want you to listen to them...or acknowledge that you hear and understand what they are saying.

Helpful Habits to Develop

- Check your lead assistant at all through balls to make sure that the play is onside.

- Make eye contact with your assistant referees at all dead balls, and check to see if either team is requesting a substitute.

- Watch behind the play to catch late contact that may lead to trouble.

- Scan the field during uncontested play to look for signs of trouble.

- Remember to use a quiet "thumbs-up" sign to thank your assistants for their help, even if you are overruling them.
- Smile and try to look like you are enjoying yourself. It will either relax the people around you, or make them wonder what you are up to.

- Move quickly toward the spot of any foul.

- Make a practice to run vigorously for the opening minutes of the game. If you are in shape, it will help warm you up, and get you used to staying close to play; if not, it will give you an incentive to do so.

- Off the field, try to do something physical every day.

- And do not let your officiating interfere with your family. Always remember that soccer should be part of your life—not your whole life.

Chapter 6

Dealing with Dissent

FOR THE GOOD OF THE GAME, the Laws give soccer referees nearly total discretion over the conduct of a match. Fouls are fouls only if the referee determines them to be "careless" at the very least, and much of what is allowed or disallowed on the field will depend upon the referee's judgment. By making the referee the final authority on the field, the Laws encourage the players to play the game rather than spend their time quibbling over fine points of the rules.

For the same reason, the Laws make "dissent" an act of misconduct. Protests or squabbles arising during a match only distract everyone from the actual game. Giving one official the responsibility to make and enforce decisions is the best way to ensure that a match can proceed without the endless procession of committee discussions that often disrupt other sports.

The fact that soccer referees are entrusted with near-dictatorial powers, however, does not free us to act like dictators on the field. Many soccer referees make the mistake of thinking and acting like they are a god when they enter the field. There is, however, at least one major difference between being God, and being a soccer referee: nobody has ever seen God strutting around heaven, pretending to be a referee.[*] The reason that soccer gives its officials such wide-ranging discretion is not that we are

---

[*] Of course, when the punishment for dissent is a lightening bolt from the sky, rather than a card made of plastic, the referee might be less inclined to overreact to protests, and less likely to suffer from a lack of self-confidence.

infallible, because we know more soccer than anyone else, or even because we have actually read the rules— but because the sport trusts each referee to use that discretion for the benefit of the players.

As with many things in life, discretion can be a burden as well as a blessing. Ironically, the very fact that so much of what happens on the soccer field falls within the discretion of the referee leads spectators and players to blame the referee whenever anything goes wrong. At the youth level, where most new officials begin their careers, the players are usually no problem. They are too busy enjoying themselves to worry about what the referee is doing, and rarely care about anything more than playing the game. Instead, it is the adults who may spoil things for everybody, and for the new official it is the coaches and parents who are likely to present the biggest obstacles to learning how to referee. While "dissent" will start invading the youth fields once the players are in their teens, it is actually the younger levels of play that place a new referee at greatest risk. It is there that the new referee will be facing the new "soccer parents," whose misunderstanding of the game is likely to be matched only by their lack of appreciation for the burdens faced by those who are still discovering what it takes to be a match official.

Among referees of all ages, but most particularly among younger officials, abuse by coaches and spectators continues to be the main reason why many decide to end their careers as soccer referees. And each brand new referee who leaves after a season or two is one less experienced referee who will be available five years later. The result is that we face an endless shortage of good, experienced referees—and, inevitably, further complaints and abuse by those whose misbehavior keeps driving good people away.

This does not mean that a new official should be afraid to walk onto the pitch, however. Knowledge is power, and it is better to be prepared for what may happen at the field than simply to hope that all of our matches will go smoothly. Our mission to see that the game is fun and enjoyable for all. This means learning how to keep everyone—spectators, coaches, and players—on a tight-enough leash so that the players can actually play the game. While we must recognize that "dissent" is punishable as a misconduct, we must also acknowledge that soccer is an emotional game, and that although the Laws may empower us to punish, they do not always make it mandatory that we do so.

The Laws tell us that "dissent" is misconduct, but common sense tells us that there is a difference between expressions of disappointment and "dissent." For purposes of understanding how to distinguish between disappointment and misconduct, it may help to think about "dissent" as occurring in different stages, each warranting a different reaction by the referee.

The Stages of Dissent

Forgivable Dissent

Human Reaction

Strictly speaking, we could consider any spontaneous, reflexive reaction to an adverse decision to be a form of dissent. Such reactions do, after all, exhibit signs of disagreement with the referee's decision. Normal human reactions to disappointment or frustration are both predictable and quite understandable, however, and do not constitute the offense of "Dissent" as long as they fade quickly, and the participant returns his attention to the game. In dealing with these reactions, it often helps to pretend you have not noticed them. Ignoring them conveys the message that you have confidence in your decision, and will not pay attention to such "trifling details."

"Quiet" Dissent

Occasionally, a player or coach will speak to you "privately," to tell you that you blew a particular call. ("He really *did* trip over the ball, Ref — I didn't touch him"; "The ball *did* deflect off Blue, Ref"; etc.). So long as the remarks are quiet, polite, and discreet, they need not be cautioned. In fact, a wise referee can use these comments as constructive feedback, particularly if they come from a player or coach whom you respect. Still, the player's "quiet word" is not always accurate, and is often a form of gamesmanship. In any case, your reaction should be the same: smile, and acknowledge that nobody is perfect.

Emotional Dissent

If the language used to express disappointment or frustration is "marginally inappropriate," or a player (or coach) is having problems bringing his frustrations under control, it may mean that the emotional reaction to your decisions is undermining your control over the game. Once again, however, the player is simply reacting, but now his emotions are making him lose the ability to focus on the game. At these times, a calming word ("Settle down, Number 6"; "Keep your mind on the game, Eleven—not on the last call"; "Coach, please keep your voice down") may help soothe tempers, and gives everyone the chance to regain their self-control before getting into trouble. When dealing with such reactions, though, you must remain calm yourself and make a special effort to avoid baiting, taunting, flaunting your authority, or doing anything to provoke a response. You are trying to *calm* the player, not yank his chain, and there is no need to prove who the boss is on the field. Your call has already shown your authority, and you want to help him accept the decision, not dare him to challenge it. If possible, calming the player without issuing a caution will mark you as a diplomat and reinforce your match control. Failing to caution him when you need to do so will cause things to deteriorate, however, and it is often hard to know exactly where the line for each game will be. Your best tool in this circumstance will probably be the ball. The quicker it is back into play, the sooner the player's frustrations will disappear and the less likely you will need to issue a caution.

Actionable Dissent

Demonstrative or Calculated Dissent—*Caution*

Once dissent passes the purely emotional stage, you need to take action. If a player or coach is complaining whenever a call goes the other way, persists in protesting a call or continues to ride you after you have asked him to stop, follows you around to argue the point, or makes an unmistakable physical demonstration of protest,* failing to issue an appropriate card will only make things worse. These actions are often calculated to unnerve you, or make you afraid to render decisions unfavorable to that particular team. When confronted with such a display your reaction should be quick and unapologetic. If all goes well, your yellow card for dissent will be like a splash of cold water in the face, and get everyone focused on the game again. At the very least, it will quiet them down for a while.

Offensive, Insulting, or Abusive Language or Conduct—*Expulsion*

Every so often, a coach or player goes beyond merely protesting a call, and loses control. If someone is hurling insults, making threatening gestures

---

*Examples include throwing or kicking the ball in anger, gesturing wildly, verbally challenging your authority, or screaming in your face.

or noises, or otherwise offending the ears and sensibilities of everyone around, you must deal with him quickly and sternly to minimize the damage to the game. While the line between a yellow and red card may be difficult to draw in the abstract, a simple rule of thumb can help draw the distinction when you are on the pitch. If, during the offender's rantings, you feel that your decision, your authority, or your control of the match is under attack, it will most likely be cautionable dissent, which you should punish with a yellow card. On the other hand, if you feel that *you personally* are under attack, then the offender's actions are probably "offensive, insulting, or abusive," and a red card is in order. Yet the first instinct of many inexperienced referees, especially young ones confronting a screaming adult for the first time, is often to retreat, and they may completely forget about the cards in their pocket. In such circumstances, assistant referees should be alert to the trouble, and quick to provide help—reminding the referee of his options, including the red card; reassuring him that it is not the official's fault that the coach is out of control; and telling him that he is doing just fine (even if he is clearly struggling), and should not let the ranting of a lunatic interfere with the game.

Drawing the Line

In the last analysis, the responsibility for match control rests with each individual referee. Therefore, each referee will have a different tolerance for dissent and may properly draw lines in different places to distinguish between types of protests to punish, tolerate, or ignore. Before a match, you should think about your own strengths and weaknesses as an official, and try to develop a sense of where your personal line will be. Each game is different, however, and you may have to adjust your approach to suit the match at hand. After all, a good referee will always try to bring out the best in everyone, even if it means adapting to the participants and circumstances. Don't be afraid to grow, or to reexamine your approach to all facets of game management, for we often learn more from our mistakes than from our successes. And even if we cannot revoke a card issued in haste or issue one that we were afraid to give in the last game, we can always do better the next time. We cannot change a call after the fact. We can, however, always change our philosophy, and our approach to the game.

Dissent and the Madding Crowd

The hardest part of being an official in any sport can be dealing with hostility from the sidelines. Jeering, heckling, and hostile comments from spectators are the most common reason that referees decide to stop working as an official in a sport they love. By an unfortunate coincidence, soccer referees are more vulnerable to this kind of abuse than most. We are closer to the sidelines than many officials; our sport is fast-paced and leads to a high pitch of fevered emotions; we must anticipate and react to developments on the field as quickly as the players in order to keep the game under control; and, most importantly, the game itself gives more discretion to the referee than any other sport on Earth.

Soccer's growing popularity in this country means that we have a desperate need for referees. While this gives many people the chance to participate, the American tradition of jeering the officials at sporting events often makes many younger referees, and a fair number of older ones, feel picked on, unappreciated, and humiliated. But because competitive soccer is impossible without referees, hostile reaction from the sidelines poses a direct threat to the continued growth of American soccer. Referees will not be available if they are chased from the field by the crowd before they learn their craft. And without skilled officials, soccer players in this country will never reach their full potential.

Dealing with hostile reactions from the sidelines is something that all experienced referees have learned to do. It is something that each new official must confront and overcome. We are not, however, helpless in dealing with tormentors along the touchline, and if we learn to relax, we will find that we have a number of tools at our disposal that can help us.

Appearance and Deportment

A professional appearance will go a long way toward eliminating many problems you may have on the field. If you are neatly dressed, in a proper uniform, signal your decisions confidently, blow your whistle *loudly*, and hustle your way around the field, you will have fewer problems than if your socks hang down around your ankles, your whistle sounds like a dying quail, and you walk through the game looking annoyed that the players are keeping you from taking a nap. No matter how uneasy or unsure of yourself you feel, if you look like you know what you are doing, and can project a "field presence" to those around you, people will be more willing to accept your decisions.

Words of Explanation

Though you are under no obligation to do so, a timely word of explanation about a call can do wonders to calm feelings on the sidelines. For example, whether or not you properly signaled "advantage" at the time, telling a coach who is grumbling about an obvious handball you let go that "I didn't call the last handball on the other team because the ball went right to your wing, and I didn't want to stop his charge on goal" will not only show that you really *are* paying attention to the game. It also tells the coach: (1) that you understand the rules better than he does; (2) that you are trying to be fair to *both* teams; and (3) that he had better watch what he says on the sidelines.

A Word to the Wise

Another helpful tactic is using a stoppage in play to jog over to the sidelines and politely ask for the coach's assistance: "Coach, please keep your voice down," or "Coach, some of your parents are bothering my linesman. Please tell them to behave themselves" are discreet ways of making your concerns known *before* the need to take action arises. This will often solve the problem for you. But if trouble persists, and you need to take sterner action later in the game, then you have done what you could to prevent it, and the coaches and parents will have only themselves to blame for the consequences.

For New Referees, Young and Old

Like other forms of wildlife, coaches, players, and spectators can often smell fear. New referees in particular often show their lack of confidence by their body language. In addition, it is only natural for younger referees to feel awkard standing up to the adults on the sidelines, or for beginning referees to feel unsure of themselves on the field. Many coaches understand this, and will go out of their way not to cause trouble. People unschooled in proper sportsmanship, however, may take this as their cue to begin screaming. Those coaches who scream at you, or allow their spectators to do so, are nothing more than bullies, trying to intimidate you into shading your calls in their favor. When this happens, take a deep breath and remind yourself:

You are in command of the field. While everyone else is *participating* in the game of Soccer, you alone *represent* the game—its history, traditions, and spirit of fair play. And it is *your* sense of fair play that governs the field, and makes the game possible. When you are serving as an official, you are entitled to respect by everyone on the field, and to deference by all the other participants.

Whatever anyone says, and however loudly they complain, you are doing nothing wrong. In fact, you are only doing your job. It is the people screaming at you who are misbehaving. They are showing not only a lack of proper sportsmanship, but ignorance of the rules and traditions of soccer.

Trying to intimidate the referee is an unfair tactic, just like pushing, holding, or tripping. You should do everything you can to make sure that it does not succeed.

You should be careful not to develop "rabbit ears," reacting to everything anybody says about you on the field. In fact, it can be healthy to let participants vent their frustrations or disappointment over their bad luck, especially if it involves a close call that has just gone against them.

However, you must try to distinguish between expressions of frustration, and "dissent." It is often wise to pretend not to overhear the sideline's reaction to a call, especially if it is a close one or if that particular side has just had a run of fouls called (or not called) against them. But do not hesitate to use your authority, including your cards, if the reaction involves more than an isolated, spontaneous outburst of emotion, if you are singled out, or if your authority is challenged. In such cases, showing the card may or may not calm them down. It may, however, convince them to keep their mouths shut.

You are not helpless if it is the fans, rather than the players or coaches, who are causing you grief. At most levels of play, you have two basic alternatives in dealing with such a problem, and the choice between them is entirely up to you. You may book or dismiss the coach for failing to keep his spectators under control, or you can suspend the game for spectator interference and refuse to resume it until the offending spectators retire to an appropriate distance. Both courses have their advantages and disadvantages, and you should warn the coaches ahead of time, not only to demonstrate your fairness but to give them a chance to bring their sideline under control. In either case, you should note any action you take on your game report.

No matter what goes wrong during a game, your soccer club is on your side. If you make a mistake, you can learn from it and try to do things better next time. But any mistake you can possibly make during a game is minor, compared to the damage that coaches or fans can do to the game by trying to intimidate you.

The Laws of the Game give referees discretion to deal with a wide range of problems. Just remember that you are there for the players, not the parents, fans, or coaches. For the players to play, they need officials who are honest, fair, and able to concentrate on the game, and who are not intimidated or frightened by everyone on the sidelines. Just as you cannot be afraid to make a call on the field in order to ensure a safe and fair match for the players, do not be afraid to take action against anyone on the sidelines who is trying to bully you.

Lastly, a thick skin and healthy ego are, like your cards and whistle, the tools of your trade, and the best officials take care to keep their egos in check and their tempers firmly under control. It is not, after all, a sign of weakness to be considerate and polite to the players, coaches, and spectators. It is, instead, the ultimate show of strength.

Thoughts for Before the Match

- Soccer is a game of passion and excitement that often leads to strong emotions.

- Since I don't care who wins the game, and may be the only sane person at the field at any given time, everyone is counting on me to keep a level head.

- Since I have all the cards, and can caution or send people away whenever I feel the need to do so, it costs me nothing to be polite.

- My skin is thicker than that of a rhinoceros.

- My ears can be selectively deaf, depending on the needs of the match.

- This being a free country, everyone is entitled to an opinion. Under the Laws of the Game, however, the decibel level allowed for freedom of expression at a soccer game is at the discretion of the referee.

- They did not give me a badge and whistle because I know more about soccer than anybody else. They gave them to me because I have actually read the rules.

- I don't much like being bullied or embarrassed by others, and it's unlikely that the players or coaches feel differently.

- It is a better use of my cards to protect the players' ankles, knees, and calves, rather than to protect my own ego; but nevertheless....

- A player who continues to argue after play has restarted should probably receive a caution.

- A player who follows me around after I reposition myself to give him the chance to cool off should probably receive a caution.

- A player who screams something that I don't think I should pretend not to hear should receive a caution.

- A player who violates one of the "Three P's"—Public, Persistent, or Personal—should receive a caution.

- And anyone who goes after a youthful or obviously inexperienced assistant referee has just bought a world of trouble.

Chapter 7

When Things Go Wrong

WHILE NOBODY SHOULD START A GAME expecting the worst, humans are imperfect creatures. Mistakes sometimes happen, problems arise, and on rare occasions things simply get out of control.

Since a little forethought can prevent most problems from turning into disasters, a wise referee will give some thought how best to handle many foreseeable events that can arise at the field. A crisis is usually a stressful time, and a little forethought can help us manage problems that might otherwise turn out very badly. Even if we never use any of our contingency plans, it never hurts to be prepared.

Of course, not all crises are created equal. Some are self-inflicted, some are nobody's fault, and some are unavoidable. Others fall into the categories of blunders by others or abuse by the barbarians who occasionally appear along the sidelines. In all cases, the most important thing is keeping your head and providing any help you can to whoever needs it. There are many ways to manage something that goes wrong. Panic, however, is usually not the preferred course of action. In dealing with any of these situations, the important thing is remaining calm and dealing with the situation. The appropriate authorities will take matters from there.

Problems For Which Nobody Will Blame You

As with life in general, issues can arise at and around the soccer field that are nobody's fault. This does not mean that we are free to ignore them, just that the explanation obviously has nothing to do with the officials. Some things may cause safety problems. Others may simply be matters of filing the necessary reports or paperwork, or simply making a telephone call:

Teams do not appear for the match

Every so often, the officials will appear at the game site on schedule only to find that the teams are nowhere to be found.

If you are the only one there, it is possible that you have made a mistake in reading your schedule, or you are the only one who did not get the word about a change in plans. If all of the officials are there, but the only other people at the field are walking the family dog, somebody probably made a mistake in scheduling, or there was some last-minute development affecting the game and nobody thought to tell the referees.

Whatever the cause, you should try to contact your assignor from the field for instructions. If there was a mistake in the schedule that sent the referees to one field while the teams went to another, you may still be able to have a game if you can get everybody to the same place. If you cannot contact the assignor, you should wait for a reasonable time after the scheduled start of the match and then, if nobody appears, you may leave. You will, however, need to contact your assignor and make a report when you get home. More likely than not, unless you are the one who made the mistake you will be paid for your appearance, once the organizers sort out what went wrong.

Inclement Weather

Living on a planet with a variable climate, we are often at the mercy of the weather. Storms pop up from time to time, making it dangerous to play or turning fields into unplayable swamps.

Once you arrive at the field, it will be your decision whether the weather is making it impossible for the game to start, or to continue. You should consult both sides before making your decision, but the final decision belongs to you. Your chief concern should always be the safety of the players, and you should not let coaches, parents, or others bully you into playing a game under conditions you know to be unsafe. Among the factors to guide your decision are the following:

Is there lightning in the vicinity? If so, the game should not continue.

Is there are reasonable chance that a storm will pass? If so, you should defer any final decision until the situation clarifies itself. A passing thunderstorm may look threatening when it is upon you, but the sky may be clear a half-hour later.

Is threatening weather widespread, or isolated? Checking the weather reports will tell you whether the storm that is upon you is an isolated pocket of bad weather or part of a broader front. If a series of storms is approaching, it may simply be a waste of time to wait. If it is the only threatening weather in the area, on the other hand, it may be worth waiting to see if it passes.

Aside from lightning, does the weather pose a risk to any of the participants? Soccer does not cancel games simply because it is raining or cold outside. But extreme conditions—gale-force winds, perhaps, or temperatures posing a risk of frostbite—may make playing inadvisable.

If you terminate or suspend a match due to the weather, you will need to report your actions to the league. Be specific about your actions, and note the game situation when play was halted, including the time, the score and the nature of any restart that would have taken place if play had resumed. Most leagues have rules that deal with weather-related stoppages, and your report may determine whether the match is deemed an official game, is replayed, or resumes from the point of the stoppage.

Field is inadequate or unplayable

Storms can leave a field wet, muddy, or littered with debris. Occasionally, sustained rains may leave it flooded, and even without the intervention of Nature, some fields are so neglected or poorly maintained that playing soccer on them is impossible.

The Laws specify the requirements for a proper field, and you should note any major discrepancies or shortcomings on your game report so that they may be corrected. You should also use your common sense and good judgment in deciding whether a field is playable. So long as a field's problems pose no risk of harm to the players, you can accommodate a great many failings through ingenuity and a willingness to help accommodate the game. On the other hand, a field with no goal posts, grass that is a foot tall, or water covering one or both of the penalty areas cannot host a soccer game without turning the match into a farce.

Referees arriving at fields that are not proper venues should decline to officiate the match, and provide full details on their game report.

Accidents and Other Misadventures

As with any contact sport, injuries are an unfortunate part of soccer. Most common mishaps are minor, and players can usually resume playing after a few moments of recovery, often with no need to stop the game. Occasionally, however, a player's injuries go beyond a minor knock on the shin or muscle cramp. When this happens, you must be able to assess the situation and help take appropriate action, which will vary depending upon the nature and severity of the injury, and the ready availability of medical help.

Stopping the Play

The Laws instruct us to let play continue despite minor injuries. When it looks like a player is seriously hurt, though, the game must stop before anyone can tell how severe the injury is, and decide what kind of treatment is called for.

While whistling to stop play for an injury is not forbidden, if you do so the restart will be a dropped ball. Complications arise if players do not know traditional soccer etiquette. The customary procedure is for the players to send the ball across a boundary line to tend to a player who needs help. If players are bringing an injury to your attention, you should direct them to kick the ball over the touch line. Note the time of the stoppage, and the appropriate restart. This may prevent embarrassment in the event that the stoppage is a lengthy one and everybody forgets how play came to be stopped. It will also help you describe the incident on your match report. As with other noteworthy incidents, significant injuries need to be reported not only to advise the league of the event, but also to help document the injury in case of an insurance claim.

It is considered good sportsmanship for the team entitled to the restart to return the ball to the team kicking it out of bounds. Reminding younger teams of the customary protocol will help educate them in proper on-field behavior. Failing to return the ball is not, however, a violation of the rules. This is the main reason why putting the ball into touch after an injury is usually better than whistling play to a halt. It results in fewer problems if the teams do not understand the traditions of the game.

Help for an Injured Player

Once play is stopped, you should go to the player to make a quick assessment of the nature and severity of the injury. If the injury needs treatment, you should summon help as soon as the seriousness of the injury is apparent. As the match official, your responsibility does not include providing medical treatment or first aid. You already have a job on the field, and must monitor and control everyone in and around the area. Tending to an injured player is a job best left to team officials, or trained medical personnel.[*]

Medical Emergencies

On rare occasions, a player or other person may collapse at the field or suffer a major trauma. If this kind of emergency crops up at one of your matches, you may need to suspend the match and wait for help to arrive. Seriously injured people should only be moved by trained medical professionals. You should do nothing to jeopardize the safety of anyone in serious need of medical treatment, even if it means suspending or abandoning your match.

If the emergency arises nearby, but not on the field where your game is being played, you should use your own common sense in deciding when and whether to continue your own match. The needs of a game will never match the life-and-death needs of a real medical crisis.

When Things Get Out of Hand

Some referees can go years without encountering an ugly incident at the field. Others seem to face them with alarming regularity. But all referees must be ready to deal with disturbances, since we never know ahead of time which games will lead to trouble. In nearly every case, panic is a greater threat to you than anything happening at the field. To prevent it from overcoming you, and keeping you from taking the appropriate action at the time, there are several things you need to keep in mind before and during each game:

- You are the authority at the field, and the Laws are on your side in any confrontation.

- Following the rules will never get you into trouble.

---

[*] Or anyone with a can of the "magic spray" used to cure a any number of otherwise crippling injuries at professional matches.

- If things get too ugly, you are authorized to terminate or abandon the match.

- You are responsible for officiating the match, not for keeping or restoring order on the field.

Understanding these basic principles, you should be able to face anything happening at the field.

Confrontations

Sooner or later, all referees will face angry or quarrelsome players, coaches, or spectators. Soccer is, after all, a game that excites the emotions of everyone at the field, and it is only natural for some to get caught up in the heat of the moment.

This does not mean that everyone at the game can taunt or heckle the officials. The Laws give you the power to do what you must in order to keep the match under control. This power includes the authority to dismiss or send off any coach or player who is out of control, and to suspend the match to allow the teams to bring order to the sidelines. You must, however, take care to remain calm yourself as you remind everyone that you have made your decision, and that it is not going to change. Doing so often diffuses the situation and helps everyone's mind return to the game; becoming angry or combative yourself may escalate the incident from a manageable problem into a major incident. Your choice of actions will depend upon whether a confrontation arises during a game or afterwards, and whether you are faced with a coach, a player, or an angry spectator:

Coaches

Coaches, like players, are participants in the match and subject to the Laws of the Game. This means that there will be disciplinary consequences stemming from any misconduct, and you will need to make a full and accurate report of any incident.

Unlike a player, however, the Laws do not anticipate that referees will ever display misconduct cards to a coach. Because there are no on-field consequences flowing from a coach's misconduct, there is simply no need to do so. Coaches are allowed along the sidelines as long as they behave in a responsible manner, and you may dismiss them from the field if they do not. Usually a system of escalating warnings—from an informal admonition, to a warning, to a dismissal—will roughly correspond to similar actions taken against a player in the form of a quiet word, a caution, or a send-off.

It is important to stay outwardly calm when confronting an angry coach. It may quiet tempers to let the coach have his say, and since you make the final decision, you may want to give the coach the last word in a discussion. Expressing frustration can have a therapeutic effect and often lets the coach return his attention more quickly to the game. This is particularly true if his show of temper stems from a particular call on the field. If convinced of the injustice of a penalty kick, or concerned about a no-call that left one of his players on the ground, the coach may simply be reacting to the excitement of the moment, engaging in "human reaction" or "emotional dissent" as we discussed in Chapter 6. In these cases, though the Laws do not require it, letting the coach voice his concerns may end the matter and lead to no further trouble. If this is the course you choose, just listen politely, rephrase his concerns in your own words to show that you understand what he is saying, and explain the way you saw the play. This turns the matter into a simple difference of opinion among soccer people, leaving the coach with nothing to do but accept your view of the play. If he keeps confronting you, then you have clearly done what you could to resolve the matter amicably and there can be no doubt that the coach is responsible for the consequences. And if the coach continues riding or taunting you afterwards, your reason for taking action will be apparent to all.

On the other hand, there are times when a coach's actions are intolerable from the outset, particularly if he keeps bellowing across the field during the run of play. When you have determined that a coach has crossed the line from harmless grumbling to actionable misconduct, your actions should be similar to those dealing with a player: isolate the offender, calmly state the action you are taking and the reason for doing so, and inform him of the consequences. In the case of a player, you would display the appropriate card. For a coach, you simply state whether you are booking him,* or dismissing him from the field.

---

*Ie, noting the incident in your game report, which would be the equivalent of a caution for a player. Unless, of course, the League itself has directed you to issue a card.

Players

Though rarely seen in games involving young children, referees often face angry reactions from the players during the course of a match. The reasons may vary, but your reaction to an angry player can set the tone for your dealings with players from both sides, and failing to act appropriately can undermine your control of the field.

As with a coach, the cause of a player's anger may determine your course of action. If it stems from a particular incident, you can give the player* a few moments to bring his temper under control. If the confrontation persists, you will need to follow the appropriate procedure for issuing a card for player misconduct.

You can often avoid trouble simply by walking away from it. Moving off the field, or changing your position to move away from an emotionally charged player, lets you to draw a line beyond which the player crosses at his peril. Moving off the field after calling a penalty kick, for example, lets you point to the end line as a boundary marker, effectively telling everyone that it is time for them to quit squawking and return to the game. Moving away after telling a player to focus on the next play shows that you are trying to avoid the confrontation. Everyone will understand that the player has earned his card if he follows you around the field to continue his protests.

Spectators

At some soccer games, crowds are non-existent. At others, the crowds are seated in grandstands or bleachers and separated from the officials by the venue's geography. In most youth games, however, parents and friends form the majority of those in attendance, and it is at these games that a referee can face the greatest risk of confrontation.

While you are under no obligation to explain any of your calls, a polite word of explanation in response to a polite inquiry after the game may keep a contact from turning into a confrontation. When facing an angry person demanding an explanation, however, the wiser course of action may be to avoid entering into any conversation at all, and suggesting, as politely as you can, that they direct any questions they have to their coach. If the contact persists, and you have no place to retreat, the entire referee

---

* Or players: often, confrontations arise in the aftermath of a critical call in the game—such a penalty kick, or a particularly nasty foul—and may lead to several players surrounding the referee in order to plead their case.

crew should remain together, both for reasons of safety and to provide witnesses to any incident that develops. You can seek refuge in a different part of the field, among spectators from the opposing side, or in a vehicle belonging to a member of the referee crew, and you are free to delay finishing the game report until you can do so without distraction.

As always, you should include any pertinent details in a supplemental match report, so that the authorities can take appropriate action. You may submit this report together with the usual paperwork for the match or afterwards, if it takes time for you to prepare it. You should, however, do what you can to identify the parties involved, in case the need for formal sanctions arises.

Referee Abuse

A problem for referees around the world is abuse by players, coaches, and spectators. Soccer raises many deep-seeded emotions, and some people are unwilling to take responsibility for their own failures. Unfortunately, referees are easy scapegoats for a team's lack of success on the pitch. On rare occasions, these feelings flare up into cruel taunts, threats of harm, or actual physical attacks.

If faced with a hostile crowd of people, you may feel small, isolated, and alone. In truth, you have many people behind you, including your colleagues on the pitch, the people on adjacent fields, and the many decent people on both sides who will be appalled to witness a display of poor sportsmanship—not to mention the hosting soccer club, and the league and State soccer associations. Though it may be difficult, the most important thing for you to do is to keep a level head and avoid panicking. Afterwards, your crew will need to gather and assess the situation and determine what to do next. While you cannot decide your precise course of action ahead of time, there are a number of alternatives open to you:

- If the crowd becomes abusive during the game, you have the option of suspending or terminating the match. Collect the game ball and advise the coaches that the match will not proceed until the sidelines are under control. You may, if you like, let the coaches try convincing the spectators to behave themselves. Or, if you prefer, you may inform them that the game will not resume until the offending parties leave the vicinity, even if that means clearing the sidelines of spectators. You do not, however, need to calm the crowd yourself.

- If you decide to clear the sidelines, you do not have to resume the game until the offending crowd has retreated to a distance far enough to suit you.

- If you decide to terminate the match, you should have the assistant referees furl their flags and join you. You can decide on further action once you are together.

- Some leagues encourage officials to hold the coaches responsible for the behavior of their own spectators, giving you the option of dismissing a coach who cannot control the team's parents. Though many referees follow this course when things are getting ugly, it has two major disadvantages. It does not deal with the offending parties; and it may well remove from the offending sideline the only adult with an incentive to keep the crowd under control. If you decide to use this option, you should treat it like any other dismissal. Inform the coach of the reason for your action and do not resume until the coach in question leaves the field. You should, however, make sure that there is an assistant coach available to take charge of the team before choosing this alternative.

- If the level of hostility is high enough, you may need to withdraw from the vicinity. If you are an adult, you have the option of driving away. Younger officials may need to seek a ride from a friendly adult. In either case, you should take all paperwork with you, including game reports and any pass cards you have collected. You can return them later, after tempers have cooled and the situation has settled down. All officials should remain together to help prepare reports of the incident.

Whether you finish the game or terminate the match, you will need to report the incident. Your state or local association may even have a special form for you to use to do so. Any report should contain the names of all referees in attendance; the time, place, and date of the match; the league and teams involved; the names of any witnesses to what happened; and a narrative account of precisely what happened, including specific quotes of anything that was said, and a list of any misconducts issued as a result. At least one copy of the report should go to your state referee administrator, who will initiate any appropriate action. You should distribute other copies according to any specific instructions you may have, and keep at least one copy for yourself.

Referee Assault

There is a world of difference between a reassuring pat on the back and a physical attack, and you should be careful not to overreact to someone who means you no harm. But by and large, unless you are injured and in need of first aid, there is no reason why anyone at the field should ever have to lay hands on you during the match. If anyone does so in anger, it escalates the incident from misconduct to a matter beyond the Laws of the Game.

The criminal law defines an assault as any attempt to engage in unwanted physical contact.* On rare occasions, there have been times when referees have been subjected to actual, physical attacks by disgruntled spectators or participants. If this ever happens to you, you should include a report of it in your supplemental report to your state referee administrator, but you should also report the matter to the police, who will take appropriate action against your attacker. Assault is a crime, and there is no room in the game of soccer for those who attack its officials.

Duties when there is a fight

Among the most frightening events that any referee can face is a general free-for-all involving the players. In venues with lights and bleachers, this may bring an onrush of security onto the field. At most fields, however, you will be on your own. Your job as a referee is to officiate the game and maintain order on the field. A brawl goes beyond your responsibilities as a sports official and into the area of law enforcement. Even so, you will have responsibilities even during a melee, and foremost among them is the duty to report what happened accurately to league officials. As a citizen, you may also have a duty to serve as a witness to what has happened. You cannot do either if you are an active participant.

On occasion, stepping between players who are showing signs of stress can prevent a fight. This is not always a wise thing to do, however, and may leave you in no-man's land between two combatants if tempers lead to fists. In addition, the primary job of an official witnessing an outbreak of violence is simply to watch, and the middle of a battlefield hardly offers the best vantage point for an observer. A better place is safely outside the

---

* *See, eg, People v. Reeves*, 458 Mich. 236, 239, 580 N.W.2d 433 (1998).
Actually, the court's definition was considerably longer. The definition in the text is a rough translation from the original Legalese.

disturbance, with notebook in hand, taking numbers and recording actions by whoever is participating.

With a full three-member crew, the officials should be able to surround the disturbance. One official—usually the assistant referee furthest from the melee, with the best long-distance view of what is happening—can assume responsibility for detecting people who enter the field to join the disturbance, especially if he is on the same side of the field as the players. If there is a fourth official at the match, this is the official who usually takes charge of the sidelines, freeing the team-side assistant, usually identified in game reports as "AR-1," to move closer to the players for a better view of what is happening. The other officials should take positions that maximize their collective view of events, ensuring full coverage of whatever is going on. All officials should clearly note which acts were performed by which players, using whatever short-hand code will record the necessary information. And each official must clearly distinguish between "brawlers" and "peacemakers," to avoid punishing those whose only offense was helping to restore order on the field:

54'   TI-B

R6 h B5 h R6

R17 h B14

R12 r R14

B11 r R17

Using this shorthand, the official can reconstruct her observations for the match report: After the ball went over the touch line, Red #6 and Blue #5 got into a fight; Red #17 also began hitting Blue #14, but the official saw the latter engage in no aggressive conduct. In the meantime, this same official saw Red #12 and Blue #11 attempting to restrain two of the combatants. In addition to recording the participants for purposes of determining who should be sent off for violent conduct, this account may help clear the two players who were trying to break up the fight, in case other officials saw them scuffling during the melee but did not see enough of the event to know what they were trying to do. The rest of the crew, recording their own observations from their different positions around the field, can add to the account, or clarify events that this official did not clearly see. If, for example, one of the other officials saw Blue #14 start hitting Red #17, that would explain how that part of the incident started and justify a send-off for the second Blue player.

Brawls can be game-ending events. Tempers may remain high, and players may be unable to return their focus to the match. Sometimes, though, sending off the troublemakers is enough to calm everybody down, letting the match resume after the dismissed players leave the area.

In the cited example, the final match report may well look something like this: "In Minute 54, a fight broke out after the ball crossed into touch. During the fight, Red #6 and Blue #5 were deliberately and violently striking each other, and Red #17 and Blue #14 were also deliberately and violently striking each other, while players from both sides were attempting to restrain the combatants. Once order was restored, Red #6, Red #17, Blue #5 and Blue #14 were each shown a red card and dismissed for violent conduct. As play was stopped at the time for a ball into touch, play resumed with a throw-in for Blue. There were no further incidents of misconduct in the match."[*]

With Friends Like These...

As a new official, you will find that most of your colleagues are happy to help you in any number of ways, whether by giving you advice or sharing their own insights about the game. On rare occasions, you may come across a fellow referee who is not only unhelpful, but whose approach to officiating makes you uncomfortable—someone who shows contempt or bias toward particular teams, or who insists upon rewriting the rules to suit the occasion.

While you should refrain from airing your differences with a colleague in public, you should feel free to bring your concerns to the attention of your assignor. Matching games and officials is a difficult job, and the assignor will probably appreciate the feedback, since it may bring to light a problem that needs correcting. At the very least, it can spare you the burden of having to work with someone whose approach to the game strikes you as unprofessional.

In rare cases, you may need to bring a serious matter of referee misconduct to the attention of your state referee administrator. If you believe that an incident warrants further investigation, you may want to talk to a trusted mentor or senior official, who can advise you on the steps to take.

---

[*] In the actual match report, it would be better to include the players' names, as well as their jersey numbers.

Owning up to Mistakes, and Learning from Them

Wisdom can result in the exercise of good judgment in trying circumstances. Of course, good judgment comes from experience—and, unfortunately, experience often comes from the exercise of bad judgment.

While nobody ever tries to blunder, soccer is a game designed and run by fallible human beings, making mistakes inevitable. With millions of players participating in thousands of games across the country, it is unrealistic to expect everyone to be perfect, and the occasional blunder is simply an occupational hazard. When something does go wrong, please keep in mind the following:

- Most mistakes are avoidable. Learn from them, and try not to make the same mistake twice.

- Veteran officials did not start out with experience. Most likely it came the hard way, from making the same blunders that others have made. If you can get them to share their misadventures, you can learn from their mistakes as well.

- When you do make a mistake, the honorable thing to do is acknowledge the error and take whatever steps you can to correct it. If correcting a serious mistake on the field is impossible—if, for example, an intervening restart prevents you from disallowing a goal or changing a poor decision on a misconduct—you may need to include a full report of the problem to the relevant authorities, so letting them take whatever remedial steps are appropriate.

- Consulting a trusted mentor may help give you perspective on any errors you have made, as well as giving you ideas on how to avoid similar problems in the future.

Common Mistakes and Pitfalls

While there are an infinite number of mistakes you can make, there are an equal number that you can try to avoid...including the following:

- Blowing the whistle upon seeing deliberate hand-to-ball contact in the PA...only to discover when bodies part that it was the keeper who was trying to block the ball from entering the net.

- Raising the flag to summon the referee's attention for an off-ball incident involving rough pushes and shoves by opposing players...only to discover that you cannot remember the numbers of either player.

- Confidently pointing direction for a free kick...only to discover that, this being the second half, you pointed in the wrong direction and the wrong team has just taken a quick free kick.

- Correcting your wrong directional signal...only to have the right team take a quick kick and score against the now out-of-position defenders.

- Confidently snapping an offside flag...only to see the ball caught by the wind and never make it to the offside player.

- Briskly sprinting upfield as an assistant referee to confirm a goal that caused the net to billow, only to see the defenders set up and take a goal kick...without protest by the other team.

- Insisting on signaling a throw-in for Red after Blue ran to fetch the ball...only to notice that all the Red players—including the one you are certain never touched the ball—are racing to change position, having positioned themselves for a Blue throw-in.

- Calling a hotly protested penalty kick from 40 yards away at the end of the first half...only to discover in the second half that attackers from both teams are now unable to stay on their feet in the penalty area.

- Loudly blowing the whistle to call a foul for a late hit following a cross...only to see, a split-second after play is stopped, a spectacular bicycle kick directing the ball into the upper corner of the net for the most memorable non-goal you have even seen.

Timelines—Real and Imaginary

Some referee literature specifies guidelines and recommended timelines for pre-game activities. These guidelines vary depending upon the nature of the match and the level of the competition—and whether the games are professional, amateur adult, or youth. All of them specify recommended times for specific events—such as inspecting the field, conferring with colleagues, meeting the teams, conducting the coin toss, and the like— and look something like this:

One hour before game time:	Referees arrive together at the game site.
50 minutes before game time:	Referees walk the field as a team, inspecting the field.
40 minutes before game time:	Pregame conference
30 minutes before game time:	Player check-in commences....etc, etc.

Invariably, these timelines conclude with a kick-off that starts the game precisely on time—which can be very important when the TV cameras are rolling and there are commercials to schedule. Such precision, however, is often unrealistic in the real world, where people have lives that include things other than soccer.

Most of these guidelines can be confusing to the new referee, and may be a cause for concern when nothing goes according to plan. To prevent any needless anxiety in your first few matches, or fears that whatever goes wrong is somehow going to be entirely your fault, here is a more realistic look at what you may encounter while trying to get your game under way:

Pre-Game Timeline—Typical Youth Game

1:10 New Referee leaves house for a 2pm match at a venue five minutes away, excited to be in the middle for the first time.

1:12 Referee, caught in traffic, frantically calls home. He tells spouse where to find his address book and asks her to contact his assigner, apologize for the likely delay, and give assurances that Referee will appear for game, even though he may be delayed.

1:13 Referee is still stuck in traffic; sister-in-law calls as spouse looks for assignor's phone number, asking about dinner plans for the following day. Spouse spends the next hour on the telephone.

1:15 Last player on home team arrives, and home team manager has finished placing corner flags. All players from both teams are busy engaging in pre-game warmups. Spouse forgets about the assignor.

1:22 Referee decides to take alternate route to field, and adjusts course accordingly.

1:23 Traffic clears, and begins flowing smoothly.

1:29 Referee, having made three wrong turns, finally begins heading in the right direction.

1:33 Referee arrives at field and notices that he is the first official to arrive. He places equipment bag in the shade of a nearby tree and jogs briskly toward the team with the blue uniforms.

1:34 Referee introduces self to home coach, gathers game fee, game ball, and team roster.

1:36 Referee checks and approves game ball, puts game fee in pocket.

1:39   Referee introduces self to visiting coach and collects rest of game fee and roster. Gust of wind arises, and Referee jogs after scattering bills and paperwork on the way back toward equipment bag. AR-1 arrives on bicycle, dressed immaculately and looking like movie version of future World Cup soccer player. Letting bike coast to a stop, he helps retrieve money en route to shady tree.

1:40   Referee, reluctant to begin pre-game conference or player check-in without the entire crew, double-checks the game ball.

1:42   Beginning to panic, Referee decides to start check-in. He and AR-1 jog toward the blue uniforms.

1:43   Home team check-in begins.

1:44   Referee finishes checking in home team, begins pre-game talk to players.

1:50   Having concluded his pre-game remarks, Referee and AR-1 jog over to visiting team to begin their check-in.

1:51   During visitors' check-in, Referee remembers that he and AR-1 have not had a pre-game conference.

1:52   Concluding visitors' check-in, Referee and AR-1 dash to shady tree to retrieve game ball and finish pre-game preparations.

1:53   Panicking Referee cannot find prepared notes for pre-game conference and decides to wing it. AR-1 retrieves set of flags from his own equipment bag, both of which are much nicer than Referee's.

1:54   During pre-game, AR-1 casually remarks that the game ball seems a bit soft.

1:55   Referee continues pre-game while frantically searching for ball pump and needle.

1:56   Realizing need for a club linesman, Referee abandons pre-game and races toward home sidelines, delegating AR-1 to prepare game ball. Referee looks to recruit club linesman from among home-team parents.

1:57   Only volunteer for club linesman is a reluctant soccer dad and former high school offensive tackle, presently 197 pounds above his prime playing weight.

1:58   Instructions to club linesman concluded, Referee realizes that he has left his whistle and cards in his equipment bag at the shady tree...along with the game ball.

1:59   Trotting across the field, AR-1 hands Referee whistle, cards, and ball, and suggests that he try to relax. Referee looks to see club linesman with back to field, chatting amiably with his buddy along the touchline.

2:00   AR-2 arrives, sporting untucked jersey, white-on-black shorts hanging down past knees, white crew socks, a backwards baseball cap, and day-glow green cleats. He retrieves flag from club linesman and waves to Referee while sauntering into position. Referee realizes that he has forgotten to conduct the coin toss. Having left his coin in his equipment bag, he directs visiting team to guess which hand is holding his whistle. Home team wins whistling contest, and captain yells to the sidelines, asking the coach which end of the field they should choose. After hearing the answer, the captain elects to attack the south end of the field, requiring the teams to change sides.

2:02   Kick-off.

Pre-Game Timeline— Typical Adult Men's Game

1:00   Referee leaves for 2 o'clock adult men's game at a venue that is 15-30 minutes from home, depending on traffic.

1:15   Referee arrives at game site.

1:16   Seeing nobody else around, Referee checks schedule to make sure that he is in the right place.

1:17   Game site confirmed, Referee takes equipment bag out of car and walks toward field.

1:18   Referee arrives at field, plops equipment bag onto ground.

1:20   Having nothing else to do, Referee begins to jog around field, noting wavy markings along touch line and checking nets along the way.

1:25   Young couple walks by field, pushing stroller on way to nearby playground.

1:26   Referee takes drink of water, begins to stretch, and has passing thought that he should remember to bring something to read to his next game.

1:31   Two members of visiting team arrive, along with home team manager.

1:33   AR-1 arrives at the field, along with three more members of the visiting team. Referee shakes hands with AR-1, then walks over to greet home team manager.

1:34   Referee introduces himself to manager, and asks for pass card, game fee, and game report. Manager, who was absent from last week's game, indicates that

"George" has the pass cards. Manager pays the game fee, but defers turning over game sheet until he sees which players actually show up this week.

1:35　Referee introduces himself to the visiting team and learns that their manager is on his way.

1:36　Referee returns to home manager and asks for game ball. He learns that all the equipment is with "Franco," who will be along shortly.

1:37　Three more players from the visiting team appear, along with one member of the home team, named "Fred." Referee begins pre-game discussions with AR-1 but concludes that he would rather not do it twice. Noticing that the field has no corner flags, Referee again confers with home manager, discovering that "Bob" will be bringing the flags to the game.

1:39　Still hoping to start the game on time, Referee conducts coin toss with Fred and random member of the visiting team. Toss is won by home team, and Fred decides to attack the north goal.

1:40　Six more players from the visiting team appear, none of whom is the manager.

1:43　Two players from the home team arrive, including Franco—who left the team's equipment bag in his trunk. Visiting team manager shows up, pays game fee, and promises to have the game sheet ready in five minutes. He defers turning over his pass cards to the Referee, since he needs the cards in order to get the correct spelling of his players' names.

1:45　Three players from home team pull up and start jeering at Franco to hurry him along with the equipment; thought of helping him tote the equipment bags is somehow lost in all the camaraderie. Remainder of visiting team arrives in a nifty-looking conversion van.

1:47　Referee collects pass cards from visiting team and gathers game ball from Franco. Worried about having to do the game with only one AR, Referee conducts pre-game discussion with AR-1 while inflating ball to proper pressure.

1:50　AR-2 appears and heads directly to the mobile sanitation unit adjacent to field.

1:51　Referee makes rounds, discreetly checking equipment and asking if anyone on the home team has seen George or Bob. His previous commitments concluded, AR-2 begins slow walk toward field.

1:55　George arrives at the field, along with six teammates. Visiting team begins stretching and slow jogging across the field. AR-2 shakes hands with visiting coach and begins conversation about mutual friend.

1:56 Remainder of home team pulls into the parking lot. Referee gets pass cards from George and loudly informs everyone that the clock will start on time, whether they are ready or not.

1:57 Home team begins stretching along the sidelines. Referee asks again about their team's game sheet and is told that it will be available soon.

1:59 Visiting team turns in game report. Officials move onto field, moving toward center circle as Referee runs through quick recap of pre-game instructions with AR-2. Referee places ball in center circle.

2:00 Referee loudly sounds whistle and announces that the clock is running.

2:01 Visiting team starts kicking soccer balls all over the north side of the field. "Bob" is still nowhere to be seen. Officials move to check report of a gaping hole on visitor's side of the field and conclude that it looks like a small skid mark left by a slide tackle. Referee reminds visiting team that they have the kick-off; home team retrieves game ball from center circle to use in their warmups.

2:02 Returning to center circle, Referee notices that game ball is not where he left it. Looking about, he sees that home team is using it to practice shots on goal.

2:03 Directing AR-1 to retrieve ball, Referee runs to home team manager to obtain game sheet and again inquires about the whereabouts of Bob.

2:04 Referee puts game sheet in equipment bag, runs to center circle and notices that game ball is now being used for juggling practice by the only apparent athlete on the home team.

2:05 Referee runs to retrieve the game ball. Loudly reminding players that the clock is running he receives obligatory complaint that the game ball is too hard. In response to question, Referee informs home team that the other team has the kick-off.

2:06 Returning to center circle, Referee blows whistle several times in vain attempt to get player's attention. Officials shake hands and move into position.

2:07 Home team keeper runs to sidelines for water bottle.

2:08 Visiting team keeper saunters onto the field. Referee blows whistle multiple times, as substitutes wander off and players slowly gather into position on the field.

2:09   Responding to questions, Referee confirms that the visiting team still has the kick-off.

2:10   Visiting team makes obligatory complaint that game ball is too soft. Visiting keeper places water bottle inside net, and begins to adjust his gloves.

2:11   Kick-off.

2:22   Bob arrives at field. After brief discussion with manager, Bob returns to his car.

2:24   Bob returns from car with corner flags and begins putting them in place.

2:37   Flags now in place, Bob returns to bench and starts to put on shin guards and jersey. Alerted to previous commitment, he halts game preparation and heads in direction of nearby mobile sanitation unit, shin guards flapping as he walks.

2:39   Bob returns to bench and resumes preparations for game.

2:40   Bob, now properly attired, stands at half-way line and alerts AR-1 to upcoming request for substitution.

2:42   At home team goal kick, AR-1 signals for substitution and confirms to Referee that Bob is properly equipped; Referee beckons Bob onto field.

2:45   Referee whistles for half-time, ignoring howls of protest by both teams.

Chapter 8

Personalities on the Pitch

IN THE COURSE OF OUR LIVES, we meet a variety of people every day: fat people, skinny people; angry people, sad people; calm people and very tense people; and people of all sizes, shapes, and personalities. It should come as no surprise that we will meet the same array of people at the soccer field. As in life, some will be easier to deal with than others, but we should be prepared to meet and cope with all of them.

Sideline Personalities of Note

At a typical soccer match, most people along the sidelines will be well-behaved and cause no particular problem. The nurturing, supportive soccer parent, the saintly coach, and the occasional well-informed soccer fan are, we hope, filling our touchlines and ready to enjoy a well-played game between two well-behaved teams.

Of course, if every match were played by angels and attended by saints there would be little need for a referee, since there would be no fouls occurring on the field and no reason for anyone to become difficult or unruly. Unfortunately, while these model citizens are certainly around, they are often overshadowed by others, who are usually the ones commanding our attention. In the belief that it is better to be prepared than caught with one's whistle down, there are several distinct sideline personalities that a referee—particularly a new referee—should be prepared to encounter.

The Psycho Coach

In Youth Soccer, most games proceed uneventfully. The teams appear, they play, one team wins, and everyone goes home. Or, in the case of very young players, the team goes out for ice cream. There is, unfortunately, a particular type of coach that can make the life of a referee difficult, which we may describe, in general terms as the "*Psycho Coach.*"

A good coach, even at the game's premier levels, is there to teach, to help his team to play their best, and to offer encouragement and advice from the sidelines. These coaches are easily recognized, even by the beginning referee. They cause no trouble, their teams (and the parents along the sidelines) are usually well-behaved, and they are polite and supportive after the game is over, even when they lose.

The *Psycho Coach*, by contrast, may be hard to spot until the game begins. Often (though not always) these coaches will be amiable and gregarious before the match starts, revealing their true nature only after the kick-off. But they cannot conceal their identities forever, and it is only a matter of time before they reveal themselves. When that happens, you will need to determine which form they will assume. While both are annoying, only one variety causes problems for the referee.

The Screamer

All good coaches, whether at the premier or recreational level, do their best to prepare their teams for the match. The wise coach, understanding that soccer is a dynamic game, is usually content to let the team play the game on the field. He will make quiet comments along the sidelines, usually to the players on the bench and to players coming off the field, and will use a loud voice only to get someone's attention for a particular purpose: to alert the referee to a requested substitution or injured player, perhaps; maybe to alert an inattentive referee that the assistant referee has flagged a play as offside; occasionally to redirect players during a stoppage.

A *Screamer* will appear most often at recreational games, and may well be a good coach during the week. Come game day, however, he sometimes confuses soccer for American football. As a result, he may be intent on controlling his team from the sidelines and unaware that screaming at players who are trying to concentrate on the task at hand rarely does anything but confuse them. Or, being a volunteer without a real under-standing of the game, he may simply be caught up in the emotions of the game and trying to be the team's loudest cheerleader.

In any event, and however confusing they may be for their own team, *Screamers* usually pose no problem for the referee. While loud, they really mean no harm. While increasing the decibel level at the field, from the referee's perspective their effect is little different than any other extraneous racket. Like any other crowd noise, it is something to be filtered out of our awareness, but no cause for real concern.

The Abuser

The same cannot be said for the other species of Psycho Coach, who is probably responsible for chasing more referees from the pitch than any other single source. The abusive coach is a real threat to referees at all levels of the game and must be dealt with severely.

The *Abuser* comes in many shapes and forms, and often takes great pains to conceal his identity. He may be unusually helpful during check-in, for example, explaining to the team the need to keep their shirts tucked in and their socks pulled up. Or he may seem warm and friendly when you introduce yourself, doing his apparent best to make you feel at ease. You will probably not realize his true nature until the first time a critical call goes against him. Then, the mask will come off, his true nature will become apparent, and he will start filling the sidelines with a running commentary about the kind of job the officials are doing that day:

- "What was that!!??? Where's the call, Ref?"

- "You've got to be kidding me!!!"

- "Ref—*Ref*!!! What was that? Are you going to allow *that*?"

- "Hey!!! Can't you see that? It's right in front of you?"

- "Are you blind??? You've got to be *joking*!"

- "You've been letting that go all day, and now you're calling it on *US*?"

- "*OFFSIDES*!!! Oh, for crying out loud—now they're not calling offsides today!"

- *Etc, etc, etc...*

Abusive coaches are a destructive force on the game of soccer. Their actions encourage similar behavior by their team's spectators and players, and are intended to achieve a single purpose—to intimidate the referee into making calls that favor their team by making it unpleasant for the referee not to do the coach's bidding. They will feed on any weakness they perceive in the officials and will be relentless in their verbal attacks until they are forced to stop. The reason for the abuse is unimportant, and it does not matter whether the coach is unhappy at home, whether he was just passed over for a promotion at work, whether his parents criticized him unfairly when he was a child, or whether someone with a whistle ran over his cat when he was ten years old. Allowing this tactic to succeed not only undermines the authority of the officials, but turns the game from a contest of skill into a shouting match, and chases many referees away from the game before they have a chance to learn the art of officiating.

Once an abuser is identified, a referee should move quickly and fearlessly to remove the problem and allow the match to proceed without interference. The offender should first be told that his behavior is unacceptable. If it persists, he should be duly warned about the consequences. And if it does not stop, he should be dismissed from the field.[*]

Unfortunately, the reaction of many officials, particularly new, young officials who are not used to dealing with angry adults, is to shy away from a confrontation. But part of preparing ourselves to be referees is recognizing that this is one problem that will simply not go away by itself, and will only get worse as the match progresses. If we remember that it is the referee, and not the coach, who controls the match—the referee, who can send people from the field—and the referee who will be filing the game report—we see that any reluctance to take action on our part is either the result of our own lack of self-confidence, or our reluctance to confront a bully and make him back down.

Since all referees are human,[**] this reluctance is understandable. But we must learn to overcome it, if we want to survive as officials.

---

[*] Under the Laws of the Game, the coach would be dismissed for failing to conduct himself in a responsible manner, since non-players do not receive cards for misconducts.

Some competitions direct referees to display misconduct cards to coaches, just as they do to players. When in doubt about the rules of the competition, the referee should use the procedures outline in the Laws. In any event, the referee should make a full report of the activities leading to the dismissal.

[**] The behavior of some coaches suggests a contrary viewpoint.

Spectators

At a typical youth match, the spectators will be divided into two main groups: siblings, who are often more interested in playing in the dirt than causing trouble; and parents,* whose interest and enthusiasm for the game often exceeds their knowledge. Parents come in two basic varieties—mothers and fathers—and finding specimens of either is no cause for concern by itself. Most are quite harmless, and are simply there to enjoy watching the children play. Often well-behaved and enthusiastic, they usually make no trouble and could very well pass without notice, except for the fact that sidelines filled with these sorts of spectators tends to make a game pleasurable and enjoyable for player and referee alike.

As with coaches, however, there are some subspecies that are known to cause trouble, which may warrant our attention:

Rabid Soccer Dad

Sometimes an accomplished athlete in his own day—though occasionally an aspiring athlete whose ambitions were frustrated by a lack of natural ability—this breed of spectator sometimes confuses soccer with ice hockey or professional wrestling. Often brought up as a fan of professional American sports, he has embraced the notion that referees exist mainly to provide entertainment for the fans by serving as the target for cruel jokes and insults. Generally disinterested in the actual rules of whichever athletic event he is watching at the moment, he deems officiating to be a simple task fit only for the morons and mental defectives who stubbornly ignore the two most important rules of any sport, and the only ones that matter to him:

(1)   Any call that favors my team is a great call.

(2)   Any call that favors the other team is the product of incompetence by the idiot getting paid to oversee this sideshow.

A rabid fan tends to be loud and obnoxious, and is usually an embarrassment to the other spectators as well as to the players on the field. Most

---

* For our purposes, "parents" include "grandparents," who come in the same sizes and assortments, and are subject to the same concerns and considerations. The only practical differences (age, physical stature, and the strength of their eyesight) tend to make grandparents less of a practical concern.

of them, in fact, wish he would simply go away. A referee who wishes to oblige them, or whose patience is simply at an end, has a number of options, all of which boil down to doing the following:

- Stopping the Clock (*ie*, noting the time to add to the end of the match).

- Having a quiet word with the coach.

- Telling the coach that the game is suspended until the "village idiot" leaves the vicinity.

- Resuming the match when—and only when—the village idiot actually leaves.

Occasionally, Rabid Soccer Dads roam in packs, and the unlucky referee may find more than one along the sidelines at any particular game. When this happens, the basic procedure remains the same. Only the number of people sent to the parking lot will change.

A referee should always try to avoid sending people away from the game, however, and an early word to the coach is sometimes enough to solve the problem before it gets out of hand. Often, however, a veteran official may show this species of fan more patience than is warranted, either because experience has taught him to filter out the rantings of lunatics along the sidelines, or because the official is tired and does not want to bother trotting all the way across the field to deal with an obvious fool. The new referee usually suffers from neither handicap, and has no reason to show the same level of patience. In any event, there is no reason for an official to feel pressured or intimidated by the presence of a loudmouth along the sidelines. In fact, the nature of the game itself suggests the obvious solution to this problem: The game actually needs the referee to continue. It does not need the loudmouth.

A Note of Caution

Sadly, while the Center Referee is likely to be the focus of attention for most troublemakers, this particular species of spectator sometimes directs his attention to the nearest body wearing a referee's uniform—which is usually the assistant referee along the sideline. Referees should pay particular attention to young referees who are forced to share the sideline with a Rabid Fan, to catch the problem early and spare young and inexperienced officials the ordeal of listening to the rantings of a disgruntled parent.

Soccer Mom from Hell

Women are not immunized by their gender against being idiots, and we have seen a growing number of soccer moms who cannot avoid causing trouble along the sidelines. On occasion, and perhaps for the same reasons, a soccer mom may become as abusive as any of the fathers. When this happens, the treatment is the same. Isolate and separate the offender from the rest of the group and, if necessary, invite the coach to allow the game to resume by convincing the troublemaker to leave.

There is another kind of Soccer Mom from Hell, however, who will appear at the field from time to time. The target of her abuse, though, is not the referee—it is her own child...and sadly enough, it is usually her own daughter who, it seems, can never play quite well enough to suit her mother.*

Women's sports have grown exponentially in the last two decades, and we see premier-level girls' and women's teams at all ages. Unfortunately, the frustration that some feel at missing the chance to compete in their own day is visited on the heads of the child fortunate enough to get the chance to participate, but unlucky enough to have to carry the disappointments of another generation on her shoulders.

This kind of parent is to be pitied, though not as much as the child. Unfortunately, there is nothing the referee can do to change human nature.

Whining Wannabees

Many people at a soccer match will loudly wonder why the referee at their games gets so many calls wrong, especially since the spectators can get all of them right while sitting in their chairs along the sidelines.

Referees, of course, know that things look different on the pitch, and that it is easy to get everything right as long as *someone else* is making the decisions. The moment that the responsibility falls on your own shoulders, you realize how much there is to observe, how fast plays can develop, and how challenging it is to make split-second calls without the benefit of slow-motion replay, or the luxury of knowing that the call should always be going in *your* team's favor.

---

*In point of fact, men are not immune from directing anger against their own children. Like their mates, however, they are more likely to direct their frustrations against the child they see as most like themselves—their sons, rather than their daughters. And it is likely that this occurs for the same reason: they are reliving their childhood vicariously.

As long as there are referees, there will be people along the sidelines complaining. We can ignore them; or, since they obviously have perfect eyesight and impeccable judgment, we can invite them to join our ranks. What we *cannot* do is allow them to rattle us.

Some sidelines chatter can help us,[*] and some of it can distract us. But most sidelines chatter is harmless. Difficult as it may be to do so, a wise referee will learn to ignore most of it.

A Field Guide to Players

As with the people along the sidelines, the personalities of the players will be infinitely varied and generally harmless. Players, for the most part, are there to play the game. They usually ask only that the officials protect them from foul play by the other side, and avoid interrupting the game needlessly. As with people everywhere, some will be excitable and passionate; others may be calm and cerebral; a select few will be able to harness the energy of their own team and, on occasion, even help the officials keep order on the field. Aside from the occasional pratfall or accidental mishap, most will be too intent on what they are doing to cause much trouble.

There are, however, some types of players who bear study, since they seem to cause more than their share of problems:

The Actor

While most soccer players take pride in their skill and ability to fend off the best their opponents have to offer, few are above taking a convenient tumble from time to time. What distinguishes the occasional bit-player from the real actor, however, is not just the frequency of their encores, but the obvious relish that a genuine thespian takes from the act of performing. Stepping from the role of brave and courageous athlete into that of a helpless and pitiable victim is not something that comes naturally to most, and a true artist will often be seen flying spectacularly through the air— almost always in or near the other team's penalty area—coming to rest with an unmistakable howl of pain, and rolling on the ground in

---

[*] If a referee misses an offside flag, for example, he usually has half the spectators eagerly telling him to "check your linesman!!!" And when a player is injured behind the play, it can be helpful to have other eyes watching the field.

agony...usually clutching a shin, knee, face, or whatever other body part is convenient. As with any art form, critics abound, and the referee who fails to appreciate the actor's craft may receive poor reviews from the other commentators in attendance, most notably members of the opposing team, who will invariably pan the performance.

During the regular season, the most talented actor-athletes appear weekly on the various all-soccer channels, though aspiring amateurs can be found locally. Every four years, the world's best gather together to showcase their acting abilities in Soccer's equivalent of the Emmy Awards, also known as the World Cup.

This type of player usually begins to make an appearance on the soccer field at adolescence. Most younger players are either too self-conscious, or too interested in playing the game to take much interest in acting.

The Temperamental Star

We learn early in life that talent often carries a price. For a fortunate few, this price includes multi-million dollar contracts and the chance to appear on television. The rest of us have to be content with using our more modest abilities as best we can.

Talented athletes, like other talented people, will often feel frustrated by teammates who prove to be less than helpful. Some may even come to believe themselves entitled to special or favorable treatment by the match officials—either by overlooking their own occasional petulance or misbehavior, or by paying particular attention to the misbehavior of their opponents, who are well aware of the dangers that a talented opponent presents on the soccer field.

A star player *is not* entitled to a referee who makes excuses or allowances for misbehavior. Talent does not carry with it an immunity from the rules, or a privilege to engage in misconduct that is not allowed among the peasantry.

A star player *is entitled*, however, to a referee who protects skillful play—one who recognizes the artistry that skilled players bring to the field, and takes care to prevent foul play from taking the place of skill in determining the outcome of a match. A referee who does this is likely to have an exciting and challenging match to officiate. One who does not may find himself in the position of punishing the victim, rather than the perpetrator of foul play, for like any other player, a star who is left unprotected by the referee will become angry when fouled time after time.

Since a team's best player is likely to be a target for both teams— whether getting the ball from a teammate,or getting whacked by an opponent— these players are likely to need special attention throughout the game.

As a referee, you will need to recognize the talented players on the field. They are the ones who make the game a joy to watch and to play, and they are the ones who are most at risk of being the victims of rough play by their opponents. Because we want the game to be an equal contest of skill, we must take special care to ensure that gifted players get a fair chance to show their talents on the field, and do not have their gifts reduced to a test of their ability to withstand pain.

The Sociopath
While most players are happy for the chance to play the game, a few seem to view sporting events as a means to amuse themselves by causing grief for their fellow human beings. Blessed with quick elbows and knees, this player's unique asset on the field is an uncanny ability to sense when officials are looking the other way. Often, though not invariably a defender, he occasionally hides among the rest of the players until he determines that the time has come to make his contribution to the match. Warning signs may include a curious lack of concern about an opponent's welfare after a particularly nasty tackle, as well as needlessly rough challenges for the ball, particularly when it is going out of bounds.

The Obnoxious Victim
Most people do not like being fouled. Fouls hurt and, even if they do not, an obviously unfair challenge offends the sense of sportsmanship that—in theory, if not always in practice—most of us bring to the soccer field.

Some people, on the other hand, appear to take great delight in being fouled, so much so that they are quick to call attention to every bump that befalls them anywhere on the field. Players of this persuasion will go to great lengths to convince everyone within whining distance that they are the oppressed victims of forces that threaten our moral fabric and, perhaps, modern civilization itself. Obviously, in their minds, the only thing that will realign the forces of nature and bring balance back to the Universe is merciless retribution by the referee.

Curiously, whatever the referee actually does never seems to be quite enough. A skeptical look at a player who seemed to trip over the line marking the penalty area will be met with outrage. A whistled foul will be greeted by contempt over the lack of a yellow card. And a yellow card is almost invariably met with cold fury, and a demand to know why the referee allows barbarians to remain on the field.

By an odd coincidence, players of this sort often regard red cards issued to opposing players as a source of amusement. This amusement, however, is never shared by their opponents.

The Disappointed Friend

This player is always delighted to see you, even if you are meeting him for the first time. He is proud to have you as the match official for the game, and eager and happy to help you in any way he can. His only goal, it seems, is to make sure that all goes well at the field and that both teams can play the game in an inspired and sportsmanlike manner.

Unfortunately, no matter how hard you try, you will invariably wind up breaking your friend's heart. You will miss an obvious foul that, he assures you, everyone else on the field saw. Or you—and, oddly enough, your assistants as well—will fail to see the blatant shirt-tugging that caused his team's forward to muff a kick inside the penalty area. Even worse, you may fall for an obvious dive by the other team's star player and award a penalty kick perhaps because, being innocent and gullible, you naively thought that the blood spewing from the other player's shin meant that the defender actually nailed the striker, rather than the ball.

Even so, no matter how many times you shatter your friend's faith in humanity, or how bitterly he chides you for ruining the game for everyone, he will always be delighted to see you the next time your paths cross.

The Psychotic

While most soccer players will get excited from time to time, and few are above the occasional display of temper, this player appears to relish making people miserable—including, it seems, himself. Perhaps a closet conspiracy theorist in another life, this player appears convinced that someone is to blame for everything that goes wrong on the soccer field, since the explanation for a poor performance cannot, to his mind, be the skills, hustle, or artistry of the opposing team. As a result, he roams the field in a state of perpetual rage, hoping that invective and abuse will exorcize the demons that threaten his team with defeat.

Ordinarily, this player is an equal-opportunity abuser, and is just as likely to be screaming at members of his own team as he is to direct his fury toward the officials. A yellow card will usually divert a Psychotic's attention away from the match officials. A deaf ear is almost as effective, but both approaches will keep his hapless teammates at ground zero, and sometimes only a red card for some unrelated ranting will rescue them.

Astute referees will be careful to distinguish this player from the typical goalkeeper. Though many players are chosen as keepers precisely because of this facet of their personality, some people who are otherwise quite normal will display similar behavior on the field, simply because it is customary and expected for those playing the position.

The Show-Stoppers

Some teams have players who excel at defense, others at attacking. Most soccer teams have a few key players, whose skill and efforts are vital to its success on the field. These players can occupy different parts of the field and often change positions during the course of the game. But they tend to fall into one of three categories, with one of three assigned roles: creating, destroying, or scoring.

Every good team will have at least one. A great team may have all three. But every successful referee must be able to recognize and deal with all of them, for they often hold the key to controlling the match successfully.

The Enforcer

Usually a sweeper or central defender, this player tries his best to give the opposing team nothing but trouble whenever they cross the half-way line. Always strong, he delights in physical play and disrupting an enemy's attack, and takes it upon himself to keep his opponents honest—with or without the referee's help. An alert official can recognize him by observing which defender is always rescuing his team from danger, and which one assumes responsibility for organizing the defense.

Ever alert to enemy attempts to bully or intimidate his teammates, the Enforcer will not shy away from retaliating against opponents who are fouling his teammates. Since he is often assigned the job of frustrating the other team's best player, his efforts in this regard may extend to exacting his own kind of "frontier justice" by avenging himself against the other side's star. A referee can often keep the match under control by making sure that a team's enforcer knows the limits of acceptable play—and, by voice or by whistle, making sure that both sides understand that they are playing by the same rules.

The Playmaker

Recreational soccer often features random kicks and mad scrambles after the ball. Competitive soccer usually involves moving the ball up and down the field, as the teams try to capitalize on temporary advantages in numbers or position. But without a player who can control events on the field, a team may find itself always on the outside, unable to penetrate the penalty area for a good shot on goal.

Great soccer teams usually have one or two players who control the play by their instincts for positioning and their uncanny ability to pass the ball to exactly the right spot on the field. They possess the knack of exploiting weaknesses that are not yet apparent—and will not materialize, except for their unique ability to sense opportunity well ahead of everyone else on the field. These players are the tactical field marshals who make the game exciting, and set up the chances for their team to score. They are the Playmakers—the creative forces that make things happen on the field.

Often positioned as midfielders, Playmakers are usually adept at maneuvering out of trouble. More interested in team success than individual glory, they delight in slotting the ball to teammates or penetrating enemy defenses by using their wits as well as their feet. Play usually flows through them—either from teammates passing them the ball, or opponents who cannot avoid an interception. For this reason, they are frequently victims of foul play by their opponents. Often, they are targeted by the defending team's Enforcer, who can sense that neutralizing the other team's Playmaker is the quickest way to disrupt an attack.

Games with gifted Playmakers tend to be fast-paced, with the action moving seamlessly from one end of the field to the other. Shutting down a team's offense by persistently fouling its Playmaker is a tempting tactic for the defense, but it destroys the improvisational creativity of soccer's most inventive players and robs the game of its soul. For this reason, all referees must learn to recognize and protect these creative players, and be alert to effect that foul play will have on the game if allowed to shut them down.

The Striker

The star of many teams is the Striker, the player who magically appears from nowhere to put the ball in the net. Sometimes a ball-hog, but always dangerous, this player is usually focused on a single task—scoring for his team—and for him, everything else fades into insignificance.

Players of this type come in many shapes and sizes. Some are big and strong, others are small and swift. All of them, however, share the unique gift of sensing when and where the ball will pop into the open—and live for the moment they can claim a goal for their team. They can often shoot off-balance with either foot, and can usually out-jump most of their opponents.

Because of their ability to score, this player is a major target for the other team's best, most physical defender. Usually so intent on scoring that he is willing and able to shrug off most contact, this player will nevertheless become frustrated if the defenders are allowed to take him out of game through an unremitting series of fouls.

As with the Playmaker, protecting this player is vital for a referee. Defending through physical play is always a legitimate tactic, but defending through foul play is not. And a referee who does not intervene to protect each team's best scoring threat is simply inviting trouble.

All three types of star players come in a variety of sizes, shapes, colors, and personalities, but their role on the field will likely remain a constant. Strikers will always try to score; defenders will always try to stop them; and playmakers will always be trying to create opportunities for their own team, while sowing danger and panic in their opponents. Recognizing each team's star players, and the unique role that each kind of star performs, is critical to understanding the challenges that each game will present, and to managing that game successfully.

Meet Your Colleagues

As we have already seen, there is no single personality that is unique to officiating soccer, and soccer imposes no ban on anyone simply because of quirks or oddities. If it did, the soccer world would be a much more boring place.

Fortunately, you will find most of your colleagues to be friendly, helpful, and surprisingly normal. Unfortunately, there will be days when all of *those* colleagues are busy on other fields. By way of introduction, and to help acquaint you with the wide range of personalities you are likely to encounter at some point in your career, you may want to start looking for the following people, whom you should be able to identify even though they will all be wearing the same uniform:

The Know-it-All

This referee is usually easy to spot. Within five minutes of meeting him, you will know that while he has had many problems in the past at his field all them were caused by somebody else. This is, by the way, the reason why you will be under strict orders not to ruin his game by calling any fouls—most particularly inside the penalty area, which he will take care of personally, in order to make sure that the game goes smoothly, thank you very much...so do not, *under any circumstances*, raise your flag for a defensive foul inside the box at his field.

The most memorable aspect of working with this official will likely be his advice to you about learning to deal with any complaints along the sidelines without troubling him about it, as well as the flak that you encounter during your game together. Especially the flak about the lack of any calls inside the Penalty Area.

Way Too Good for This Game

You are, indeed, fortunate to be able to work with this official, who once stood in the same men's room waiting line as Esse Baharmast. He does not, after all, like to do any games below Division I. And before the game starts both assistant referees, and most of the players, will know that how lucky they are that he decided to do this game as a personal favor to the assignor...since he is, after all, a Division I referee.

You will, he is sure, be able to learn a lot just by watching him, because he is on track for his National Referee Badge, just as soon as he can get enough Division I matches under his belt. But given his vast experience, you will come to understand why he looks so bored during the match. Still, you may find yourself wondering why a National Referee would be twirling his whistle from its lanyard as he strolls about the pitch. And you'll be happy to help him clear out right after the game, as he rushes through the paperwork so he can leave in time for his next match later that day—a Division I game that he'll barely have time to get to before kickoff. This is why he may need to delegate to you and the other assistant the task of distributing the pass cards and game sheets to the teams so he can hurry off to his next game.

Unfortunately, his early departure may leave a number of unresolved questions in your mind. Such as why a Division I-level referee would keep missing so many offside flags during the game. And how in the world anyone could mix up the scores on both game reports.

The Couch Potato

Coaches spend many a sleepless night praying that they can go another season without encountering this referee at one of their games. Not that he lacks experience. On the contrary, he has spent the last ten or fifteen years refereeing soccer. This gives him nearly a year's worth of experience, repeated ten or fifteen times.

Still, you will note, the coach's worries are not entirely accurate. He actually does run a full diagonal, from one end of center circle to the other. And he does not, as the coach was grumbling to his assistant, have a habit of coming to games out of uniform. As you can plainly see, he has quite a nice uniform. He just has trouble keeping his jersey tucked in over his belly.

He does, however, do his best with what he has. He usually stays within 50 yards of play at all times, despite being afraid of dropping his whistle. And he is adept at compensating for any problems he has seeing the ground around his feet. Along with more than his share of more tangible delicacies, however, he seems to have thoroughly digested at least one aspect of the Laws of the Game, for among his pre-game remarks to you was a reminder that under the rules the referee is deemed "part of the field." From what you can see, this is what probably has led him to his belief that since he's part of the field, it's everyone else's job to go around *him*. Curiously, he seems very surprised every time he collides with the ball or a player in the center circle.

The Shrinking Violet

We can recognize this referee by two primary clues: body language, which indicates a preference to be someplace else; and whistling technique, which runs the gamut from inaudible to non-existent.

This type of referee often tries hard to please everyone. Unfortunately, doing so guarantees nothing, except that everyone will end up angry and upset. Like many politicians, this official's hallmark is a strong, if unspoken desire to make everyone happy. Such an approach usually leads us to disaster when taken by our public leaders. It tends to achieve the same result on a soccer field.

Way Too Cool

Disdaining the advice of others that the game is about the players and not the referee, this official often appears sporting colorful jewelry, though he is usually careful about tucking it inside his jersey before telling the players that it isn't allowed on the field. Appearing just in time for the opening kick-off, he often pulls up on his motorcycle, sporting a stylish leather jacket and reflective sunglasses. He usually remembers to put his sunglasses in his referee bag, though...while complaining to his colleagues about having to weave his way through a pesky funeral procession on the way to the field, which delayed his arrival by several seconds.

During the match, this official will often be seen making faces and winking at his assistants along the sidelines whenever a player's pratfall and or blunder strikes him as amusing. Occasionally, he may offer a running commentary during the match about dinner plans with his newest romantic interest.

He typically exits in grand style, performing a wheelie on his bike on his way out of the parking lot. After he leaves, it is not uncommon for the coaches to complain to the AR's that the referee forgot to sign the game sheets. And that they think he drove off with everyone's pass cards.

Clueless...but Enthusiastic

This referee is always ready with a friendly word of encouragement to anyone on the field who seems to need one. He loves everything about being an official. He loves his uniform, and he adores his whistle. And he practices nightly, signaling fouls and giving stern but insightful lectures in front of a mirror. He is mystified why everyone at the soccer field is always mad at him.

He does, after all, know the rule book backwards and forwards...even if he does have trouble recalling the rules under stress, and hasn't quite deciphered the section dealing with "slouF." And he takes great pride in staying close to play, even if he is reluctant to interfere with the game by blowing his whistle.

The Hippie

Usually an older referee, this referee's heart, though not his day job, belong to the halcyon days of the 1960s. Often sporting longish hair and a beard, he has been known to appear at games with guitar in hand, serenading his teenaged crew with what they regard as Greatest Hits from the Dark Ages. Too free-spirited to be weighed down by a faceless bureaucracy like FIFA, he applies what he regards as his Common Sense and innate sense of Justice liberally at his games, often reaching different results than a review of the Laws of the Game might otherwise suggest.

The Autocrat

Convinced that civilization has been doomed ever since the Spanish Inquisition stopped burning people at the stake, this referee thinks that soccer has been going downhill ever since the dark day that FIFA elected not to make red cards punishable by death.

Often heard whistling *"Ride of the Valkyries"* while strutting to the spot of a foul, he takes particular delight in his specialty—whistling six-second violations, which he times to the 1/100th of a second. As a spectator, he judges the referee's performance by the ability to call fouls invisible to the naked eye. For himself, he takes pains to maintain his career average of ten minutes between cards for dissent, and takes great pride in the fact that he enforces the same rules at every field and in every game, under all field conditions.

Though unconfirmed by eye-witness accounts, he is rumored to have given a red card to a four-year old player last season for tripping an opponent closing on goal by stooping to pick up a dandelion blossom to give to her mother during a game. And he has been known to reduce grandmothers along the sidelines to tears by threatening to banish them from the field unless they move their walkers back an additional 3-½ inches, in order to give his assistant referee more room to run along the sidelines.

Resolute and courageous, this referee has definite ideas on how the game of soccer should be played. He will see to it that the game is played properly, even if neither team is left with enough players to finish the match.

The Social Worker

This referee is the true idealist of the profession, whose belief in human perfectability simply will not allow him to give up on trying to reform lawbreakers on the soccer field, no matter how long it might take him.

Believing that soccer could be a beautiful game again if only everyone would try to get along, he tries his best to convince the players to change their ways, believing that if mere words won't make a player simmer down, then more words might. He is always surprised when nasty players turn out, in the end, to be...well, nasty players.

The Good Ol' Boy

This referee is friendly and gregarious, and delights in taking care of his friends on and off the soccer field. He seems to know everybody in the world, and is still friends with half of them. Unfortunately, however, one of the two sides at the day's game always seems to be among the other half.

Proud of his sense of humor, this official can never resist the urge to make a joke about any topic, no matter how tasteless. He especially loves to flirt with female players when he does women's games, invariably making both teams mad.

Oddly enough, jokes about his officiating, or about fouls he's missed, tend to fall flat on his field.

The Guardian Angels

Finally, we also have three other primary referee types—who come in both genders, many sizes and shapes, with varying styles of officiating and many different and distinct personalities. They usually work quietly in the background, magically appearing out of nowhere in all corners of the pitch, calibrating their calls precisely to match the players and conditions of play, and solving most problems on the field by preventing them before they arise. As is their habit on the field, they often appear when people least expect them. You will, however, know them when you see them:

The Watch Dog

This quiet, unassuming referee seems to hide in the shadows. Outwardly mild-mannered, he is usually reserved and invariably polite. At times, however, he can become quite fierce and menacing—usually out of the blue, often just as tempers start rising on the field, and invariably before things get out of hand. Though his quietness is often mistaken for aloofness, he is a good teacher and always willing to share his knowledge and experience. And though he often passes unnoticed by others, somehow he always seems to be there, precisely at the spot of trouble, whenever he is needed.

The Facilitator

This referee is more outgoing than his quieter colleague, and is always trying to pass along what he knows, sometimes even to those who don't share his interest or commitment. Like his two companions, he possesses a vast knowledge of the game and appreciation for its traditions, but is something of a chameleon, adapting himself to those around him—often becoming jolly and helpful when doing younger games; calm and reassuring when that is what is required; or, at other times, ferocious and strong, depending on what will help the players for both teams play at their best.

The Dutch Uncle

Like the Facilitator, this referee has the capacity to project himself onto the field at will. But unlike his more amiable colleague, he (or his equally austere sister, Aunt Mildred) displays a gruff, often menacing exterior to the world. Yet despite an almost military bearing, careful observers notice an unexpected flexibility when encountering trouble, and his solutions to problems on the field are always accepted by everyone as sensible and fair. Though he can be stern and demanding, it is never without a clear purpose: to ensure his own command of the field which, somehow, always seems to help players win by skill rather than foul play. Often disappointed in his assistants, he may seem distant and unapproachable, but when convinced that a new assistant is dedicated to learning the craft, he can be among the most dedicated, fiercely loyal mentors any new referee could ever hope to have.

All three share a deep knowledge and affection for the game, as well as a resilience and mental toughness that helps them persevere through any pressures they encounter. They possess the ability to remain calm during games that other referees would see flying out of control. Oddly enough, if you happen to encounter them more than once, you may be surprised to see that they sometimes change from one to the other in the interim. And ironically, after you meet one, you may find that he simply fades into the background, and does not always share his wealth of knowledge without prompting. Though other referees respect them, and a new referee can often recognize them at first sight, they do not always recognize themselves.

Chapter 9

The Beautiful Game

SOCCER IS UNDISPUTEDLY THE MOST POPULAR sport on Planet Earth. It is also among the oldest. A game played with a ball and feet is of ancient origin, and we can trace its roots to many different places scattered around the planet, from Asia to the Americas. In various incarnations, the sport has ranged from wild communal free-for-alls* to a handful of players kicking at vaguely spherical objects made from whatever materials might be at hand.** Known by various names throughout history—called "*tsu chu*" by the ancient Chinese, "*harpastrum*" by the Romans, "*tlatchi*" by native Americans, and "*calcio*" by the time of Renaissance Italy—this simple sport has endured throughout history because it has enchanted people across cultures, and through the ages.

Instinctively understood and inexpensive to play, the sport's universal appeal comes not only from the joy each child experiences upon discovering that round things will roll, but also from the combination of athletic skill, mental quickness, and physical exuberance that comes from chasing after a ball. The modern game took its present form in mid-19th Century Britain, spreading from there around the globe. The rules have been streamlined ever since to make it simpler, more enjoyable, and easier to play and to understand.

---

* In some parts of the world, the early game consisted of a mob, a ball, and no actual rules.

** These materials varied from place to place, and included rubber, spherical fruit, animal bladders, stuffed cloth, and the skulls of defeated enemies. Today, we use an inflated ball, usually made of leather.

Today, soccer is played on every continent, and in nearly every country. The World Cup is probably the most-watched, most-anticipated sporting event in the world, and every day, millions of people savor all aspects of the game, either as players or spectators.

By helping to referee what the legendary Pelé dubbed "The Beautiful Game," you are joining the ranks of thousands of others, in this country and around the world. All share a love of the game, and a desire to help keep the sport safe and let it remain a source of joy for everyone. But referees are often soccer's invisible participants. When an official is performing well in a match that is going smoothly, nobody notices. It is only when the referee makes a mistake, or otherwise becomes a dominant feature of the match, that the conversation turns from the great plays and exciting game to a discussion about the officiating. This is not by accident, however. It is simply an extension of the game's philosophy: the game of soccer is for the players.

You will, over the course of your career as a referee, hear frequent mention of Law 18. Though soccer has only seventeen laws, Law 18 is probably the most important unwritten rule in sports—the Rule of Common Sense. As the World's Sport, soccer can vary with the players and the venue; all anyone needs is a ball. And though formal, competitive soccer needs standardized rules to make the game accessible to everyone, the traditions of the sport make it truly a "people's game." It belongs to the players, and referees are merely its guardians. For this reason, if you do not know or cannot remember the rule for a particular situation—or if something odd happens during a match that is simply not covered by any Law or tradition that you know about—you can always find your answer in Law 18. Consult your own sense of fair play, decide to do whatever seems like the most sensible thing to do under the circumstances, and then let the game proceed from there. If it turns out that you are mistaken—and that you did, in fact, apply the wrong rule—then you will have learned something to enrich your understanding of the game. But in the meantime, you will have solved whatever problem confronted you in a way that was equitable for everyone, and the players will have had some fresh air and exercise. In other words, whether you were right or wrong, sportsmanship will have triumphed.

Many sports, particularly American sports, are "rule-bound." This means that the rules define the game, and the official's task in many of them is largely to monitor the players to see that they conform to the rules. A basketball official, for example, will whistle a foul (or, on occasion, many of them) in the dying seconds of a basketball game, even though doing so lets the fouling team recover possession of the ball and gives them a chance to win. This is because the rules define the game and have a significance that extends beyond the interests of the players. As a result, the rules exist to be enforced and everyone expects the officials to blow the whistle unfailingly, whenever an infraction occurs.

In soccer, by contrast, the traditions of the game are quite different. The Laws of the Game describe soccer, rather than define it. More importantly, referees are trained not only to avoid interfering with the game needlessly, but also to avoid becoming accomplices to foul play by letting a team gain a tactical advantage by committing a foul. This is the purpose and rationale of soccer's "advantage" rule, and it is a basic feature of the game's philosophy. The referee is there to ensure the *safety* of the players, the *enjoyment* of the players and spectators, and ensure the *equality* of the participants by preventing one side from winning by cheating, or by turning what should be a contest of skill into combat by foul play.

An experienced soccer referee will distinguish between fouls that must be called, fouls that could be called, and trifling fouls that should be ignored unless they threaten to disrupt the game. This lets the game flow without any needless interruptions, while giving the officials the freedom to intervene as needed to keep the match under control. In fact, one of the hallmarks of a skilled soccer referee is the easy flow of the game, which seems to proceed without any stoppages that do not seem natural or "organic." This is possible only if the referee has learned the nuances of the game and is attuned to the needs of the players on a particular field on a particular day.

A beginning referee, however, faces different challenges. A player who has just been kicked sharply in the calf knows instantly that he has been fouled. The referee who is watching will often need a moment to process the image from his senses. If he delays too long before blowing the whistle, he may still be deciding what to do while play rushes merrily along, leaving both the referee and the smoldering resentment of the victim behind. This leads most new officials to whistle very quickly upon recognizing a foul, hoping to avoid missing something important. And in a larger sense, this is how it should be, for the new referee will usually be officiating a game of new or inexperienced players, who are also learning what is accepted on the field, and what is a foul.

Soccer can be a "beautiful game" at all levels, from the raw beginner to the accomplished and skillful artiste, and can accommodate differences in officiating as well as an infinite variety in styles of play. To succeed, the referee needs only a willingness to learn, the flexibility to adapt to changing circumstances, and a devotion to the good of the game. In the end, the referee is the guardian not only of the laws of soccer, but also its spirit. And for many, in all corners of the world, the Spirit of the Game—Courage, Honor, Joy, and Sportsmanship—is just as important as the game itself.

RESOURCES AND REFERENCES

BIBLIOGRAPHY
AND SUGGESTED READING

Ager, David. *The Soccer Referee's Manual*, 4th ed. London: AC Black, 2004.

Baay, Dirk. *Blowing the Whistle: A Referee's View of Soccer*. Colorado Springs: Halftime Press, 1997.

Baer, Al, ed. *Take Charge Soccer Officiating*. Franksville, WI: Referee Enterprises, 1993.

Burtenshaw, Norman. *Whose Side Are You On, Ref?* London: Arthur Baker, 1977.

Evans, Robert, and Edward Bellion. *The Art of Refereeing: Techniques and Advice for Every Soccer Referee*. London: AC Black, 2005.

Harris, Paul E., and Larry R. Harris. *Fair or Foul? The Complete Guide to Soccer Officiating*, 6th ed. Manhattan Beach, CA: Soccer for Americans, 1995.

Hill, Gordon. *Give a Little Whistle*. London: Souvenir Press, 1975.

Howell, Denis. *Soccer Refereeing*. London: Pelham Books, 1977.

Klein, Abraham. *The Referee's Referee: Becoming the Best*. Manhattan Beach, CA: Soccer for Americans, 1995.

Lover, Stanley. *Official Soccer Rules Illustrated: A Quick Reference for All Coaches, Players, and Fans*. Chicago: Triumph Books, 2003.

————. *Soccer Rules Explained*, rev. ed. Guilford, CT: Lyons Press, 2005.

————. *Soccer Match Control*, rev. ed. London: Pelham Books, 1986.

Mathurin, D. C. Emerson. *In Search of Fair Play: The Soccer Writings of D. C. Emerson Mathurin*. Spring City, PA: Reedswain, 1996.

————. *Linesmanship*. Spring City, PA: Reedswain, 1996.

Rouse, Sir Stanley, and Donald Ford. *A History of the Laws of Association Football*. Zurich: FIFA, 1974.

Schwartz, Carl P. *Soccer Officials Guidebook*. Franksville, WI: Referee Enterprises, 1999.

Stern, Jeffrey, ed. *Thinking Soccer: Officiating Success Techniques*. Franksville, WI: Referee Enterprises, 1996.

Taylor, Jack. *Soccer Refereeing: A Personal View*. London: Faber and Faber, 1978.

————. *World Soccer Referee*. London: Pelham Books, 1976.

United States Soccer Federation. *Advice to Referees on the Laws of the Game*. Chicago: USSF, 2006.

————. *Cautions and Cautionable Offenses, 2006*. Chicago: USSF, 2006.

————. *FIFA Laws of the Game, 2006/2007*. Chicago: USSF, 2006.

————. *Guide For Fourth Officials*. Chicago: USSF, 2001.

————. *Guide to Procedures for Referees, Assistant Referees, and Fourth Officials*. Chicago: USSF, 2006.

Weinberg, Robert S., and Peggy A. Richardson. *Psychology of Officiating*. Champagne IL: Leisure Press, 1990.

SELECTED HELPFUL WEBSITES:

The American Soccer History Archives. http://www.sover.net/~spectrum

Big Soccer. http://bigsoccer.com/forum

The Corsham Referee. http://www.corshamref.net

Federation Internationale de Football Association. http://www.fifa.com/en/index.html

Soccer Learning Systems. http://www.soccervideos.com

Socref-L. http://pete.uri.edu/archives/socref-l.html

United States Soccer Federation. http://www.ussoccer.com

The Watch and Whistle. http://www.watchandwhistle.org/#offthefield

GLOSSARY

Added Time: Time added to the end of a half to compensate for playing time lost to injuries, substitutions, time-wasting, or other any other cause for which the referee deems appropriate. Also called "stoppage time"or "injury time."

Advantage: A decision by the referee to allow play to continue, despite witnessing an act of foul play, when doing so would benefit the fouled team.

AR: An assistant referee

Assistant Referee: An official positioned along the touch line, who communicates with the referee by means of a flag signal; formerly called a "linesman."

Attacker: A player who is in the opposing half of the field; or any player whose team is in possession of the ball.

Backpass: The common name for the technical offense of a keeper handling the ball following a deliberate kick or throw-in to him by a teammate, punishable by an indirect free kick.

Caution: A formal warning by the referee to a player or substitute whose behavior or play has become unacceptable, signified by the display of a yellow card.

Center Circle: A circle marking the ten-yard radius from spot of a kick-off.

Charging: Bodily contact undertaken against an opponent in order to win or obtain possession of the ball. If done unfairly, it is a penal foul.

Club Linesman: A non-neutral official, pressed into service on one of the touchlines due to the absence of a qualified assistant referee, and asked to signal when the ball goes out of play.

Coach: The team official allowed along the sidelines, who is entitled to pass tactical advice and instruction during the match; sometimes called the manager.

Competition Authority: The organizing league or agency which is organizing a soccer competition.

Corner Arc: A one-yard quarter circle from the corner of the field, marking the spot for a corner kick.

Corner Kick: The restart of play occurring when the ball passes over the end line after last being touched by a defender.

CR: The referee (or "center referee").

Dangerous Play: A technical foul, consisting of any act considered by the referee to be dangerous to an opposing player.

Defender: A player on his own half of the field; or a player whose team is not in possession of the ball.

Direct Free Kick: A free kick from which a goal may be scored, awarded as a result of a penal foul.

Dissent: A form of misconduct consisting of protesting a call by any of the officials, punishable by a yellow card.

Dropped Ball: A means of restarting play after a stoppage caused by something other than an offense by a player. Also called a "drop ball."

End Line: The boundary line at each end of the field, upon which each set of goals rests. Also called a "goal line" or "bi-line."

Extra Time: The additional period or periods of play to obtain a result at the end of a match that ends in a draw, usually during the later stages of tournament play where the match requires a winner.

Free Kick: A kick awarded to a team due to an infraction committed by the opposing team, free from interference by the opponents.

Fourth Official: An extra official appointed by the competition authorities to assist at the match and serve as a substitute official for the referee or assistant referee.

Game Report: The official account of a match, including the score and any misconducts issued, prepared by the referee.

Goal: (1) The targets of both teams, consisting of two uprights and a crossbar, placed at the end line on opposite ends of the field and defended by each respective team. (2) A score, occurring when the ball passes entirely over the end line and into the goal.

Goalkeeper:	The player on each team designated as the one entitled to handle the ball inside its own penalty area and required to wear a distinct jersey, different from the rest of the team.
Goal Line:	The end line; usually, the end line between the goal posts.
Goal Posts:	The physical boundaries of the goal, usually made of metal or wood.
Half-time:	The period of time between the end of the first half, and the beginning of the second half of a soccer game.
Half-way Line:	The physical line marking the center of the field.
Handball:	Another name for "handling."
Handling:	A penal foul, consisting of the deliberate use of the arm or body to control the ball. A goalkeeper cannot be guilty of handling the ball inside his own penalty area.
Holding:	A penal foul, consisting of unfairly hindering or restraining the progress of an opponent, usually by means of the arms or hands.
Impeding:	The act of physically obstructing or impeding the progress of an opponent. Also known as "Obstructing."
Indirect Free Kick:	A free kick which requires a touch on the ball by a second player before a goal may be scored, awarded as a result of a technical or non-penal infraction.
Jumping:	The act of leaving the ground under one's own power by leaping. If directed at an opposing player in an unfair manner to prevent the opponent from making a play on the ball, it is a penal foul.
Keeper:	A goalkeeper.
Kicking:	A penal foul consisting of unfair contact against an opponent by means of the foot or leg.
Kick-off:	The means of starting the match, or restarting the game following a goal, taking place from the middle of the center circle.
Kicks from the Mark:	A means of obtaining a result following a draw, where the rules of the competition require a winner, consisting of a series of penalty kicks.

Misconduct: An act deemed by the referee to be unsporting, reckless, violent, or flagrantly in violation of the laws and spirit of the game, and punishable by a caution (and yellow card) or a send-off (and red card).

Offside Line: An imaginary line signifying the furthest point downfield that an attacker may be without risk of being penalized for being offside.

Offside Offense: The act of participating in play from an offside position. Also "offside infraction."

Offside Position: A position in the attacking half of the field in which a player is closer to the opposing goal than (a) the ball, as well as (b) the next-to-last defender.

Obstructing: The act of physically obstructing or impeding the progress of an opponent. Also known as "impeding."

Outside Agency: Any force acting on or influencing a match which is not part of game.

Penal Foul: An infraction resulting in a direct free kick.

Penalty Arc: The marked arc extending outside the boundary of each penalty area, marking 10 yards from the penalty spot.

Penalty Area: The marked area around each goal, measuring 18x44 yards, within which the defending keeper has the privilege of handling the ball, and inside which a penal foul by the defensive team will result in a penalty kick.

Penalty Kick: A direct free kick from the penalty spot, pitting the attacker taking the kick directly against the defending keeper.

Penalty Spot: The marked spot 12 yards from the middle of each goal, from which penalty kicks are taken.

Persistent Infringement: The misconduct of continuous or repeated foul play, punishable by a yellow card.

Pitch: Another name for the soccer field.

Player: A competitor at a soccer game.

Pushing: A penal foul resulting from the unfair use of the arms or body to push, shove, or otherwise force an opponent into changing position or direction.

Red Card:	The misconduct card shown to a player who is being sent off either for a serious act of misconduct, or for receiving a second caution.
Referee:	The match official responsible for supervising and controlling a soccer match; also called a "Center Referee" or "CR." Often called other names, as well.
Restart:	Any method of resuming the game after a stoppage of play.
Result:	The final outcome of a soccer match, whether a draw, or a victory by the team scoring the greater number of goals.
Send-off:	The dismissal of a player following the display of a red card, either for a serious act of misconduct or for receiving a second caution in the same match.
Serious Foul Play:	A misconduct, often violent, which consists of the clearly disproportionate use of physical force against an opponent during a contest for the ball on the field, and while the ball is in play.
Spitting:	A penal foul, consisting of the deliberate attempt to direct bodily fluid from the mouth onto the person of someone else. It is also an act of misconduct, punishable by a red card.
Striking:	A penal foul, most often resulting from the unfair use of the hands or body to hit an opposing player, or to hurl an object that strikes an opposing player. If done intentionally, it is usually a misconduct, often a form of violent conduct.
Stoppage Time:	Time added to the end of each half at the discretion of the referee to compensate for lost playing time; see "Added Time."
Substitute:	A non-participating player along the sidelines, who is eligible to replace a player on the field.
Tackle:	An attempt to obtain possession of the ball by using the feet. If a tackle results in contact with an opposing player before contact is made with the ball, it is a penal foul.
Throw-in:	The method of restarting play after the ball has gone out of bounds over a touch line.
Touch Line:	The boundary lines marking each side of the field.
Tripping:	The penal foul of tripping an opponent.

**Unsporting
  Behavior:** The most common form of misconduct, consisting of conduct or play which the referee deems to be unacceptable. Consisting of a wide range of misbehavior, it is punishable by a yellow card.

Violent Conduct: A misconduct consisting of a violent act against any person at a soccer match, punishable by a red card.

Yellow Card: The misconduct card shown to a player who is being cautioned by the referee for an act of misconduct.

INDEX